NATIONAL
SECURITY
DILEMMAS

RELATED TITLES FROM POTOMAC BOOKS

Iraq and the Evolution of American Strategy
—Steven Metz

War and Diplomacy: From World War I to the War on Terrorism
—Andrew Dorman and Greg Kennedy, editors

Diplomacy Lessons: Realism for an Unloved Superpower
—John Brady Kiesling

NATIONAL SECURITY DILEMMAS

Challenges &
Opportunities

COLIN S. GRAY

FOREWORD BY LT. GEN. PAUL K. VAN RIPER,
USMC (RET.)

Potomac Books, Inc.
Washington, D.C.

Chapters 2–7 were originally published as monographs between 2002 and 2007 by the Strategic Studies Institute of the U.S. Army War College. As individual pieces, they are works of the government and are not subject to the copyright claimed herein, which pertains to the work as a whole. These chapters nonetheless have been thoroughly revised and updated by the author.

Library of Congress Cataloging-in-Publication Data
Gray, Colin S.
  National security dilemmas : challenges & opportunities / Colin S. Gray ; foreword by Lt. Gen. Paul K. Van Riper, USMC (Ret.).
     p. cm.
  Includes bibliographical references and index.
  ISBN 978-1-59797-262-8 (hbk. : alk. paper) — ISBN 978-1-59797-263-5 (pbk. : alk. paper)
  1. National security—United States—21st century. 2. Military doctrine—United States. 3. United States—Military policy. 4. Military art and science—United States. 5. Strategy. I. Title.
  UA23.G7788 2009
  355'.033073—dc22

                              2008042709

Printed in the United States of America on acid-free paper that meets the American National Standards Institute Z39-48 Standard.

Potomac Books, Inc.
22841 Quicksilver Drive
Dulles, Virginia 20166

First Edition

10 9 8 7 6 5 4 3 2 1

To the memory of Donald G. Brennan and Herman Kahn

The responsibility of statesmen . . . is to resolve
complexity rather than to contemplate it.

—Henry Kissinger, 1994

CONTENTS

FOREWORD

Americans are by inclination problem solvers. In general, they also value an engineering approach to solving problems. For this reason, they tend to favor rational and quantitative "tools" over qualitative ones. While strategy occasionally requires the use of metrics, it is principally the realm of judgment. It is fundamentally more art than science. This dichotomy—a partiality for linear decomposition and analysis vice holistic reasoning—has produced tension within the U.S. national security community for many years. These disparate ways of dealing with important strategic questions reflect two views of war, one essentially Jominian and the other Clausewitzian. For reasons I will explain, these two views seem to cycle alternately to the forefront of official American military thinking. We have witnessed several turns of this cycle over the past half-century and today we appear to be at another.

From World War II through the Vietnam War, American leaders placed mounting faith in systems engineering methods and technological means as they sought to understand and meet the challenges of national security. This led senior officers and civilian academics during the 1950s and 1960s to devalue study of the past. As a result, military history—for some two centuries viewed as "the school of the soldier"— nearly vanished from the curricula of the service academies, command and staff schools, and war colleges. In his 1961 *Military History*, the noted historian Walter Millis wrote, "It is the belief of the present writer that military history has largely lost its function."[1] Many in uniform accepted this argument, falsely believing that new technologies made the past moot, if not completely irrelevant. Over the same period, these leaders also allowed knowledge of the classical theorists to fade away. The ideas of Carl von Clausewitz eventually were unknown to most officers—as were those of other classical theorists, such as Sun Tzu, Alfred Thayer Mahan, and Julian Corbett. Leadership instruction too fell by the wayside. Increasingly, management science and analytical techniques took a central position in the programs of military schools. Strategy became largely the province of those who thought about nuclear weapons. The term "strategic" lost its proper meaning as it was equated more and more with the nation's nuclear arsenal, as illustrated by the designation for the organization given charge of the United States' long-range bombers and ballistic missiles, Strategic Air Command.

The American military went to war in Vietnam with confidence that its modern means and methods of waging war would assure success. Despite the dedicated efforts of leaders on the ground the war proved unwinnable. The officer corps returned from this bitter experience disillusioned and highly critical of the professional thinking it had taken into the war. With the support and mentorship of a handful of senior officers, many younger officers began to ponder why things had gone so wrong. The more insightful soon put away any notion that a liberal media, unsupportive public, or ineffectual civilian leadership were at the heart of the shortcomings they had observed. These officers realized they did not understand how war related to policy and strategy or how to truly practice operational art. They recognized they lacked sufficient knowledge of the historical contexts with which to compare the challenges they faced. In short, because military institutions of the 1960s were blinded by the claimed advantages of rule-based decision-making techniques and an unshakable faith in technology, instructors of the period neglected to teach officers the basics of the profession.

Grasping that they had no real appreciation of the truths of war, a number of officers in the 1970s returned to studying military history, classical military theory, and strategic thought. They soon came to understand that employing operations and tactics outside of a strategic framework—a framework that itself was tied to well-thought-out policies—was at the root of the difficulties they confronted in the Vietnam War. With the absence of a foundation provided by meaningful policy and a considered strategy, the nation had sent them on a fool's errand. These officers learned as well that their lack of historic context denied them the needed insights to the operational dilemmas they encountered. Most importantly, they rediscovered the power and the timelessness of the thoughts of Carl von Clausewitz. The 1976 publication of a much-improved English translation of his opus, *On War*, by Michael Howard and Peter Paret, greatly aided the efforts of these new students to discern the Prussian theorist's most profound thoughts. In addition, this book significantly influenced revisions of professional military education programs as well as the rewriting of key doctrinal publications.

It took some fifteen years for a new generation of officers to undo the damage done by the previous four decades of neglect. The results were impressive: military schools at all levels restructured their courses to reflect an appreciation of history; intermediate-level schools introduced officers to the essentials of operational art; war colleges examined how national leaders properly develop policy and strategy; and a solid new doctrine emerged in publications, such as the U.S. Army's *Operations* field manual and the U.S. Marine Corps' *Warfighting* manual. As a consequence, a growing body of officers well grounded in history and the fundamentals of strategy and operations soon found its senior members assigned to key positions within high-level service and operational staffs and at the Pentagon. Several served as members of the National Security Council and three became the assistant to the president for National Security Affairs, General Colin Powell being the most influential.

From these positions of considerable responsibility, they were able to put their recent education to effective use. One deficiency they sought to overcome was the absence of a written national security strategy. What strategy existed was customarily derived from other official documents, such as the Secretary of Defense's Annual Report to Congress and the Defense Guidance. This changed, however, when the Goldwater-Nichols Department of Defense Reorganization Act of 1986 mandated that the president "transmit to Congress each year a comprehensive report on the national security strategy of the United States."[2] The first two reports did not meet the requirements of a true grand strategy, but in March 1990, the White House published a fairly sophisticated strategy. This strategy was soon put to the test when Saddam Hussein's army invaded Kuwait in summer 1990.

The American Armed Forces that drove the Iraqi Army from Kuwait were a far cry from the broken military that departed Vietnam a decade and half earlier. Obvious were the superb quality of personnel, the cutting-edge weapons and equipment, and the high level of training. Not as evident, but more significant, were the intellectual tools brought to the fight by leaders all the way from the chairman of the Joint Chiefs of Staff to the young noncommissioned officers leading from the front. Critically, as the secretary of defense's *Conduct of the Persian Gulf War: Final Report to Congress* noted, the "clear statement of goals helped instill confidence and eased the formulation of military objectives."[3] Unlike in the Vietnam War, field commanders were certain of their missions. An unambiguous logic ran from the *National Security Strategy* through President Bush's August 5, 1990, statement on national policy objectives for the region and the secretary of defense's promulgation of theater military objectives to the missions the theater commander assigned to his operational units. Policy, strategy, and operations were coupled appropriately. Clausewitz would have recognized the reasoning underpinning the directions that flowed down the chain of command, perchance observing that "war is nothing but the continuation of policy with other means."[4]

Pundits often say that "success breeds success." Reasonably then, one might expect that American military leaders aware of what had allowed the United States to prevail in Operation Desert Storm would work to build on that success. Surprisingly, this was not to be the case. From the early 1990s through the mid-2000s officers who had participated in the intellectual renaissance of the 1970s and 1980s frequently were not selected to fill the most senior positions. Too often in their stead came officers whose backgrounds were narrowly technical or excessively political. These officers brought a renewed emphasis on the science of war rather than the art. Some saw war as only a targeting problem. Others made the absurd claim that information technology would change the very nature of war. Among the multitude of incredible assertions for the power of technology, none was more astonishing than that of the vice chairman of the Joint Chiefs of Staff in 1996 who, promoting new surveillance systems, declared, "If you see the battlefield you win the war."[5] Astoundingly he went on to declare that "[t]he smartness of the way we do warfare . . . will change the nature of warfare so that people such as Sun Tzu, Clausewitz and Mahan, may well now be wrong."[6] Of course, with this sort of leadership the doctrinal and educational gains made in the years after Vietnam began to erode. New defense publications talked of a so-called military technical revolution or revolution in military affairs. Slogans and unsupported assertions about the power of technology displaced real intellectual content. Time devoted to the study of strategy, campaigns, and military theory in professional schools gave way to instruction on concepts like "network-centric warfare," "effects-based operations," and "system of systems." The cycle had made a full turn, and to the great distress of the true warrior-scholars, many of the gains made between the end of the Vietnam War and the Persian Gulf War were tossed aside.

Widely read officers of the post-Vietnam War era were familiar with the books Dr. Colin S. Gray had written on strategy and defense in the 1970s and 1980s. Those who read his work could relate immediately to his thoughts, for they reflected the reality of war as these officers had experienced it. He offered no pretentious or exaggerated gibberish; his words were to the point, acknowledged war's inherent uncertainty, and spoke of history's value. His grasp of strategy was unsurpassed and he straightforwardly laid out a sound case for its relevance to officers of every service. His original admirers—among which I include myself—would return to Professor Gray's writings often as they argued against the purported visionaries' technically focused plans for the future force. Professor Gray's study *The American Revolution in Military Affairs: An Interim Assessment*, published by the British Joint Services Command and Staff College, sounded an especially prescient warning about the dangers of contemporary thinking and the "tons of nonsense" it would produce. Nonetheless, a relentless drumbeat continued to support the alleged "dominance" that new and emerging technology would confer on American forces. As it so often has in the past, a new conflict would again expose the faults of those who describe war as they wish it to be, rather than war as it really is.

Clausewitz warned all who would listen that, "In war more than in any other subject we must begin by looking at the nature of the whole, for here more than elsewhere the part and the whole must always be thought of together."[7] The Global War that President Bush asked the nation to embark on after the attacks of September 11, 2001, demanded a global strategy—a strategy that looked at the nature of the whole. Also essential were supporting campaign plans for the areas of the world where he intended the American military to fight that war. These were the parts of the whole strategy that American defense leaders should have—nay absolutely must have—"thought of together." Regrettably, the president's administration produced only operational plans. One of these plans—the one for Operation Iraqi Freedom—enabled U.S. and coalition forces to capture Baghdad, which caused the subsequent collapse of the Ba'athist regime. However, in developing the plan, the authors failed to think through the nature of the whole problem and account for the aftermath. Moreover, the Pentagon and the United States Central Command produced no overarching strategic blueprint that adequately clarified the relationship of the fighting in Iraq to the larger war. As damaging was the fact the United States military was prepared to fight only one kind of war, it had forgotten "the nature of the whole."

In Iraq in 2003 the American forces employed an improved version of the operational concept they had used in 1991. In the years between these two operations, senior leaders maintained a single-minded focus on combat between similar forces that sought to gain a position of advantage while bringing fire on the enemy, what some call "regular war." These leaders neglected to keep in mind the admonitions of Clausewitz that "War is more than a chameleon that slightly adapts its characteristics to the given case"[8] and that "the aims a belligerent adopts, and the resources he employs . . . will also conform to the spirit of the age and to its general character."[9] Thus, neither they nor the units on the ground were prepared fully for the insurgency they soon faced. Doctrine was wanting as were proper counterinsurgency training and the necessary organizations and equipment. War, as "more than a chameleon" and conforming "to the spirit of the age," had turned from "regular" to "irregular." American forces on the ground now faced the difficult and dangerous task of reforming their doctrine and restructuring their organizations at the same time they were engaging a cunning enemy.

Five years of fighting an insurgency that the United States was not adequately prepared for discredited the "revolutionary" prophets. Gradually they passed from the scene to be replaced by leaders who understood war as the uncertain, chaotic, and dangerous phenomenon that those with a penchant for scientific certitude appear unable to see. As the cycle moves once again in the favorable direction, American leaders have to take steps to ensure it never again swings back the other way. They must accept war on its own terms, educating subordinates to its awful dimensions while developing the doctrine, organizations, and weapons needed to prevail no matter the character or form of the next trial of arms.

With more than twenty books and hundreds of scholarly articles to his credit, Professor Gray is well equipped to help guide the thinking of American leaders with regard to war, strategy, and military history as they again rediscover their intellectual roots. There are hopeful signs that his contributions are becoming ever more recognized. His *Modern Strategy*, *Strategy for Chaos*, and *Another Bloody Century* are in the personal libraries of numerous military officers. Several of his books are on required reading lists of military colleges. Professor Gray's unique *Fighting Talk* has found its way to the desks of a number of senior defense officials as well as more than a handful of generals and admirals. One U.S. combatant commander has made it required reading for all of his officers. The book you now hold in your hands offers another distinctive and penetrating look at strategic and defense issues that need be of great concern to those entrusted with America's security. Undoubtedly, readers will find Professor Gray's *National Security Dilemmas* provides keen insights to those issues, issues that Americans and their elected and appointed officials must make sense of and suitably resolve. I find his arguments on how they might do so persuasive!

Paul K. Van Riper
Lieutenant General, USMC (Ret.)

PREFACE

National Security Dilemmas addresses the major issues of policy and strategy that have consumed public attention in the twenty-first century. The U.S. Army War College's Strategic Studies Institute originally published chapters 2–7 between 2002 and 2007. The chapters were written to explain the structure of their varied subjects, rather than to serve as advocacy analyses. Given this helpful basis, it has been a relatively easy task to update and reissue these chapters so as to ensure that they do not show unhelpful signs of aging. Readers can be confident that the author has thoroughly and comprehensively revised the monograph texts reprinted here.

In summary, *National Security Dilemmas* provides an education in policy and strategy as they bear on the principal dilemmas, the challenges and opportunities, that have both preoccupied Americans thus far in the twenty-first century and continue to cause trouble. The book opens with a newly written analysis of the recent and current condition of national and international security (chapter 1). Next, the book proceeds to grapple with the enduring challenge of how to define and achieve a conflict outcome worth calling "decisive victory" (chapter 2). Chapter 3 explains the arguable past, troubled present, and necessary future of the former centerpiece of U.S. strategy, deterrence. In chapter 4, the book tackles the recurring defense-planning dilemma posed by strategic surprise. The problem is analyzed in the context of another major challenge, the ongoing commitment to implement an information-led transformation of the armed forces. Chapter 5 addresses a challenge and perceived opportunity that has excited many Americans for at least fifteen years, the idea of revolutionary change in warfare or Revolution in Military Affairs (RMA). The text explains "the sovereignty of context." In chapter 6, the book moves from consideration of regular warfare to irregular varieties. Warfare against enemies who fight irregularly is considered in the light of the "essence of strategy." Chapter 7 confronts a hot topic of the twenty-first century, whether and/or when to "preempt." It is particularly concerned with distinguishing between "attacking first in the last resort," which is to say preemptively, and "shooting on suspicion," which is to say preventively. The final chapter, 8, presents a brief new analysis of "the merit in ethical realism." This discussion advances and defends the proposition that policy, strategy, and action perceived by stakeholder communities to be unethical has a way of proving self-defeating. We are moral beings.

I am grateful to a number of good friends for the encouragement and advice that led me to assemble, edit, and add to elements that comprise the core of this book. In particular, I would like to express my thanks to Antulio J. Echevarria II of the Strategic Studies Institute (SSI) at the U.S. Army War College. The monographs that are the basis for chapters 2–7 were all written and published under the auspices of SSI, to which excellent institution he is the SSI's director of research. He is a first-rate Clausewitzian scholar, as well as the possessor of a lethal pen and computer on the subject of the less robust contemporary strategic pretensions. I am grateful to Tony for pointing me toward Potomac Books, Inc., as well as for his other offerings of good advice. Also, I am much indebted to Steve Metz of SSI, the scholar who first ushered me into the Army War College's research and publishing fold. Steve's new book on American's recent and current course in Iraq truly is a landmark work.

Why reprint and edit these monographs? The answer is that they comprise a body of analysis that expresses a coherent strategic approach across a wide range of topics central to national security. While chapters 2–7 began life as monographs that were published to stand alone, they can serve as well, I believe better, when they are presented together. Also, I have welcomed the opportunity to revisit every argument, often in excruciating detail, to interrogate my reasoning of only a year or two ago. I hope that readers will agree with me that it is a worthwhile effort to reproduce, update, and assemble coherently this body of substantial analyses.

I am very grateful to Lt. Gen. Paul Van Riper, USMC (Ret.), for agreeing to write the foreword. He speaks for common sense from an extensive personal experience of war and preparation for war. I am indeed honored to have this book graced by his words. Paul is an outstanding American soldier whose opinions command universal respect.

Finally, I wish to thank both my excellent computer/manuscript preparation person Barbara Watts, who performed her now customary magic, and my ever-suffering family. I tell Valerie and TJ that I write books for their well-being, but I suspect that they believe I just have a bad habit.

Colin S. Gray
Wokingham, UK
April 2008

1

PORTRAIT OF AN ERA

Whatever we do we are sure to be wrong.
—General Sir Neil Macready, 1920[1]

Small-scale failures can be produced very rapidly, but large-scale failures can only be produced if time and resources are devoted to them.
—Isabel V. Hull, 2005[2]

INTRODUCTION: SNAFU

This book is about control. It analyzes our attempts to control a rival or enemy, as well as our efforts to control ourselves. Decisions to seek control lie in the realm of policy, while its design and execution are in the zone of strategy. The great strategic thinker, Carl von Clausewitz, and the finest theorist of the last hundred years, Rear Adm. J. C. Wylie, USN, gave pride of place to control as the capstone concept in their respective theories. Clausewitz states that "[w]ar is thus an act of force to compel our enemy to do our will,"[3] or in other words, our instrumental goal in war is to secure control over the enemy. Wylie advances the same proposition: "The aim of war is some measure of control over the enemy."[4] This book discusses national security dilemmas that flow either from loss of such control, or from reasonable anxiety that control could well be absent in the future. The vulgar popular term "snafu" fairly characterizes the post-9/11 era. Although the U.S. national security's contemporary condition could be far worse than it appears, the situation nonetheless is deeply unsatisfactory. The United States now has antagonistic relations with the Russian Federation and troubled ones with mainland China, remains deeply mired in conflicts in Afghanistan and Iraq—that are unlikely to have happy endings, despite recent optimism over the latter—and is on the losing side of long-standing diplomatic confrontations with the Democratic People's Republic of North Korea and the Islamic Republic of Iran. These examples cite only the leading U.S. policy and strategy dilemmas. It would be a mistake to surrender to the seductions of "presentism"—the conviction that the future will closely resemble the present—and believe that the current crop of national security dilemmas is either uniquely perilous or exceptionally numerous: it is not. Great powers normally face diverse challenges simultaneously, some of which are without ready solution or even notable alleviation. For this reason, "snafu" suitably describes the contemporary U.S. national security context.

A TRAIN THAT LEFT THE TRACKS?

What has gone wrong for U.S. national security in the twenty-first century? Perhaps one can best answer the question rhetorically with a further question: "What has gone right?" Malign events around the world, especially in the Middle East and Central Asia, indicate that al Qaeda is not yet a spent force, though certainly it has suffered much damage. However, there has been no follow-on spectacular to the Twin Towers atrocity. Many of the less tractable dilemmas for U.S. national security in the twenty-first century either have yet to happen—which is no great claim, given the very early date—or may never occur at all. This book's secondary title, *Challenges and Opportunities*, suggests that the latter tend also to be the former. Although there are impossible missions for national security policy and strategy, all is not doom and gloom. However, the second Bush era has not been a happy time for the nation. Aside from domestic troubles with the economy, especially the growing mountains of public and private debt, leading to the great credit crunch and awesome crisis of financial confidence of September 2008, the global political context for American statecraft has come to be contested, as have the country's choices in national security strategy, defense planning, and military behavior.[5] Is the metaphor in this section's title correct? Did the United States leave the tracks of sound policy? Or, were there no well-engineered tracks to leave? Overall, is it plausible to suggest that what appears to have gone wrong in the 2000s comprises simply an unhealthy combination of statecraft's "normal accidents" multiplied in the severity of their consequences by the injection of a few large errors.[6] Since politics, policy, strategy, and its implementation are human enterprises and subject to error as such, it is not especially insightful or helpful to cite American public mistakes. "Stuff happens," to quote then secretary of defense Donald H. Rumsfeld. However, some of American policymaking's recent damaging errors should have been avoidable. Alas, the policy vehicle driven by policymakers comes only with rearview mirrors. "'It seemed like a good idea at the time' is the epitaph to human actions," writes Bruce Fleming all too persuasively.[7] After the fall of the Third Reich, it was hard to find a Nazi in Germany. Apparently, all the evil deeds of the erstwhile regime had been committed by the führer and his henchmen, or for a more inclusive indictment, by the Schutzstaffel, commonly known as the SS. The ordinary citizens were "good Germans," or so they maintained. Moving to the present, for many Americans the George W. Bush administration has served as their SS alibi. More exclusively still, blame for much of America's national security trouble in the twenty-first century has been conveniently laid at the doorstep of a neo-conservative clique who allegedly hijacked administration policy. This book does not assign blame for the arguable train wreck that is American national security. Suffice it to say, serious mistakes were made, as they always will be, and that some were truly gratuitous, again as ever is so. Since the national security dilemmas addressed in these chapters cover ongoing issues, there would be little point in drawing conclusions susceptible to falsification by future events. Instead this analysis explains the structure of key national security dilemmas and assesses those that are generically enduring, rather than inherently transient.

We cannot replay the second Bush era in search of a better performance and outcome. We should, though, be willing and able to learn what recent events can teach us. Six candidate "lessons" beg for recognition and authority. First, personality, the quality of individual judgment, and personal relations are vital ingredients to policy and strategy. Intellectual, moral, and political pygmies did not abundantly people George W. Bush's administration: quite the contrary. The administration was made up of exceptionally strong personalities hugely experienced and with different agendas attributable in part, of course, to their distinctive responsibilities. Those who have poured scorn on the country's more recent federal executives need to recover a little empathy if they are to comprehend what has occurred in Afghani-, Iraqi-, and Sino-American relations. By way of a usefully bold step, it helps to consider the axiom: "There but for the grace of God go I." Most apparent errors in recent U.S. statecraft stem from domestic cultural traits, universal human frailties, and sheer bad luck. They have not been the product of venality and stupidity. If anything, with reference to possible moral judgment, the Bush administration and the America for which it acted have been punished by the nature of politics for their good intentions.[8] It has been claimed, alas correctly, that "hope is not a course of action."[9] To hope for better things to come is normal. But, if policy and strategy substitute hope for feasibility assessment, disaster is sure to follow. For reasons that seemed sufficient, America's recent leaders suspended their critical intelligence, while their hopes, dreams, and good intentions occupied the driver's seat and accelerated hard into the bandit country of "Dilemmaland."

Second, recent events should have reminded Americans that their proclivity to crusade for democracy, freedom, and open markets needs to be subordinate to the need to craft policy and strategy fit for foreign cultures that do not emphasize these values as heavily.

In the early twenty-first century, the Bush administration chose to transform the challenges it faced from unfriendly regimes in Kabul and Baghdad into a grand opportunity to improve Afghanistan and Iraq by the use of military force and good intentions. To the administration, swift defeat of the "bad guys" then in charge would liberate a populace eager to be freed. Beyond the prompt military act of liberation lay the hazy vision of a revolutionized Arab, perhaps even Islamic, world. This new order would resemble America writ larger. It is difficult to understand how the administration's realists could have allowed themselves to staple serious hopes for such an improbable outcome in Iraq to what was an inherently high-risk foreign policy adventure.[10] In hindsight, the theory of a spark in Baghdad igniting a great benign conflagration in the Middle East and beyond appears absurd. However, it did not seem ridiculous to many key Americans back in the hubristic year, 2002–3.

Third, by 2004 it was quite evident, not least to American soldiers, that the country had slid into the conduct of counterinsurgency (COIN) operations without having troops trained, organized, equipped, and guided by the doctrine "Fit for purpose." Because the U.S. Army did not like COIN, it had not seriously prepared for its possibility. Unfortunately, in the twenty-first century, the more active of America's enemies have practiced irregular, not to say unrestricted, modes of warfare. The U.S. Armed Forces have relearned one of strategic history's oldest lessons—the necessity for flexibility and adaptability.

Fourth, the Bush administration has rediscovered that making and stabilizing a peace is often more difficult than winning a war. Because war is not solely about fighting but also about the peace that follows, detailed, though flexible, planning for the post-war context is vital. Peace stabilization is not achieved miraculously by some hidden hand, nor can it be improvised from scratch in the absence of careful preparation. If America neglects to equip itself so that it may shape its wars' political, inter alia, aftermath, unfriendly elements are certain to fill the vacuum and perform the shaping role instead. If the United States does not punish an errant, roguish regime and then immediately withdraw such expeditionary forces as had been committed on the ground, it will discover that it "owns," and therefore will be held accountable for, local governance.

Fifth, contemporary America is rediscovering the eternal lore of international politics. Former and aspirant greater powers accept and tolerate an adverse balance of power and influence until they have a practicable policy alternative. Neither China nor Russia, nor probably the European Union, are going to join a hegemonic United States as junior partners in global ordering. They are rivals for influence. In the cases of China and Russia, the rivalry already is serious and could spark great-power warfare. Beijing understands that the alternative to being "number one" in the world power stakes, a position the United States firmly occupies at present, is to be "number two" or lower. As Thucydides wrote 2,400 years ago, states fight primarily out of "fear, honor, and interest."[11] Increasingly, all three motives will be actively in play to bedevil Sino-American relations in the twenty-first century. Whereas U.S. military rivalry with China is real—but still mainly to come in the future—that with Russia is far more immediate. What is so dangerous about U.S.-Russian relations is that they have an explicitly military continental focus along, indeed across, a strategic frontier between NATO and Russia that is very much in live contention. Russia's brief spat with Georgia in September 2008 needs to be regarded as a reliable sign of severe dangers to come.

Sixth, the twenty-first century should teach Americans that although it is expedient to conduct a capabilities-led defense transformation, strategy, which is to say intelligent design and direction, tends to fall victim to this approach. When one focuses on what one can do, rather than on why one might want to do it, the outcome tends toward an essentially purpose-light modernization. Given the diversity of potential U.S. military tasks against a wide range of enemies who wage warfare in both regular and irregular modes, there is a good deal to be said in praise of a flexible and adaptable U.S. defense establishment. Certainly the United States cannot prudently decide to be capable of waging only regular or irregular warfare. Nonetheless, even in the absence of a dominant threat, even class of threat, America has an acute need for strategy. As this book argues, time after time, a persisting U.S. strategy deficit translates into lives and billions of dollars wasted, as well as unattained foreign policy goals.[12]

NATIONAL SECURITY DILEMMAS: UNWELCOME GIFTS OR FOOLISH CHOICES?

The question posed in this section's secondary title highlights the principal sources of security angst. Of course, the question presents a false alternative. National security dilemmas are the product of existential challenges and opportunities, as well as errors in policy and strategy. In the latter regard, as just observed, the United States is inclined to suffer from the consequences of the major self-inflicted wound of strategy deficit. Wylie reminds us of the practical meaning of strategy in application. He claims incontestably that strategy is "[a] plan of action designed in order to achieve some end; a purpose together with a system of measures for its accomplishment."[13] While in some respects Americans are the authors of their own insecurity, in larger part they are the fairly innocent victims of recalcitrant realities. When assessed through the conceptual and policy lessons provided by the idea of national security dilemmas, the main subjects addressed in this book reveal an essential unity in structure and consequence. It is a cultural characteristic of pragmatic Americans to examine separable problems in isolation and not as a whole, as a *Gestalt* the Germans would say.[14] In practice, there is virtually no limit to the extent to which national security problems can be subdivided for isolated attention. Despite the military's "jointness" ideology, much talk of integration, and episodic bureaucratic reorganizations always touted under-convincingly as reforms, the U.S. government quintessentially is a medieval patchwork of competing principalities. This overall condition is mirrored faithfully within each semi-sovereign polity with its rival fiefdoms.

It is not much use railing against the difficulties of achieving and maintaining unity of public purpose, because the Founding Fathers, obviously while not anticipating government's appalling growth, succeeded in writing a constitution that balanced power among the state's chief institutions. When we add consideration of the cultural elements to the political and legal structural features, we appreciate how the domestic context of American policy and strategy making is likely to thwart strictly rational behavior. Americans behave as Americans are inclined culturally to behave, in ways shaped by their homegrown agencies and procedures, in response to external stimuli. Americans must approach the foreign-sourced prods to behavior, the principal reasons for U.S. national security dilemmas, as conditions to be endured and survived, not as problems that can be solved. The next few paragraphs explain the nature of the national security dilemmas analyzed in chapters 2–7. In the twenty-first century, the United States has been reminded of the age-old conundrum of defining victory. It waged two agreeably brief and cheap campaigns against roguish state enemies and, of course, won them both handily. However, it then discovered that its missions had not really been accomplished. The victories achieved against enemies fighting in a regular mode counted for little to nothing in the warfare yet to come. Indeed, some of the U.S. military's virtues as a regular fighting machine were shown to be a liability once conflict assumed a largely irregular character. A Global War on Terror (GWOT) was proclaimed grandiloquently after 9/11, a struggle open-ended both in geographical scope and, of belatedly recognized necessity, time. Being a hugely sports-minded nation, America is culturally programmed to think in terms of winning and losing and of episodes of hostilities that have a beginning, middle, and end. For Americans, the notion of a war without a predictable end, moreover one that is unlikely to present clear evidence of success, let alone eventual victory, has been culturally hard to grasp and digest. The dilemma entails the challenge of devising strategies that might succeed against terrorists, especially when strategy is not one's long suit and the enemy in question is not a single targetable foe. Today, the "guys in black hats" are an indistinct, globally networked array of different organizations with different capabilities and motives. The dilemma of knowing how to define and achieve some conclusion to hostilities worth calling decisive victory is as old as history itself and by no means unique to the United States today. Every war presents the questions: "How do we define victory?" and "How do we win?" The character of international security's contemporary context renders this dilemma especially acute.Next, while the modern theory of deterrence was invented and translated into strategic practice for the purpose of controlling and exploiting nuclear danger, the idea and relevant associated behavior have been around forever. There is a central dilemma for the intending deterrer that no theoretical sleight of hand or manipulation of the military balance can resolve. The deterrer needs to know what is likely to deter a particular rival or enemy from taking certain unfriendly actions. The dilemma for the deterrer lies in the much underappreciated fact that he cannot answer his all-important question with complete confidence. An important reason why many states choose to go to war is because they believe that they cannot place sufficient trust in a strategy of deterrence. The problem is that deterrence only succeeds if the potential deterree agrees to cooperate, under duress admittedly—and be deterred. From the 1950s until the present, many American theorists and officials have sincerely believed that deterrence can be guaranteed, assured, and, as the term of art has it, stabilized. Thanks to faith in rational choice theory, these theorists and officials provided the country with what appeared to be a healthy comfort zone of deterrence stability. How did they achieve this? By persuading themselves that deterrence is a science, at the least that rational behavior governs its function, and that its requirements can be determined reliably, if not necessarily, in precise detail.

With respect to nuclear deterrence during the Cold War, the absence of a dreaded explosive conclusion seemed to verify the truth in the dominant Western theory of stable deterrence. However, despite the negative evidence, which suggested to the trusting that nuclear deterrence works reliably, we do not and cannot know why the Cold War ended without a big bang. What some among us do know is that the modern formal theory of deterrence is fatally flawed by the conflation of rationality and reason. A rational enemy, one who carefully and purposefully matches ends with means, need not be reasonable in American estimation in his choice of political ends. Furthermore, deterrence can never be thoroughly reliable, because it is always a human exercise attempted by imperfect people in organizations that reveal particular bureaucratic pathologies. And, need one add, there is the potential for accident as a result of potential sources of "friction" that are ever ready to impede performance.[15]

An existential dilemma for America's national security strategists is the future's strict virtuality and non-existentiality. Because we do not know what the future will bring by way of policy demands for military support, how can we plan in such a condition of ignorance? This is a perpetual dilemma. Even a national security budget as large as the American—currently running in excess of $600 billion a year in total, including supplementals for the warfare in Afghanistan and Iraq—cannot bear every burden that threat analysis suggests it should. A defense planner's challenges are to try to make only modest and correctible mistakes and to hedge prudently, which is to say adaptably, against the worst effects of surprise. Given that strategic surprise is a condition, not a problem, of national security, protection must be provided to negate the dire potential effects of "bad cases." No country, including the United States, can purchase total security. Such an attempt would be foolish and impossible. The U.S. defense community should have learned the old lesson that national security is more than a narrowly military responsibility—it needs to be provided by genuinely "joined up" thinking, organization, planning, and behavior. The necessary "joining up" is achieved by strategy. The information revolution remains inevitable and unstoppable. There is no dilemma for America's defense planners with regard to a fundamental commitment to exploit new information technologies. Most of the technical advances have not been achieved for purposes of national security; they arrived for reasons of their own technological momentum and because they promoted commercial profit. But given that U.S. national security must exploit technical progress in information technologies, the extent of the consequential military dependence remains discretionary. Furthermore, it is not self-evident that the arguable information-led Revolution in Military Affairs (RMA), though radical in its implementation, must have revolutionary strategic consequences. Defense planners and other strategists cannot evade the dilemma of comprehending what should be achievable and, more important, what the anticipated progress should mean. To cite a few historical cases of this enduring national security dilemma, strategists have had to make sense of: gunpowder weapons; food canning; steam engines and the railroad; steam propulsion for ships; the electric telegraph; heavier-than-air flight; the atomic, then the hydrogen, bomb; and the computer. While an ongoing, if contestable, information-led RMA yields a dilemma in understanding, as well as deep uncertainties over preferable modes of exploitation, it was ever thus with major technological change.

This text proceeds to consider the American military establishment's dilemma of how to adapt to a contemporary reality dominated by the needs of irregular warfare, when its culture and favorite capabilities are profoundly regular. Properly gripped and applied as strategies, the general theory of strategy provides essential education.[16] For particular cases, however, such as Somalia, Iraq, or Afghanistan, the strategies selected have to be tailored to local contexts. While needing to be obedient to the general lore of strategy, this tailoring has to be effected and then applied according to the general theory of strategy for warfare against irregular enemies. Thus there are no fewer than three relevant levels of strategy: the general, the general for irregular (or for regular) warfare, and the tailored for a particular episode.

Is war so awful that one should never choose to begin it? Or, are there circumstances so impregnated with menace for national security that moral, if not necessarily legal, qualms and reservations must be set aside? The twenty-first-century debate over the advantages and disadvantages of a "preemptive" strategy has addressed yet another recurring dilemma in statecraft and strategy. With weapons of mass destruction (WMD) proliferating among states and, predictably before long, among non-state political entities, traditional niceties about when and how one should and should not go to war appear ever less relevant. When dozens of countries possess short- and medium-range ballistic and cruise missiles, the first strike option has to enjoy wide strategic appeal. If one waits to be certain that an enemy is attacking, it may be too late to achieve anything other than revenge by retaliation. In some countries' cases, a decision to strike second would risk not striking at all. For the United States, as for every other political community, no dilemma should attend a decision to preempt. This statement is valid only if preemption is defined restrictively, which is to say properly, as military action taken in response to an attack that either is already underway or on certain knowledge is imminent. The dilemma for national security arises when one believes that a menace is growing and can be arrested by the application of force on our initiative now or soon, but has yet to reveal itself unambiguously. This is the category of action known as preventive war. It amounts to a decision to shoot, or refrain from shooting, on suspicion. Since the United States has stated repeatedly on the highest authority that because of 9/11 and other lesser atrocities it considers itself "a nation at war," the issue of preemption cannot apply in counterterrorism, at least strictly.[17] Preventive war is as controversial as preemptive war is not. The strategic attractions of going to war today, to prevent the emergence of an intolerable threat in the future, has to be balanced against multidimensional costs. Before the anticipated, feared event, demonstrating that a war cannot be avoided is impossible. Yet again, this is a dilemma residing in the existential column for statecraft; it is not a passing issue only for the twenty-first century.

CONCLUSION

A major problem for the United States today is that it is a hegemonic power without a hegemony, an imperial state bereft of empire and imperium. As the sole superpower, the United States is hegemon by default, insofar as contemporary world politics can accommodate the leadership that hegemonic status implies. Practical constraints on American international behavior, especially on its forceful exercise of hegemony, are beneficial for international order and the United States. In this view, to be the sole superpower is to be granted awesome opportunities to do harm. The harm will be inadvertent, the product of operation of the law of unintended consequences, but harm it will be. America's critics point with undisguised satisfaction to the undeniable, continuing mess in Iraq as proof of U.S. incompetence. At worst, the condition of Iraq is taken as evidence of U.S. greed and ambition.

A central dilemma for American policymakers is that while they appear to have, or until recently certainly thought they had, the power to reshape local, regional, and even global security environments, they have lacked the needed authority. As the sole superpower extant, the United States is the only candidate for global sheriff. How active should the United States be on the world stage? The primary, and often only, ordering power must protect those who need protection from regional predators, even when those predators have a cover story for their predatory behavior. It is well to remember that disorder need not refer, 1990s-style, simply to lack of governance. Instead it may be created by entirely purposeful state aggression for gain. Russia and Georgia in 2008 are a classic example. Do U.S. national interests oblige U.S. national security policy to be so concerned about disorder in distant places that intervention is always a possibility? How powerful is the United States? More to the point, how selective should the country be in drawing on its huge, but still limited, assets in efforts to influence, let alone reshape, the international security environment? These are not questions of episodic transitory significance.

2

DEFINING AND ACHIEVING DECISIVE VICTORY

The political object—the original motive for the war—will thus determine both the military objective to be reached and the amount of effort it requires.
—Carl von Clausewitz, 1832[1]

President Bush marked five years since ordering the invasion of Iraq by proclaiming yesterday that American troops had achieved "undeniable" success and predicted that the war "will end in victory."
—*London Times*, March 20, 2008

In war there can be no substitute for victory.
—General of the Army Douglas MacArthur, 1951[2]

The idea of victory, let alone decisive victory, was very much out of style during the Cold War. The theory and practice of limited war in the nuclear age was more concerned with minimizing the risks of escalation to nuclear holocaust than to winning the conflict. That changed dramatically with the end of the Cold War—indeed so much so that from 1991 to late 2001, from Kuwait City to Kabul, with the painful exception of Somalia, the United States knew only victory in its exercise of military power. I challenge the view that war lacks the power of decision. Instead I argue that even when it does not conclude with clear success for one side, war still has the power of decision. This chapter discusses the idea of decisive victory with reference to different levels of analysis—the operational, strategic, and political. It suggests that the concept of decisive victory needs to be supplemented by two ancillary concepts: strategic success and strategic advantage.

The discussion explores the means and methods most conducive to achievement of decisive victory. It explains that objectively
better armies tend to win (war may be the realm of chance, but the
dice are loaded in favor of the militarily competent); that there is
no magic formula that guarantees victory (not even today's information-led American style in warfare, which tends to equate precise firepower with war); that technology is not a panacea, the
answer to all military and strategy difficulties; that the complexity
of war and strategy allows for innovative, even asymmetrical, exercises in substitution as belligerents strive to emphasize strength and
conceal weakness; and that it is essential to know one's enemies,
especially if one requires them to cooperate in a deterrent or coercive relationship. They need to be persuaded in order to be deterred
or more actively coerced.

The concept of decisive victory is meaningful and important.
Also, different enemies in different wars require the application of
different military means and methods. One size in military style
cannot fit all cases. One should not think of decisive victory in
terms of a simple either/or. Strategic success or advantage may serve
the goals of policy well enough. Among Western states at least,
the United States today is unique because of its interest in the
idea of, and capability for, decisive military victory. America's
European allies do not discern any serious military issues as clouds
on their peaceful horizons. With its prevalence of irregular combat, the strategic history of the twenty-first-century has alerted
strategic thinkers as well as politicians and soldiers to the fact
that the concept of victory is not simple. In practice its opacity
is only matched by its importance. Unless one can define victory for a particular conflict, it is always going to be difficult to
know when or whether one has achieved it. Victory is not necessarily an objectively self-evident end-state to hostilities. When
fighting irregular enemies, one is likely to exercise considerable
discretion in policy choice over the identity of an outcome plausibly describable as sufficiently victorious. In some wars there
will be no doubt when victory is secured, yet in others, hostilities

will be run down and the ending will not mean the enemy's utter destruction or surrender. The range of possible conditions of war termination is a military and political complication of great significance.

INTRODUCTION: VICTORY MATTERS

The justification for this analysis was explained succinctly in French scholar Raymond Aron's brilliant essay written forty years ago. "Strategic thought draws its inspiration each century, or rather at each moment of history, from the problems which events themselves pose."[3] After September 11, 2001, it was open season for many to grapple with the deceptively simple concept of victory. Journalists and other commentators penned analyses with titles such as, "The Elusive Character of Victory" and "What Victory Means."[4] If "victory" unadorned is hard to corral intellectually, what sense can one make of "decisive victory"? Is the concept a theoretical artifact from a past age or does it retain vitality, particularly for a hegemonic United States? I argue that decisive victory is a meaningful and important concept.

Before we plunge into the muddy waters of definition, it may be useful to recall a little history. Although since 1991 victory has come back into fashion as a proper outcome to be expected of the use of American arms, for the duration of the Cold War it was most emphatically one of yesterday's ideas. For reason of the sensible fear of an escalation to nuclear holocaust, the only kind of conflict that the United States dared wage in the nuclear era was limited war. Writing at the tail end of the golden decade of modern American strategic thought (1955–66), Thomas C. Schelling argued that

> "victory" inadequately expresses what a nation wants from its military forces. Mostly it wants, in these times, the influence that resides in latent force. It wants the bargaining power that comes from its capacity to hurt, not just the direct consequence of successful military action. Even total victory over an enemy provides at best an opportunity for unopposed violence against

the enemy population. How to use that opportunity in the national interest, or in some wider interest, can be just as important as the achievement of victory itself; but traditional military science does not tell us how to use that capacity for inflicting pain.[5]

To strategic sophisticates in the 1950s and 1960s, victory was an atavistic notion. American theorists found the Clausewitz they wanted to find in *On War*, which is to say the post-1827 Clausewitz who revised some of his manuscript to balance his discussion of "absolute war" with consideration of "real war" for limited aims.[6] But on the first page of Book One, chapter 1, Clausewitz insists that "[w]ar is thus an act of force to compel our enemy to do our will."[7] He rams the point home by writing that "to impose our will on the enemy is its object [the object of the act of force that is war]. To secure that object we must render the enemy powerless; and that, in theory, is the true aim of warfare." Of course, in the sentences quoted, the great man is explaining and exploring the nature of war, not offering advice on its conduct. However, Clausewitz's admirably terse summary of the nature and object of war did not find much intellectual favor in Cold War America. After all, in a nuclear age would it not be dangerous in the extreme, even perilously irresponsible, to attempt "to compel our enemy to do our will"? Has not Michael Quinlan written persuasively that "a nuclear state is a state that no one can afford to make desperate."[8] To extend Quinlan's point, a nuclear state is a state against which no one can afford to press for victory.

Readers can imagine the shock and horror that resulted when in 1980 I published (with Keith B. Payne) an article on nuclear strategy bearing the exciting title, "Victory Is Possible."[9] A year earlier I had expounded at length on "Nuclear Strategy: The Case for a Theory of Victory," but the pages of *International Security*, or my dense prose, probably were too forbidding to attract non-academics.[10] While I was trying to inject strategic reasoning into debate over what passed for nuclear strategy, others made a similar complaint about extra-nuclear matters. For example, in a characteristically robust essay of 1982 vintage titled "On the Meaning of Victory," Edward N. Luttwak recorded a similar view:

> The West has become comfortably habituated to defeat. Victory is viewed with great suspicion, if not outright hostility. After all, if the right-thinking are to achieve their great aim of abolishing war they must first persuade us that victory is futile or, better still actually harmful.[11]

In the mid-1980s, and in good part to help offset the belligerent façade of earlier talk of the United States "prevailing" in a nuclear war,[12] Secretary of Defense Caspar Weinberger repeated the sensible-sounding mantra that "a nuclear war cannot be won and must never be fought."[13] He had earlier aired the following thought, which, despite its honesty and commonsense logic, had not played too well politically: "You show me a secretary of defense who's planning not to prevail, and I'll show you a secretary of defense who ought to be impeached."[14]Luttwak's 1982 judgment that "[v]ictory is viewed with great suspicion, if not outright hostility" was to be vindicated on the grand scale a decade later when most Western scholars of the subject insisted that although the Union of Soviet Socialist Republics (USSR) had lost the Cold War, the United States had not won it.[15] Victory had fallen so out of strategic fashion that the decade 1991–2001 should have caused traumatic shock among professional pessimists. With the exception of the Somalia debacle of 1993–94, the United States enjoyed a decade of unalloyed strategic success. From the Gulf War in 1991, through Bosnia in 1995, to Kosovo in 1999, concluding (after a fashion) with Afghanistan in 2001–2, the United States achieved plausible facsimiles of victory.[16] Given the absence of such evidence from 1945 to 1991, this was a notable reversal of strategic fortune. Had the U.S. military machine improved dramatically, or had its political masters at last been able to select cooperatively inept foes? Wherever the truth may lie, and I suspect it reposes in a combination of professional military excellence, technological superiority, and enemy incompetence, victory became a habit, indeed was the expectation—at least until the early

Afghan and Iraqi triumphs metamorphosed into protracted nightmares.

The decade that opened with victory over the USSR and a campaign in the Gulf, memorialized immodestly and contentiously for the U.S. Army by Maj. Gen. Robert Scales in a book titled *Certain Victory* and by Norman Friedman for the U.S. Navy in *Desert Victory*, closed with what appeared to be another brilliant success, this time in Central Asia.[17] For the fourth time in ten years, American airpower delivered military success, especially in Afghanistan (2001–2) with a style of joint warfare as novel as it was appealing to a country still nervous of committing large forces on the ground in distant climes. America's friends and foes noticed a certain military triumphalism about U.S. policy. The George W. Bush administration, in particular, was the beneficiary and the victim of military success. It benefited from a recently acquired reputation for military effectiveness, suitably enough for the contemporary hegemon. As with Rome in its early imperial centuries, America is unchallengeable in regular warfare. Also, as with Rome, however, a mixture of unusual incompetence, bad luck, and a smart enemy can produce the occasional imperial disaster. Happily, Mogadishu in 1993 was only a minor embarrassment compared with Publius Quintilius Varus's loss of three legions in the Teutoberger Wald in 9 AD. Those whom the gods destroy they first make overweeningly proud. The miscalled "war against terror,"[18] a conceptual and linguistic atrocity, was launched by an understandably vengeful American hegemon that fell victim to the heightened self-esteem that followed its recent military successes. America succumbed to the fallacy that in practice the age-old lore of strategy can be short-circuited by high technology.

Osama bin Laden and the elements he represents have shown up contemporary, leading American attitudes for what they are, as examples of what historians have called "victory disease."[19] Germany in 1940–41 and Japan in 1942 indulged in the illusion of their own invincibility, an illusion fed by the misreading of the causes of their early successes. A new American way of war was demonstrated in Afghanistan, one that married long-range airpower, space systems, special operations forces (SOF), and local allies. But success in Afghanistan informed us more about the hapless Taliban in 2001 as a then-regular style of belligerent, than it did about a high road to victory in future conflicts. Ironically, America's strategic education was to continue, unhappily, in Afghanistan itself. Preeminent in the most advanced ways of regular warfare, a hegemonic United States has twice been thwarted strategically: first after 1945 by its own nuclear discovery,[20] and today by asymmetrical enemies. The long nuclear stand-off challenged traditional understanding of victory as goal and descriptor. The new stand-off between the asymmetrical strategic cultures of hegemonic superpower and transnational terrorism similarly throws into question the meaning of victory and the sense in its pursuit as a goal of high policy, grand strategy, and operational art.

THE BIG IDEAS

In *The Age of Battles*, Russell F. Weigley argues the case against war as an instrument of decision. Quoting Walter Millis, Weigley writes, "If 'its power of decision' was the 'one virtue' that war had ever had, then war never had any virtue."[21] Referring to the strategic history of 1631 to 1815, "the age of battles" from Breitenfeld to Waterloo, Weigley offers an uncompromising condemnation. "If wars remained incapable of producing decisions at costs proportionate to their objects even then, consequently the whole history of war must be regarded as a history of almost unbroken futility. So it has been."[22] Or has it? I will argue that Weigley is fundamentally wrong. There may well be wars that the belligerents wished they had never entered, but that is another matter entirely. The issue pertains strictly to the alleged futility of war.

Historically, well-educated persons, certainly those raised in some variant of the "realist" school of statecraft, know that one cannot wage war to end all war, or to establish a permanent universal empire and imperium.[23] Hitler's prediction of a "Thousand-Year Reich"

fell 988 years short of the declared ambition. War is a social institution, employed and abused by flawed people for a host of reasons,
praiseworthy and otherwise. Any rapid foray into the morass of scholarship on the subject of the origins or causes of war impresses with
the near unmanageable richness of variety in the subject.[24] Though
war is certainly the most extreme among Man's behaviors, its history does not suggest that it is beyond the pale of reason, or useful
instrumental achievement, in high policy. For all his high reputation as a military historian, Weigley was monumentally in error—
for then, for today, and for the future—when he took issue with
Clausewitz in the following way:

> War in the age of battles was not an effective extension of policy
> by other means. With partial exceptions encompassing those pow-
> ers that like Great Britain could sometimes remain on war's pe-
> riphery and even fight it by proxy, war was not the extension of
> policy but the bankruptcy of policy.[25]

- World War I (the numeral was employed, pessimisti-
  cally, as early as 1920) *decided* that Wilhelmine Germany
  would not secure European hegemony. Germany did not
  go to war in pursuit of such a dominant position, but
  that would have been the consequence had the Central
  Powers been victorious. The conflict also *decided* definitively the fate of the Austro-Hungarian, Russian, and
  Ottoman empires.

- World War II *decided* that the Nazi adventure in racial
  hegemony would come to an abrupt and well-merited
  conclusion after only twelve and a quarter years.

- The Korean War, 1950–53, *decided* that forcible unification of the peninsula was not attainable at bearable
  cost to either side. It would not be correct to claim that
  three years of war—actually one year of quite intensive
  combat followed by two years of negotiating and fighting—simply confirmed the *status quo ante*. Prior to June

1950, North and South, and some among their backers abroad, could reasonably aspire to redraw the local frontier along more favored lines.

- The American war in Vietnam, 1965–73, *decided* that South Vietnam would not sustain itself as an independent polity. Although America's dependent ally eventually lost the military decision, the protracted U.S. involvement had the effect of *deciding* that communist victory would be delayed by ten years. Though ultimately unavailing for South Vietnam, that delay may have played a vitally positive role in the stability and development of most of Southeast Asia. The history of this region subsequent to 1975 suggests that, for once in its experience, the United States lost the war but won the peace.

- The Cold War, the virtual World War III, *decided* that the great communist experiment would self-destruct, admittedly with no little assistance from American statecraft. The outcome of this conflict also *decided*, by geopolitical elimination, that the United States would enjoy globally hegemonic status for a while.

- The war over Kosovo in 1999 *decided* whose writ would run in that Yugoslavian province. In its consequences, it decided also that Slobodan Milosevic and his appalling family would cease to reign and rule in Belgrade.

- The war against the Taliban and al Qaeda in Afghanistan in 2001 *decided* that that country (speaking loosely) would have a change in central government and probably a return to traditional warlordism, Afghan-style.

These examples of wars demonstrating a significant power of decision are not exceptions that prove a rule to the contrary affirming war's futility. Naturally, war is apt to be futile, or more likely worse, for the losing side. But the thesis that war either has lost its presumed erstwhile power of decision or, following Weigley, never had such power is thus easily shown to be absurd. I would not sound the trumpet so loudly on this point were it not so central to the Big Ideas that must organize this analysis. After all, I contend: (a) that wars can be won or lost (admittedly on a sliding scale of completeness, perhaps "decisiveness"); and (b) that wars' outcomes typically have a significant power of decision, if not always the decision intended, even by the victors. War remains not merely useful, but essential as a tool of statecraft for which there are no close substitutes. Further, it matters greatly who wins and who loses.

Our North Star is the composite idea(s) of decisive victory. Thus far, we have chosen to treat this very Big Idea relatively low key, requiring of it only that it recognize the likelihood of wars having winners and losers and the strong probability that the outcomes of wars will, through strategic and political effect, achieve noteworthy decisions. So much should not be in contention among reasonable people. However, there will always be a rump of idealists who resist the idea that war is an instrument of policy.

The Big Idea of decisive victory can be disaggregated where it is interpreted as referring to the ability of success and failure in war to enable issues to be decided (e.g., who runs Kosovo, Iraq, Europe, or the world). This approach to the concept should not be unduly controversial. More challenging, perhaps, is a strict focus on the adjectival modifier. What do we think we know, not about the ability of victory to facilitate important, say geopolitical or ideological, decisions, but rather about the decisive quality of victory? Braving the risks of damage by some critic wielding Occam's razor, we can argue, following Clausewitz in his belated recognition of real war, that at least three related concepts require recognition. These are not fine academic distinctions, but real-world conditions apt to be encountered, indeed enforced, by American superpower. The concepts are decisive victory, which is our organizing Big Idea, strategic success, and strategic advantage. They make up a three-level view of relative military achievement.

The concept of decisive victory can be employed with operational, strategic, or political meaning. At the operational level, decisive victory should refer to a victory that decides the outcome to a campaign, though not necessarily to the war as a whole. Decisive victory in one theater might be offset by decisive defeat in another. In contrast, a strategically decisive victory should be one that decides who wins the war militarily. Such a victory or defeat need not be effected by a single climactic clash of arms, but may rather be the outcome of an attritional struggle. Some historians have commented that there were no decisive battles in the two world wars, of necessity both were conducted as long wearing-out processes.[26] This view probably is an exaggeration, though it points correctly to the great resilience and depth of modern societies' mobilizable assets. It is tempting to identify the German defeats on the Marne in 1914, in the Battle of Britain in 1940, in front of Moscow in 1941, at Stalingrad in 1942, and at Kursk in 1943, at least as candidates for "decisive" status. Each of the defeats arguably had far-reaching influence over subsequent military events. Politically understood, a decisive victory should be a favorable postwar settlement. Since soldiers do not make policy, whether or not a military victory leads to a political victory is above their pay grade. However, the responsibility of the soldier is to advise policymakers as to what military power can and cannot accomplish. Also, it is important that war should not be conducted in such a manner as to subvert the prospects for lasting peace.[27]

Victory and defeat register on a sliding scale of possibilities. However, a simple axis would miss much of the relevant action. Note Michael Howard's plausible opinion that "a war, fought for whatever reason, that does not aim at a solution which takes into account the fears, the interests and, not least, the honor of the defeated peoples is unlikely to decide anything for very long."[28] Decisive victory probably is sought, because one intends to shape the postwar environment for a tolerably good fit with one's idea of an international order that provides a lasting condition of peace with security. Though, one must admit, decisive victory also may be sought for the dominant—though not sole—reasons of national honor and revenge, as in the U.S. case after September 11, 2001.

Although the concept of decisive victory in principle is distinguishable from strategic success or strategic advantage, in practice either of the two more modest achievements can be positively decisive. One may not, indeed generally will not, need to "render the enemy powerless" in order "to impose our will on the enemy."[29] After all, and notwithstanding its declamatory appeal, a decisive victory strictly refers to favorable military achievement that forwards the war's "political object." Strategic success or strategic advantage, accomplishments that can fall notably short of the forcible disarmament of the enemy, may qualify for the label of decisive victory. Most belligerents seek an end to hostilities well before the point where their power to resist is totally dismantled.[30] The idea of decisive victory, therefore, should not be equated necessarily with the enemy's military obliteration. All that it requires is a sufficiency of military success to enable achievement of whatever it is that policy identifies as the war's political object.

MILITARY DECISION FOR POLITICAL DECISION

Given that most wars are not waged for unlimited goals, whether or not military victory proves politically decisive will be an issue for the (somewhat) defeated party to resolve. North Vietnam and its southern proxies were defeated militarily in 1968 and again in 1972, but in neither case did Hanoi choose to regard the defeat as decisive.[31] In 1940–41, Germany won a succession of military victories that appeared to many people at the time, not least to the Germans themselves, to be strategically, rather than merely operationally, decisive. North Vietnam in 1968 and 1972, Britain in 1940 (in continental warfare), and the USSR in 1941, all declined to define military failure as political defeat. British and Soviet geography and U.S. policy guidance for rules of engagement allowed the losing side to rally, recover, and return to fight again. These historical examples illustrate a structural problem for the strategist.

Strategy is, or should be, a purpose-built bridge linking military power to political goals.[32] If the political aim in war is a total one—the enemy's overthrow—then it has to be matched with a military effort intended to achieve the complete defeat of the foe. One may argue about the respective merits of some apparently contrasting styles in warfare, alternative modes designed to succeed by maneuver, attrition, or paralysis. However, one will be in the relatively straightforward realm of military science. One will not be attempting to coerce a reluctant and culturally alien enemy, rather one will be applying such military means as should prove necessary to remove his power of resistance. As I have argued, an important reason why strategy is difficult to do well is its very nature as a bridge between military power and policy.[33]

Defense officials have to pretend that they know "how much is enough," so that they may justify the precise numbers proposed in budget requests. Except for the Pentagon's leading luminaries of the McNamara years, however, American strategic thinkers have rarely been confused over the fact that estimates of "sufficiency" owe more to art than to science.[34] The carefully calculated drawdown curves of the endless vulnerability analyses that accompanied the competition in strategic arms were exercises in a spurious precision. Those U.S. Cold War strategic calculations were as fundamentally flawed as was Graf von Schlieffen's great final memorandum of December 1905, which neglected logistics, numbers, the French railroads, and Russian recovery from its contemporary low ebb. At least one scholar has claimed that the so-called Schlieffen Plan was in fact nothing more than a speculative think piece, a *Denkschrift*.[35] Unsurprisingly other scholars disagree.

It is an inconvenient fact that "[w]ar is nothing but a duel on a larger scale." Clausewitz explains that

> [i]f you want to overcome your enemy you must match your effort against his power of resistance, which can be expressed as the product of two inseparable factors, *viz. The total means at his disposal and the strength of his will* [emphasis added]. The extent of the means at his disposal is a matter—though not exclusively—

of figures, and should be measurable. But the strength of his will is much less easy to determine and can only be gauged approximately by the strength of the motive animating it.[36]

The meaning, perhaps meanings, ascribed to decisive victory assumes huge significance in the light of Clausewitz's words. By way of an elementary, two-dimensional cut at the issue, the quest for decisive victory may focus either on the apparent completeness of the military success—meaning that a victory is militarily decisive—or on the quality and quantity of political decision that that military victory enables. Although the former must underpin the latter, a focus on victory as contrasted with the political fruits of victory desired by policy translates all too readily into the situation where war obeys the dictates of its own nature. "That while the purpose of war is to serve a political end, the nature of war is to serve itself."[37] Military victory becomes an end in itself and policy is shaped to assist the war effort, rather than vice versa. Because strategy is a highly imprecise art, albeit one subject to material discipline (e.g., with reference to logistics), calculation of what is required to deliver victory is never going to be better than guesswork. In principle, at least, a proximate goal of military overthrow does usefully simplify matters in that the overriding problems should be strictly military in character. However, if policy specifies limited political goals, which logically should require the application only of some military power, the full challenge to strategy is easily comprehended. Defined as the use that is made of force and the threat of force for the ends of policy, strategy is not always a bridge in good repair. Although strategy is neither the use of force nor the ends of policy, somehow, mysteriously, it is the employment of the former to satisfy the latter. The more modest the policy goals, and hence the more measured the military action, presumably the greater the policy discretion an enemy enjoys.

There is not much about war that is literally, as opposed to merely rhetorically, calculable. Logistical problems are, indeed have to be, calculable, though there was a Napoleonic and later German approach to the challenge of supply and movement that transcended boldness and ventured far into irresponsibility.[38] Even the sums of the logisticians, however, are subject to practical refutation by the action of "friction" of many kinds—for example, bad weather, mechanical breakdown, unexpectedly unfriendly terrain, including insect life and disease[39]—and particularly to harassing efforts by the enemy. It is surprising how many otherwise impressive examples of military planning betray a pervasive failure to recognize that war is, alas, a duel.

The strategist must cope with an uncertain exchange rate between military effort and political effect. If the overthrow of the enemy is not the policy goal, the strength and durability under pressure of his political will must be a crucial determinant of whether or not a decisive victory is achievable at tolerable cost. One may be denied practicable attainment of decisive victory if the enemy chooses not to be coerced into acquiescence by the amount and kinds of military pressure that one allows oneself to apply,[40] which was the U.S. problem in Vietnam. The logic of decisive victory in limited war is generically identical to the logic of success in deterrence. In both cases, the enemy has to choose to cooperate, albeit under duress, if one is to claim a variant of decisive success. He can choose to fight on, calculating that the political decision we seek will be judged by us not to be worth the human, economic, and political costs of protracted, possibly more intense, combat.

Before we turn to consider how decisive victory is likely to be achieved, three broad propositions need stating. First, decisive victory, and indecisive victory even more so, is hard to translate into desired political effect. Clausewitz rightly insists that "at the highest level the art of war turns into policy—but a policy conducted by fighting battles rather than by sending diplomatic notes."[41] He does not dwell, however, on the difficulties that beset the strategist on the bridge between military power and policy. The concept of strategic effect usefully conflates the consequences of the threat and use of force of all kinds, so that we have a common currency for the value of all forms of military power.[42] What we do not have, to repeat the point, is an agreed exchange rate between apparent military success and political reward. "War" comes in many shapes and forms, has many different contexts, and is subject to diverse cultural influences. As Victor Davis Hanson explains, culturally asymmetrical belligerents are apt to disagree on the definition, feasibility, and consequences of so-called decisive victory.[43] British historian Jeremy Black registers the same argument when he claims that "war and success in war are cultural constructs."[44]Second, decisive victory is best viewed as a range of possibilities rather than as a stark alternative to the failure to achieve such a success. The enemy can be understood to have continuing powers of resistance on a sliding scale. Decisive victories come in many guises and sometimes mislead the winner. While Cannae (216 BC) was the tactically decisive victory straight from the textbook, its strategic and political consequences were trivial.[45] Roman civic militarism produced fresh legions. Hannibal could win battles; indeed, for a long period, he and his veteran mercenaries and barbarian allies were tactically invincible, but he lacked a convincing theory of victory in war as a whole. Centuries later, Jutland in May 1916 was a material, though not tactical or operational, victory for Germany's High Seas Fleet. It was a strategically decisive victory for the Royal Navy, however, because its very occurrence and course demonstrated to the German government that its fleet could not challenge Britain in the North Sea for the right to use the seas. At the time, Jutland was widely interpreted in Britain as a significant defeat. In May–June 1940, the Wehrmacht won what most contemporary commentators regarded as a decisive victory over France and Britain. The victory decided that France, if not its empire, was definitively *hors de combat* and influenced German self-evaluation and the Fuhrer's self-confidence as warlord. Germany would now judge itself militarily unbeatable in continental warfare. The planning for Operation Barbarossa, and then the (mis)conduct of that campaign from June to December 1941, showed the effect of the "decisive" victory of May–June 1940.[46]

Third, even if we affirm that decisive victory is our doctrine and military intention, in practice a number of degrees of decisiveness are likely to prove acceptable. That may not be the case if we are waging a total war keyed to the goal of enforced regime change—though even then a change in regime leadership effected by internal convulsion might tempt us to moderate our strategic goals. One size does not fit all when conceptualizing about "war," or estimating the likely military effectiveness of particular capabilities. Again to quote Jeremy Black, war has "multiple contexts."[47] A style in warfare that worked well against the Taliban in 2001, though less well against al Qaeda, has not been applicable in other contexts. Wars against Saddam Hussein's Iraq, in post-Ba'athist Iraq, against the Taliban in Afghanistan, and against terrorism worldwide are all notably distinctive enterprises. If regime change in Baghdad and Kabul counts as decisive victory—to ignore the political difficulties that followed such successes—what would constitute decisive victory over al Qaeda, let alone terrorism in general? Decisive victory is possible against some terrorists, but it is not of a kind for which Americans can practice in the California desert. Doctrine for, and metrics of, success have to be tailored to the character of warfare extant.

ACHIEVING DECISIVE VICTORY

I reject as nonsense the view expressed on September 3, 1939, by British socialist and pacifist George Lansbury that "in the end force has not settled, and cannot and will not settle anything."[48] For example, it is not entirely true to argue that a bad idea can only be defeated by a better idea. There are times, as from 1939 to 1945, when a particularly bad idea—Hitler's vision of a racially pure Thousand Year Reich—needs to be shot. Nazi ideology could not be tamed by any peaceful process of political or cultural engagement.[49] If occasionally force must be used, it is important to win—and to know how to win. War may be the realm of chance, as Clausewitz advises,[50] but victory or defeat are not recorded historically as random outcomes. There is an approach to war that maximizes the decisive victory's prospect of achievement, whatever outcome one decides is sufficiently decisive and adequately victorious. This approach is best expressed in five propositions; these can be phrased negatively as caveats or positively as advice for action.

1. *Better armies tend to win.* Contrary to Clausewitz's simile, war is not like a game of cards.[51] One's military "hand" is not dealt at random. While friction and surprise by enemy moves certainly can render campaign plans obsolete, armies that understand the nature of war expect to have to adapt in real time to circumstances that could not have been forecast with precision long in advance. There are objectively superior and inferior armies. Armies that recruit with high standards, train hard, and realistically, keep tight discipline, equip intelligently, enjoy some measure of luck, and study their variety of opponents each on its own terms will tend to win. Because surprise is always possible, even probable, an important quality in a better army is its ability to find a way to win, to adjust its capability and style to unexpected events when plans are rendered obsolete by the independent will of the foe. The principal value of military planning is not to produce ahead of time the perfect plan, but rather to train planners who can adjust and adapt to changing circumstances as they emerge. While the achievement of decisive victory at bearable cost can rarely be guaranteed, one can raise and maintain an army objectively superior in relevant quality and quantity. A good army is not one developed for its specialized excellence in a particular scenario, unless, that is, a country's defense planners are sufficiently fortunate to have a truly dominant threat in their present and confidently anticipated future. Because war is not solitaire, even an excellent army may fail to deliver victory. Policy may ask too much of its military instrument, or it may hamstring military operations with damaging political constraints. The German Army in both world wars set the contemporary standard for tactical and operational excellence. But, in war after war, German policy asked its soldiers to accomplish the impossible. To try to win against a coalition greatly superior in resources, in circumstances where dazzling operational maneuver is infeasible, means

condemnation to a lengthy struggle. When war is protracted, military skills tend to equalize among belligerents, and numbers count for more and more as the smaller side is less and less able to absorb casualties. In both world wars the Germans trained their enemies. By the summer and fall of 1918 the British Army was at least as competent tactically as the much weakened Germans, especially with respect to the scientific use of artillery;[52] while by 1944–45 the Soviet Army arguably had taken operational art to a level not attained even by the Wehrmacht at its peak.[53]

2. *No magic formula for victory.* War is so serious, complex, and uncertain an undertaking that its practitioners and interpreters are always on the alert for a "key" to victory, a philosopher's stone for military art. Antoine Henri de Jomini's popularity with nineteenth-century soldiers is entirely understandable. Instead of the opaque Clausewitzian strictures about friction and chance, Jomini offered a delightful certainty. "Correct theories, founded upon right principles, sustained by actual events of wars, and added to accurate military history, will form a true school of instruction for generals."[54] At the heart of Jomini's system, at least of his reading of Napoleonic practice, was what he called the "one great principle underlying all the operations of war—a principle which must be followed in all good combinations."[55] The principle was the injunction, *inter alia*, to throw superior force at inferior force (at the "decisive point" and at the decisive time). Even if numerically superior overall, the enemy can be defeated in detail and his main line of communication (i.e., retreat) threatened. A problem was that on a good day Napoleon Bonaparte could be inventive. Sometimes he would attempt his signature *manoeuvre sur les derrières*, and sometimes he would not. Napoleon did not have a doctrine, a formula, for victory.

The quest for the key to certain victory can lead strategists astray. Alfred von Schlieffen's approach was founded on meticulous timetabling and a faith in the outflanking turning movement sufficient to allow him confident projections of the operational endgame.[56] This German School of General Staff thinking was not interested in political context, logistical problems, or the need to improvise and adapt should the enemy not behave as expected. In his brilliant essay on Jomini, John Shy noted that modern American strategic analysis had located the certainty it craved.[57] In the spirit of Jomini's "one great principle," American arms controllers had found universal strategic truth in a formula for strategic stability. Every strategic weapon system could be analyzed according to whether or not it contributed to, or detracted from, stability. Though bereft of political or common sense, this stability theory was revealed truth to many in the 1970s and 1980s. More recently much of the enthusiasm for the concept and attempted practice of an information-led Revolution in Military Affairs (RMA), or military transformation (as the preferred term of art), stemmed from the same yearning for military certainty. The 1991 Gulf War model of decisive action appeared to demonstrate how total victory could be achieved reliably in the future. Events in the succeeding decade did little to shake faith in the ideology of victory through applied technology. Although Somalia in 1993–94 might have prompted more soul searching than occurred, Bosnia in 1995, Kosovo in 1999, Afghanistan in 2001, and the swift defeat of the Iraqi regime in 2003 were interpreted as evidence confirming the soundness of the new American RMA's way of war. Strategic history tries to tell us that wars come in a wide variety of forms and are waged in all manner of terrain. Because all wars are duels, eventually technological formulae, indeed any formula, for decisive victory will fail. The failure will be the result of tactical ineffectiveness in specific circumstances (e.g., in an urban setting), or operational and strategic negation by an enemy who behaves as Edward N. Luttwak predicts in his masterwork on strategy.[58] The paradoxical logic of conflict states that what works today will not work tomorrow, because it worked today. Formulaic military behavior can be deadly when the foe is intelligent and moderately capable.

   3. *Technology is not a panacea.* The attractive proposition that the United States currently enjoys an unassailable military technological lead that has sharply reduced the value of allies and can deliver decisive victory to order is fragile or wrong on all counts.[59]

Technology is only one of strategy's dimensions, and it is by no means the most important. The Fulleresque belief that relative technological prowess is the prime determinant of strategic success has a substantial problem with the historical record in all periods.[60] It is difficult to find clear examples of decisive victories in war achieved because of a superiority in weaponry. One must hasten to add the necessary caveats: either the belligerents were technologically in touch with each other (i.e., not assegais against maxim guns); or, even if they were truly far apart in mastery of war's machines, the materially challenged party sought and found effective asymmetrical offsets. I recognize the circularity in this second caveat, but still the flawed point is too important to neglect.

When a capability appears almost too good to be true, especially when it pertains to an activity as complex and uncertain as war, the odds are that indeed it is too good to be true. If technology gives us an edge, then by all means let us welcome and exploit it. The U.S. military record from 1991 to the present provides convincing evidence of eternal verities of warfare. Most particularly, bombardment, no matter how precise, is not synonymous with war as a whole. History provides a large strike against the belief that a transformed U.S. military, the global leader by a country mile in providing information-led and well-networked forces, has unlocked the secret of decisive victory. Technology is only one among the many dimensions of strategy and war. American optimists should be sobered by the datum that weapons do not win wars, not excluding superior weapons. Further, even when new technology is weaponized in appropriate quantity, employed by intelligently tailored organizations, and is directed by suitable doctrine, it is still no guarantor of decisive victory. The reasons lie in the complexity of war, the difficulties that can thwart strategy, the options probably open to the enemy, and that hardy perennial, friction. There can always be a first time for an important development, but it is difficult to identify a war, let alone a succession of wars, wherein exploitation of a technological lead plainly was chiefly responsible for victory.

What matters most is how weapons are used and by whom. The United States is riding for a most painful fall if it is firmly confident that its military hegemony is secured for decades to come by its current military technological lead. The U.S. Army should recall the limited, albeit still real, utility of its bright and shiny new air mobility concept in Vietnam in the 1960s,[61] while the Soviet Army did not fare much better in Afghanistan in the 1980s.[62] The tools of war are important, but typically they are not the drivers to victory. Alfred Thayer Mahan provided a wise comment for the ages when he wrote:

> Historically, good men with poor ships are better than poor men with good ships; over and over again the French Revolution taught this lesson, which our own age, with its rage for the last new thing in material improvement, has largely dropped out of memory.[63]

Technophiles should ponder also the culturalist thesis advanced by Victor Davis Hanson, though they can take some comfort from his argument.

> [T]he Western way of war is grounded not merely in technological supremacy but in an entire array of political, social and cultural institutions that are responsible for military advantages well beyond the possession of sophisticated weapons.[64]

A defense community that rests its faith for future success in a lasting technological lead will be vulnerable on several counts. Specifically, technological prowess will tend to equalize among polities over time, especially when, as today, much of the frontier technology is civilian in origin and can be acquired off the shelf;[65] asymmetrical doctrines and practices of war can reduce the value of high technology weaponry quite sharply; the political and geographical contexts of conflicts may demand manpower-intensive operations rather than precise firepower; a technological hubris could encourage an army to lose its adaptability to different conditions; and bombardment can become an end in itself with the conduct of war reduced to the application of firepower.

4. *The complexity of strategy and war is the mother of invention.* Strategy and war have to be approached holistically; all of their dimensions, or elements, are always in play, though not always of equal importance. Nominally, indeed measurably, much weaker armies than the American will search for areas of strength to offset their near certain deficiencies in technology.[66] Americans should be well-schooled by their own national history to be alert to the power of smart substitution among war's elements. How and why did the colonists defeat the might of the British Empire?[67] Why did Confederate resistance last as long as it did and come close to validating by battle the assertion of secession and independence?

There are problems with the concept of asymmetry in strategic affairs; essentially it is an empty box bereft of identifiable meaning.[68] However, for all its opacity, the concept does usefully alert people to the potential strategic rewards that can accrue to those who dare to be different. For the time being, the U.S. armed forces, rather like the Roman legions in their lengthy heyday, have taken regular symmetrical ways in war out of the active plans of potential enemies. Only seriously psychologically disturbed, martyr-bound enemy leaders are going to tempt American military power with the inviting prospect of "certain victory." Because strategic effectiveness is the product of behavior across all of strategy's dimensions, America's enemies will strive to find and exploit areas of relative strength for the leveling, or better, of the playing field.

In their pursuit of decisive victory, the U.S. armed forces will be opposed not only by inept bad guys picked by central casting to play the role of helpless victims of American military excellence. In addition to the rag, tag, and bobtail of fairly regular, and some irregular, forces who presented themselves for defeat and who played a vitally cooperative role in what became known somewhat prematurely in 2001–2 as "the Afghan model" of future warfare, the United States will confront smart enemies who understand and can exploit agents from the full range of grand strategy.[69]

The complexity of strategy, the fact that strategic effectiveness is the conflated consequence of behavior and attributes on many dimensions, can work to America's advantage as well as disadvantage. Asymmetrical conflict is a game that two can play.

5. *Know your enemies.* Respect for the enemy and his way in warfare has not been strongly characteristic of the American military experience. For example, Robert M. Utley's studies of the U.S. Army in the Indian Wars show a military establishment that made few concessions to the practical needs of the conduct of war against irregular foes.[70] In the twentieth century, the U.S. Army entered both world wars overconfident in its ability to teach Germans and Japanese (in World War II) the errors of their ways. More recently, initially at least, the enemy in Korea was not highly rated, while in Vietnam the possibility that the North Vietnamese Army and its southern proxies might prove a worthy foe was not taken as seriously as it should have been.[71] Somalia in 1993–94 is another obvious and painful example of this phenomenon. Probably the only historical example of the U.S. Army showing an undue measure of respect for its enemy was in the Eastern theater during the Civil War.[72]

Good armies are flexible and adaptable to a wide variety of combat conditions. Before World War I, the British Army was notably short on general doctrine beyond what could be gleaned from the Field Service Regulations, because as a force with literally global duties, it had to be able to move and fight in all kinds of terrain against vastly different, generally irregular, enemies.[73] The Romans and the Byzantines faced the same problem.[74] The British Army had to be competitive in mountain warfare with tribesmen on India's north-west frontier, while also capable of waging a mobile campaign (largely as mounted infantry) against Boer commandos on the high veldt of Southern Africa.[75] For their part, the Roman legions of the first and second centuries AD proved adept at waging guerrilla warfare, a form of combat socially, logistically, and culturally impracticable for their German enemies.[76]

Sun Tzu advises as follows:

Thus it is said that one who knows the enemy and knows himself will not be endangered in a hundred engagements. One who does not know the enemy but knows himself will sometimes be victorious, sometimes meet with defeat. One who knows neither the enemy nor himself will invariably be defeated in every engagement.[77]

Just as tactics are easier to perform satisfactorily than is strategy, so the material instruments of war, though essential, have a way of deflecting attention from the vital human element.[78] For a leading example, consider the challenge to a deterrence policy. Frequent reference may be found in official, popular, and even scholarly literature to "the deterrent." Deterrence, which by definition is a relational variable, is equated with the military machines procured for its intended achievement. Decisive victory for deterrence, however, can be secured only with the admittedly coerced cooperation of the targeted deterree. The path to decisive victory through successful deterrence is likely to lead less through bulking-up an arsenal and rather more through detailed understanding of the intended deterree, so that menaces are precisely aimed at values revered by the enemy. Deterrence will always be an uncertain and unreliable behavior that can fail for reasons beyond the control of rational defense planners.[79] Nonetheless, taking the enemy seriously as a unique political and strategic cultural entity must enhance the prospects for achieving decisive success. A succession of easy victories, such as the United States achieved from 1991 to 2001, from Kuwait City to Kabul—with the exception of Somalia—encourage a misleading technological triumphalism. Being sensibly conservative and prudent when offered novelty (transformation and the like), military establishments seek and apply the lessons gleaned from recent conflicts. The somewhat autistic tendency understandable in the defense thinking of a superpower is pregnant with peril. The issue can be simplified as a complex question: "Did Iraq/Serbia/the Taliban lose the war, or did we win it with a new model of warfare?" It is, I believe, a fact that the United States could not have lost the 1991 Gulf War, the war over Kosovo, the war against the Taliban regime in Afghanistan, or the war to unseat Saddam Hussein. The winning was not always elegant, and the consequences of decisive success often left much to be desired politically, but the prospects for victory in regular warfare were as certain as they could be for the realm of chance that is war.

Any formula for military success invites potential enemies to emulate, evade, and offset. Future foes more competent than those encountered in the conflicts just cited will not perform the role of largely passive victims for the American way in war on the "Afghan model," or according to any other falsely identified template. Also, churlish though it can seem to mention it, the victories recorded after 1991 were achieved despite serious errors of omission and commission that may have proved costly against more worthy opposition. The 1991 Gulf War was poorly conducted operationally, with far too much of the regime's Republican Guard being permitted to escape. In 1999 the air campaign against Serbia over Kosovo was a mixture of strategic irrelevance, operational misconception, and tactical failure. The success in Afghanistan in 2001 should not be allowed to obscure the fact that joint and combined military operations fell woefully short of reasonable expectations.[80] Aside from the elusiveness of Osama bin Laden, U.S. and allied forces permitted far too many al Qaeda fighters with heavy equipment to escape from Kandahar.

The point is not the trivial and ungenerous one that mistakes are made in war. Rather, the purpose of the discussion is to remind Americans that for a decade they flexed military muscle in exceptionally permissive strategic contexts. Because outcomes reasonably describable at the time as decisively successful were achieved in 1991, 1995, 1999, 2001, and even 2003, courtesy of an airpower-led "transforming" U.S. military, it did not follow that future conflicts necessarily would follow the same pattern. The complex "wars after the war" in both Afghanistan and Iraq in the twenty-first century have demonstrated the adaptability of America's foes.

CONCLUSION

As a military objective, decisive victory is not controversial. Whether or not the decision sought needs to be conclusive, if not necessarily quite of a Carthaginian character (*Carthago delenda est*), is a matter initially for policy to decide and then for political-military dialogue as events unfold. The quest for decisive success in the twenty-first century will carry more and more the risk of yielding only a painful Pyrrhic victory, as some of America's enemies prudently equip themselves with weapons of mass destruction. Desperate dictators, recognizing that they stand helplessly on the brink of personal and regime oblivion, may prove to be beyond deterrence or compellence, should the United States give them the choice. The commonsense strategic logic of the U.S. commitment to homeland missile defense, as well as to mobile theater missile defense, should require no advocacy here.

This exploration of decisive victory's meaning and achievement yields four claims that merit elevation as concluding thoughts. First, decisive victory is both possible and important, though it is never guaranteed, not even by military-technological excellence. The assertion that war never solves anything, that it is inherently indecisive, is simply wrong. All of history reveals the decision power of the threat or use of force. In a moral sense it may be preferable to talk rather than fight, but the West is unduly inclined to talk when it should be fighting. Bosnian Serbs, Serbs in Kosovo, and al Qaeda were all enemies who should have been addressed militarily long before they actually were.

Second, one size cannot fit all in the deterrence or conduct of war. If the United States were to find in the decades ahead that once again it faced a clearly dominant threat from a great power,[81] probably China or, less plausibly, China and Russia in close alliance, it might need to improvise in real time. From the Gulf to Iraq, via the Balkans and Afghanistan, U.S. military power was granted the initiative as well as time to correct for early errors, at least where such correction was feasible. Styles in war lack universal applicability. Blitzkrieg worked well enough in restricted terrain against French and British armies that committed disastrous operational errors.[82] It worked less well in Russian terrain against an enemy who declined to acknowledge decisive defeat.[83] If the American way of war becomes formulaic, albeit technologically impressive, it invites smart enemies to wage the kind of conflict wherein U.S. strengths would be at a heavy discount. Any belief that U.S. military power, somewhat transformed by the exploitation of information systems, can plan to fight almost without regard to enemy preferences and abilities, should be hastily buried.

Third, decisive victory, though a meaningful concept, is not a clear-cut alternative to defeat, or even to indecisive victory. Both decision and victory register on scales that allow for more and for less. If the ideal type of military encounter that should yield a decisive outcome was the brief but bloody clash of arms between the citizen hoplites of the Greek city states,[84] then the war on which the United States today claims it is embarked is at the opposite end of the spectrum of potential for decision. In words attributed to Mao Tse-tung: "There is in guerrilla warfare no such thing as a decisive battle."[85] Decisive victory needs to be supplemented with the less imperial notions of strategic advantage and strategic success. It is characteristically American to believe that wars should be unmistakably militarily winnable and to be intolerant of apparently indecisive operations.[86] As much as the U.S. defense community had to come to terms with the unique constraints imposed by the emergence in the 1950s of a strategic context of mutual nuclear deterrence, so today it must cope with the frustrating realities of the struggle, arguably the "war," against transnational terrorist organizations. While America's information-led RMA certainly has utility in the war against terrorists particularly for surveillance and targeting, it is not going to deliver strategic success. Should success be achieved, and there are grounds for optimism, technology will be only a contributory factor, not the decisive one.

Fourth, and finally, the fact of continuing U.S. interest in the concept of decisive victory is politically and culturally revealing. It is difficult to imagine this topic arousing any interest whatsoever in any NATO member other than the United States. The comfortable assumption of a coalition context for all military issues renders the concept of decisive victory a throwback to less happy times for

Europeans, despite the character of NATO, which is still a collective defense organization. Until very recently, America's European friends and allies inhabited a universe that posed no serious military questions. It is true that Kosovo in 1999 was a NATO undertaking, but that episode and the post-Yugoslavian story of the 1990s showed how far NATO-Europe had traveled down the road to military impotence. Little about the contemporary NATO performance in Afghanistan encourages high confidence in the Alliance's future potency in matters that do not bear directly on security in and for Europe. The Georgian crisis of 2008 reminded Europeans that military strategic problems could return to their continent, and indeed may never really have departed.

There is a time and sometimes a place for insistence on decisive victory. Snake-bitten by two world wars "at home," Europeans are less than intrigued by means and methods to achieve such military success. When Americans encounter honest but culturally alien European disinterest in the capability to achieve decisive victory, they are naturally inclined to suspect allied motives. Meanwhile, they breathe a sigh of relief that their preferred way in war does not require the complication of much non-American assistance (local allies are another matter). The United States increasingly finds itself strictly in a league of its own, wherein it listens to little but the echo of its own domestic debate about the use of force. America is an insular culture.

3

MAINTAINING EFFECTIVE DETERRENCE[1]

Regardless of the "strategic balance," when the challenger is not dispassionate, well-informed, or reasonable, as frequently has been the case in historical experience, deterrence cannot be assumed to function predictably. It cannot be "ensured" under any circumstances, and manipulating the force balance may be of trivial significance.
—Keith B. Payne, 2001[2]

Deterrence has fallen on hard times. From being the proudest intellectual achievement of the U.S. defense community in the Cold War and as policy, strategy, and doctrine, deterrence today looks much like yesterday's solution to yesterday's dominant problem. Times have changed, and each strategic context promotes the popularity of ideas that seem best suited to help cope with the challenges of the period. Although the George W. Bush administration did not formally retire deterrence as concept or policy, observers would not doubt that in the global war the administration declared against terrorism in 2001, deterrence generally would be left on the bench. Whereas deterrence appeared to be resoundingly successful through forty-plus years of Cold War, its utility in the very different conditions of the twenty-first century is highly problematic at best.

The purpose of this analysis is to explore the state of deterrence now, and to see what can and should be saved from the wreckage of what once was the keystone in the arch of American strategic thought, policy, and strategy. The discussion begins by explaining how and why deterrence fell out of fashion. Next, it proceeds to detail the main elements in what fairly can be termed the current crisis of deterrence. Finally, the text outlines practical measures that should maximize the prospects for deterrence, admittedly in truly demanding circumstances.

Two strong beliefs that warrant labeling as assumptions inform the chapter. First, it rests on the conviction that deterrence, though diminished in significance, remains absolutely essential as an element in U.S. grand strategy. Second, it reflects the belief that landpower often must make a vital contribution to such success for deterrence as may be achievable.

Some of the criticisms of deterrence, including those that are valid and indeed replayed here, are apt to be silent on the problems with deterrence's policy and strategy rivals. It is true that deterrence is inherently unreliable. Unfortunately, as Clausewitz reminds us, "war is the realm of chance." One reason why deterrence has to be rescued from its current condition of semiretirement is not so much because it offers great prospects of success, but rather because the leading alternatives suffer from severe limitations of their own. Military prevention and preemption are necessary options as occasional stratagems. However, they cannot possibly serve generally as strategies of choice (see chapter 7). In addition to military uncertainties, the domestic and international political demands on a preemptive strategy are much too onerous. If preemption can be only a minor, if still vital, player, while military prevention must ever be highly controversial, the principal alternative would be a strategy of accommodation. Positive inducements have their place in grand strategy, but there is nothing especially magical about their historical record of success (as experience with North Korea illustrates all too clearly). Though preemption and accommodation have roles to play, if the burdens placed on them are to be kept within sensible bounds, deterrence needs to handle much of the traffic.

The difficulties that can attend a political and strategic necessity to define victory are especially acute when there is a need to know whether a strategy of deterrence has succeeded. Since the United States has permanent call on the potential services of such a strategy, what do we really know about what succeeds with deterrence, and why and how?

INTRODUCTION: STRATEGIC IDEAS AND POLITICAL CONTEXT

As theory, policy, and strategy, deterrence has seen better days. Once the intellectual unchallenged core of Western security and certainly the proudest achievement of the modern American strategic enlightenment, this concept is now under assault from several directions. Scholars have had a long field day subjecting the familiar nostrums of deterrence to elaborate quantitative tests as well as to tests of logic and historical evidence, though for obvious reasons the latter are notoriously difficult to conduct convincingly.[3]After all, episodes of successful deterrence are recorded as blanks in history book pages. Furthermore, deterrence may work most efficaciously when it can rely not on the potency of explicit threats, but rather on the fears of publicly undesignated deterrees who are discouraged from taking action by their anticipation of the threats that adventurous behavior would bring down on their heads. Deterrence can be so internalized by policymakers that it will be at work for security even when it is nowhere visible, at least not in the form either of vulgar threats or even of subtle hints of superpower displeasure.[4] Notwithstanding its manifest general attractions—preeminently the prevention of hostile acts without the actual resort to force—deterrence more and more resembles yesterday's strategic concept for yesterday's strategic context.

Deterrence as an idea is probably as ancient as human society. The proposition that antisocial behavior can be discouraged either by threats of punishment or by a highly plausible capability physically to thwart it is not exactly a novel, if sometimes contentious, insight of recent times.[5] Those times did, however, provide the concept with its lengthy strategic moment of supreme historical glory. Strategic ideas rise and fall in popularity as the small community of strategic theorists responds to the needs of the period. Strategy, including strategic theory, is a distinctly pragmatic concern.[6] The story of the elevation, even coronation, of deterrence, especially of stable deterrence, is familiar and need not be repeated here. Suffice it to say that in the strategic context of the great nuclear-shadowed Cold War, the concepts of deterrence and a strategic stability, resting on the mutuality of such conferred by secure second-strike capabilities, were the master concepts.[7] The nuclear war that must not be fought and could not be won, as the mantra of the day insisted, had to be deterred. That mission appeared eminently feasible. Writing soon after the Cold War's close, Britain's eminent military historian and frequent strategic commentator, Sir Michael Howard, ventured the bold claim that "beyond doubt we effectively deterred the Soviet Union from using military force to achieve its political objectives." He capped that confident if unprovable assertion with the somewhat complacent judgment that "we have become rather expert at deterrence."[8] While he may have been right, he claimed more than he knew for certain. Since there was no Soviet-American war from 1945 to 1991, and I decline to view either Korea or Vietnam truly as proxy conflicts, self-evidently it was the case that whatever may have needed deterring in those years was deterred. More than that one cannot claim with complete confidence. Henry Kissinger has described deterrence's ascendancy in the Cold War with characteristic acuity:

> The nuclear age turned strategy into deterrence, and deterrence into an esoteric intellectual exercise. Since deterrence can only be tested negatively, by events that do not take place, and since it is never possible to demonstrate why something has not occurred, it became especially difficult to assess whether the existing policy was the best possible policy or a just barely effective one. Perhaps deterrence was even unnecessary because it was impossible to prove whether the adversary ever intended to attack in the first place.[9]

The rather abrupt, though mercifully nonviolent, end of the Cold War cast the U.S. defense community conceptually adrift. In the 1990s, the strategic intellectual capital of the previous five decades seemed less and less relevant. Despite brief alarmist speculation about danger from Japan, a speculation that did not long survive the growing evidence of Japan's structural economic problems, and rather more plausible if distant predictions of future conflict with China, a survey of the international horizon revealed little in obvious need of discipline by deterrence.[10] The occasions when deterrence might have been a potent strategy, in the several wars of Yugoslavian succession for example, were structured unhelpfully by the fact that the United States perceived no vital national interests at stake. It did not take murderous ethnic cleansers of several persuasions long to realize that Americans did not really care about the Balkans. The 1990s, the no-name post-Cold War era, saw the Clinton administration indulge in occasional belated, punitive military muscle flexing, but there was no national military strategy, or guiding strategic concept, worthy of the name. As a well-respected historian observed of the period, "'RMA [Revolution in Military Affairs] has replaced TQM [Total Quality Management] as the acronym of choice' among members of the armed forces."[11] Identification of the need to be able to cope near simultaneously with two major theater wars (MTWs) as the standard for postural adequacy was not very imaginative, though with the benefit of hindsight from the vantage point of 2008, the two-war standard was not obviously foolish. Iraq and North Korea were, of course, the most anticipated foes.[12] Somewhat encouraged by the successful demonstration of airpower over Bosnia in 1995 and Kosovo in 1999, the armed forces were not thinking about strategy.[13] Instead they were deeply embroiled in exploiting the information-led RMA. Given that money was tight, or worse—that the RMA story was distinctly debateable; that the forces seemed to be busier than ever deploying to support the country's foreign policy; and that an overarching policy concept to guide strategy was noticeably absent—the 1990s was an unusually difficult decade for the defense planner. This was only to be expected, since it was an immediate postwar period and, logically and historically, also an interwar period. To be blunt, in the 1990s, the U.S. Armed Forces did not know what they were doing or why they were doing it, but they did know that they were busy, while resources of all kinds were in ever-shorter supply.[14]

In 1968, Raymond Aron wrote that "[s]trategic thought draws its inspiration each century, or rather at each moment of history, from the problems which events themselves pose."[15] That wise observation explains the rise and (relative) fall of deterrence theory, more or less in step with the attempt to practice it during the Cold War. Aron's words help explain also why the post–Cold War decade was a period bereft of much strategic thought, innovative or otherwise. Those years did not present the kind of problems to American professionals that inspire strategic thinking. September 11 changed all that and effected a brutally sudden end to the brief post–Cold War era.

Unquestionably, September 11 was a wake-up call to an American superpower that previously had given the appearance of understanding neither its responsibilities for international order nor what might threaten that order with such seriousness as to warrant a U.S. strategic response. Unfortunately, when policymakers went to the strategy store in the immediate wake of September 11, they discovered that the "golden age" of American strategic thought had terminated in the mid-1960s. The shelves were well stocked with dusty variants of the dominant concepts of Cold War vintage, deterrence in particular, but were almost embarrassingly empty of persuasive-sounding concepts for dealing with the shocking new realities of post-modern terrorism. Of course, the strategic theory that should help structure national security policy has been hampered in its potential for organizing understanding by deep uncertainties over the character and future of the international political context. Was September 11 a singular and probably unrepeatable spectacular in a campaign that inevitably would lose drive and political significance as its perpetrators and their supporters suffered attritional damage at the hands of the guardian of the current international order?[16] Or was September 11 the Pearl Harbor for World War III?[17] Is the conduct of war against the forces of global terrorism—a hugely diverse enemy—the defining activity for American national security for the next decade and more? Indeed, is this struggle best understood as a war?[18] With impeccable sagacity, Clausewitz advised that

> [t]he first supreme, the most far-reaching act of judgment that the statesman and commander have to make is to establish by that test [of policy] the kind of war on which they are embarking: neither mistaking it for, nor trying to turn it into, something that is alien to its nature. This is the first of all strategic questions and the most comprehensive.[19]

The conflict with global terrorism, even in its more restricted guise of the well-networked al Qaeda, bears more resemblance to a protracted hunt than it does to what most people understandably call a war. The cutting edge of the counterterrorist effort is intelligence, especially multinational cooperation on intelligence, and muscular police work. All of which is fairly plausible, but it is by no means certain that U.S. national security strategy reduces to chasing terrorists of no fixed abode. Even though terrorists and their backers provide targets for military action, the jury will long be out on just how significant a challenge they pose to American vital interests, including the world order of which the United States is the principal guardian.[20]

This chapter is about deterrence, not primarily about countering terrorism. However, bearing in mind Aron's words, if terrorism is the defining characteristic of the post-September 11 era, we would expect and indeed require the fashion in strategic thought to reflect that fact. Superficially, at least, the extended defense community has responded as expected. From being a marginal pursuit to the mainstream of concern, counterterrorism, especially when linked in a diabolical potential marriage with weapons of mass destruction (WMDs), is the expertise that suddenly is in most demand. In the 1950s and 1960s, almost any work on nuclear deterrence could find a financial sponsor and a publisher, virtually no matter how ordinary the analysis; while in the 1970s, the consumers of wisdom from the strategic cognoscenti seemed to have a boundless appetite for deeply technical studies of strategic arms control. The 1980s were a thin period for American strategic thought, probably because the political context failed to yield a defining problem or two that could serve as a magnet for those who typically ride to the sound of the guns, meaning the strategic challenge of the moment or, less generously, the chink of cash. It should not be forgotten that strategic thought, at least the aspiration to such, is a business as well as a patriotic duty. In the early and mid-1990s RMA was the coming big concept. It happened to be profoundly astrategic, but hardly anyone noticed at the time.[21] The strategic innocence about RMA occasioned scarcely a ripple, because the U.S. government in the 1990s was not really interested in strategic questions. In that decade the outside world did not present America with problems that demanded an immediate strategic response. Certainly the Clinton administration was concerned about WMD proliferation, just as it was genuinely worried about global and homegrown terrorism. Also, it was sincerely troubled by the policy conundrum of how best to deal with a rising China; what was the prudent balance between cooperation and containment?

Overall, though, and in some respects for honorable reasons, in the postwar decade of the 1990s the United States gave every appearance of being more than somewhat lost strategically. Obviously, it wished to do good in the world. Provided the cost in anticipated American casualties would be close to zero, the country eventually could be prevailed upon to provide the intelligence, logistics, and generally, the aerial muscle that only it possessed.[22] Feckless allies and incompetent international organizations made a habit of presiding over, certainly permitting, the eruption of repeated crises in the Balkans marked by a barbarism notable even in that vicious neighborhood. But it was ad hoc, unless a rather vague globalism and a commitment to a "national security strategy of engagement and enlargement" are judged to be serious ideas for the guidance of operational policy and strategy, as contrasted with being simply noble general sentiments.[23] From the end of the Cold War until September 11, 2001, American security policy lacked a theme. This condition did not escape the notice of Henry Kissinger, who, writing shortly prior to September 11, noted censoriously, but accurately, that "[a]t the apogee of its power, the United States finds itself in an ironic position. In the face of perhaps the most profound and widespread upheavals the world has ever seen, it has failed to develop concepts relevant to the emerging realities."[24] Harsh, perhaps, but on balance true. At least it was true beyond serious contention before September 11.

Strategic ideas tend not to be developed—or have the cobwebs knocked off them because there are no new ideas—until official or industrial clients face problems to which those ideas appear to be relevant. In the political context of the 1990s, the great, life-or-death deterrent task lacked even for a convincing half-life, which was the leading reason why the slow-motion START process became a subject of distinctly minor notice. It is hard to sustain much interest in a "strategic balance" that lacks a convincing political context. Residual deterrence duties were acknowledged as a permanent feature of America's somewhat uncertain role in the world, but there was general confidence, outside of academe (and officials typically did not read the scholarly literature that was dissecting deterrence theory), that, to repeat Howard's proud claim, "we have become rather expert at deterrence." And, dare one say it, even if deterrence were to fail in the globalized, post-Cold War world, so what? The stakes would be vastly more modest than had attended the genuinely nightmarish possibilities of the 1950s, 1960s, 1970s, and 1980s.[25] Surely a concept, doctrine, strategy, and policy that either kept us safe, or at least plausibly contributed usefully to that end in seemingly the most stressful contexts, should have no difficulty speaking effectively to the minor league challenges of the brave new globalizing world after the Cold War? If the enemy was a roguish state whose misbehavior in action would come with a return address conveniently supplied for retaliation, then the mainstream

American confidence in deterrence was understandable, even if unwise. The problem was that the new phenomenon (in recent times) of religiously motivated transnational terrorism did not appear to provide rich pickings for that previous North Star for the guidance of security policy, deterrence.[26] This seemed to be true, particularly when it was considered in the light of trends in the ever greater availability of information on WMD.

While the George W. Bush administration did not formally retire deterrence as concept or policy, it left observers in no doubt that deterrence generally would not play a starring role in the global war it had declared against terrorism. The administration's capstone strategy document could hardly have been clearer:

> It has taken almost a decade for us to comprehend the true nature of this new threat. Given the goals of rogue states and terrorists, the United States can no longer solely rely on a reactive posture as we have in the past. The inability to deter a potential attacker, the immediacy of today's threats, and the magnitude of potential harm that could be caused by our adversaries' choice of weapons, do not permit that option. We cannot let our enemies strike first.

The document went on to contrast the effectiveness of deterrence when "we faced [post-Cuba, 1962] a generally status-quo, risk-averse adversary" with the situation today.

> But deterrence based only upon the threat of retaliation is less likely to work against leaders of rogue states more willing to take risks, gambling with the lives of their people, and the wealth of their nations.[27]

One may be excused for reading those words as a thumbnail character sketch of a certain Iraqi. As if the rogue state challenge is not sufficiently severe for the policy and strategy standing of deterrence, the new terrorism is proclaimed to be quite outside its domain. The president announced, uncompromisingly, that "[t]raditional concepts of deterrence will not work against a terrorist enemy whose avowed tactics are wanton destruction and the targeting of innocents; whose so called soldiers seek martyrdom in death and whose most potent protection is statelessness."[28] The principal solution to the new character of threat is advertised as a determination to shoot first in the face of an imminent threat. This well-respected and long-established legal doctrine of justifiable preemption was stated with unparalleled clarity and authority by then secretary of state Elihu Root in 1911. He spoke of "the right of every sovereign state to protect itself by preventing a condition of affairs in which it will be too late to protect itself." In law, in theory, and in the practice of states, preemption is by no means the novelty, let alone the aggressive novelty, claimed by much of the commentary hostile to the president's announcement. For once, fact was less exciting than fiction. Secretary of Defense Donald Rumsfeld explained the preemptive demands of the new political context with a signature eloquent directness: "People are used to a different century. People are used to Pearl Harbor. They are used to being attacked and then responding."[29]

There are, of course, problems with preemption (see chapter 7). Suffice it to say for now that, as policy, doctrine, and operational strategy, preemption needs all the assistance that it can garner from effective deterrence. The danger is that it could be required to bear a burden that must be far beyond its competence, not to mention the political tolerance of the American people and the political acquiescence of what is termed with irony the international community.

Preemption will be useful, even essential, as a very occasional stratagem against rogue polities, and it must be standard practice, whenever feasible, against stateless foes. Nonetheless, it cannot serve as the master strategic idea for this new political context. Its demands of America's political, intelligence, and military resources are too exacting. The case for striving to maintain, or newly achieve, effective deterrence rests nontrivially on the manifest limitations of the alternatives. If preemption is useful, though flawed, what should one make of the other big concept of the era, the one that replaced RMA as the fashionable big idea—

asymmetry? Unfortunately, asymmetry, employed effectively to characterize threats or strategy, is of scant operational value.[30]

To be asymmetrical means to be different. It has no inherent meaning. One cannot study asymmetrical threats or strategy, except in relation to those symmetrical with our expectations. It is a useful and important idea, particularly for the design of policy, strategy, tactics, and force posture, keyed seriously to efforts to deter. But it is only a vital, if obvious, insight; it cannot grow into a guiding concept, let alone a strategic doctrine. Because war is "nothing but a duel on a larger scale," as Clausewitz wrote on his classic text's first page, one must take the enemy seriously and on his own terms.[31] Given that deterrence can only work, when it does, in the minds of enemy leaders, it is their worldview, not ours, that must determine whether or not deterrence succeeds. If the concept of asymmetry encourages a healthy awareness of the differences among security communities and their probable attitudes and preferences, then it is useful.[32] To repeat, however, asymmetry has, can have, no inherent meaning. It is not a candidate for the short list of "big organizing strategic concepts" that might unlock the mysteries of how best we should strive to cope with this strange new century, with its elusive, complex menace of global apocalyptic terrorists. Although deterrence has lost its status as the conceptual centerpiece for the guidance of American strategy, it remains a vital necessity, in part to reduce what otherwise could be a wholly insupportable burden placed by default on the sometimes shaky prospects for preemptive success. However, having written that, I argue it is important to realize that not all is well with regards to deterrence.

DETERRENCE IN CRISIS

It is difficult to argue with a historical record of more than forty years that appears to demonstrate a monumental success for the theory and practice of deterrence. We can never know for certain whether or not deterrence theory and doctrine—ours and theirs (which was rather different)—made the difference between war and peace, was essentially irrelevant, or potentially contributed to the possibility of the war's outbreak. Since World War III did not occur to terminate the Cold War, however, we can be sure that our theory and practice of stable deterrence, which was, after all, the dominant strategic concept of the era, at least was consistent with a protracted condition of nonwar. Plainly it was compatible with "the long peace."[33] The Cold War's inherently ambiguous record of deterrence is of more than mere antiquarian interest. The modern theory in exploitation and elaboration of the concept was forged, elaborated, and applied for forty years. It educated all save the youngest of today's strategic thinkers and defense analysts, and it appears to have provided the ideas that kept Armageddon at bay for all those many years.

When theorists and officials today pass judgment, which typically leans toward the negative, on the contribution that deterrence can make to national security, their dominant template necessarily is the theory, doctrine, and practical approaches familiar from the Cold War. This is unfortunate. The distinctly Jominian school of stable deterrence, which reigned supreme in the United States for several decades, was dangerously unsound and risked impairing a more intelligent approach to influencing reluctant, culturally alien minds.[34] The point urgently in need of wide dissemination and appreciation is that deterrence, notwithstanding its honorable and prominent, if inherently uncertain, Cold War record, is not a fixed, settled, and now long-perfected intellectual product.[35] When commentators and policymakers discuss the notably limited role for deterrence in the much changed political and strategic context of the twenty-first century, do they have an accurate understanding of what they are discussing? My contention is that deterrence is not as well understood as it needs to be. Significant illusions persist about how to promote its success, as well as whether one should be pessimistic over its prospects. Also, as a consequence, the United States risks selling short a concept and strategy that the country direly needs as senior partner to a doctrine of preemption and prevention that, though necessary, is fraught with extraordinary political and military hazards.

What follows are definitions of important concepts, though the analysis thus far has not seemed to need the added clarification.

- *Deterrence* has the negative object of persuading an adversary not to take action that it might otherwise have done. Whether or not the intended deterree decides he is deterred is a decision that remains strictly in his hands. There is an obvious and undeniable sense in which that decision is made in a context of coercion, but still the intended deterree may refuse to allow foreign menaces to control his policy. Deterrence theory has offered many important distinctions, such as: deterrence by defense or by punishment (the former should deter by the threat to defeat the inimical action); general or immediate deterrence (the former refers to a diffuse deterrent effect deriving from one's capabilities and reputation that helps shape the international security environment; the latter to efforts to discourage specific behavior in times of crisis);[36] and extended and central deterrence (the former alludes to endeavors to extend deterrent coverage over friends and allies; the latter to the deterrence of attack on one's homeland).[37]

- *Compellence,* or perhaps coercion or coercive diplomacy, has the positive object of persuading an adversary at a minimum to cease and desist from current misbehavior, and more likely to retreat from positions seized and to surrender assets illicitly seized by force (if the actions in question involve the use of landpower, of course). Compellence/coercion is not the same as defense. A compellent strategy is relevant only after deterrence failed or was not attempted explicitly. It carries the promise to inflict an escalating weight and perhaps character of damage, unless our policy demands for the enemy's retreat are met.[38]

- *Dissuasion* is a current American term, lifted usefully from the French, and it points to the aspiration to "dissuade future military competition."[39] The DoD Annual Report for 2002 was admirably plain in stating the intention of "dissuading future military competition." Secretary Rumsfeld explained that

[t]hrough its strategy and actions, the U.S. has an influence on the nature of future military competitions. U.S. decisions can channel threats in certain directions and complicate military planning for potential adversaries in the future. Well-targeted strategy and policy can therefore help to dissuade other countries from initiating future military competitions.[40]

To the uncertain degree to which dissuasion helps structure respect for, even fear of, American military prowess, policy demand for deterrent effect should be reduced. Those dissuaded from competing with the superstate guardian should not need to be deterred. Dissuasion is a reasonable goal for a policy effect from military primacy, but nonetheless it is likely to disappoint. As so often with the American articulation of strategic ideas, the problem is an unconvincing treatment of the political context. While a dissuasive strategy should serve to discourage military competition from those currently far behind, it would be a mistake to underestimate the intensity of international dissatisfaction with the current American hegemonic role. If history is more arrow-like than cyclical, then Steven Metz and Raymond Millen may speak to our future when they write, "decisive war between major states is rapidly moving towards history's dustbin."[41] However, if history really is more cyclical than arrow-like, we should expect state-centric enemies to attempt to organize resistance to American hegemony and, in particular, to work hard in search of strategic means and methods that might negate much of our dissuasive strength. Of course, they may not succeed. However, we must assume that the political motivation will be strong and persistent. As a final point on this popular notion of dissuasion, it is worth noting its close relation to Patrick Morgan's long familiar concept of general deterrence, introduced earlier. Both dissuasion and general deterrence lack specific addressees, formally at least; they are directed for the attention of "those whom they may concern." Whether or not the dissuasive or general deterrent message is received, understood, believed, and acted on is, of course, an issue that transcends the competence of the would-be dissuader-deterrer. As always with dissuasion and deterrence, the final word lies with the intended deterree.

- *Inducement* is the flip side of the coin from deterrence. Both are strategies for influence, the one with negative sanctions, the other with positive. Much as deterrence should work to reduce the necessity for prevention, let alone preemption, except as a quite extraordinary measure (against state-centric forces, that is; stateless rogues are another matter entirely), so inducement, or bribery, should help diminish the demand for effective deterrence. A state may be beyond deterrence, but not beyond persuasion-by-reward for good behavior. General theory is of little assistance here. As a broad proposition, it is important, indeed vital, to be alert to the potential efficacy of positive sanctions. Whether or not an inducement strategy, or—more likely—a combination of deterrence and inducement, stands a realistic prospect of succeeding in any particular instance is a question that can be answered only with reference to the unique details of the case at hand. Consider the post–Cold War history of U.S. relations with North Korea over the past decade and a half as a record that illustrates the hazards, and potential benefits, of an inducement strategy.[42]

- *Preemption and prevention*, strictly regarded, are alternatives to deterrence. To endorse these concepts in a general way is to claim that one can envisage circumstances wherein confidence could not be placed in the reliability of deterrence. It should be needless to add that the U.S. government, sensibly, embraces these ideas *and deterrence*. Facing off against enemies of many kinds, motivations, and capabilities, the global superpower requires policy, strategy, and forces that are flexible and adaptable. A preemptive strategy, hopefully with a national, active missile-defense backstop, would make sense against a minor state that had only token long-range striking power. If, though, that global superpower were up against a major regional power, perhaps even a returning great power, let alone an aspiring superpower, preemption would probably be a desperate gamble, vastly more dangerous than an admittedly unreliable deterrence. The concept of preemption could hardly be clearer, at least in principle. It means to attack first in the last resort, in the face of truly compelling evidence of imminent threat. When the Bush administration talks of preemption, by and large it means prevention instead. The difference between the concepts is simply that of timing. A preventive attack is intended to strike before an identified menace becomes an imminent threat. Israel's blow against Iraq's nuclear reactor at Osirak in 1981 was plainly preventive, not preemptive, as also was the assault on Iraq in 2003. A doctrine of preventive assault, particularly in the context of the policy and strategy of dissuasion discussed, invites critics of many stripes to charge the United States with being trigger happy. To be fair, a doctrine of prevention, despite its preemptive cover story, must hover close to a willingness to shoot on suspicion. Just how strong that suspicion would need to be is a topic riven with political dangers for the American sheriff of world order.

If we are to maintain effective deterrence, we must frankly recognize the more important misapprehensions and deficiencies in the traditional American approach. My shortlist of discontents with the American "way of deterrence" is by no means identical to the most probable reasons why senior officials in the Bush administration expressed strong reservations about the concept's relevance in an era when transnational terrorism appears to be the defining threat. If the "new terrorism" is not deterrable, a popular as well as an official assumption that has merit, then improving the American way of deterrence is not likely to accomplish much of value. Though I am respectful of that view, I do not share it in its entirety. The proposition that we face undeterrable foes seems at best a half-truth. Moreover, it is a half-truth that, when accepted as revealed wisdom for our time, could discourage us from improving our policy, strategy, and force structure for deterrence.

The problems I shall outline briefly are not so much difficulties with the logic of deterrence. Rather they are troubles self-inflicted by a U.S. defense community that is much in need of revisiting the concept, its requirements, and its prospects. Five broad points capture the contemporary inclination to marginalize deterrence, though not all of these are recognized widely in the terms in which they are presented here.

First, deterrence is inherently unreliable. Although it is conceived and executed as a coercive strategy intended to control unfriendly behavior, it is a control that has to rest on the voluntary consent of the deterree. The control achieved by that consent is vastly inferior in quality to the control secured by (successful) military action that removes from the enemy the power to make the wrong choice. Although this argument is not at all controversial and is fundamental to the very structure of deterrence, it is not as well understood as it should be. American defense discourse abounds with references to "the deterrent." It makes no logical difference whether the deterrent is held to comprise the nuclear-armed "existing triad" (of ICBMs, bombers, and SLBMs) or the "new triad" (non-nuclear and nuclear strike forces, defenses, and supporting infrastructure).[43] Deterrence is a relational variable; it is not, it cannot be, a quality or a quantity immanent in particular forces. The fact that our nuclear forces were referred to for half a century as "the deterrent" was not an unreasonable error to commit, but it was an error. Whether or not U.S. nuclear-armed forces deter is a question that only foreigners can answer (aside from the phenomenon of self-deterrence). I confess to being uneasy with a chapter title that may suggest too confidently that deterrence can be effective, but my disquiet is reduced by the conviction that this is a feasible aspiration. What would not be feasible would be the wish to achieve "reliable deterrence," "certain deterrence," "assured deterrence," or any similar formula that literally contradicts the subject's nature. While it should be possible to identify and purchase armed forces that encourage would-be foes to decide to be deterred, there can be no removing the power of decision from those foreign leaders. The United States cannot purchase a truly reliable deterrent. In common with love and happiness, deterrence is not a benign condition that can be bought directly. A persisting feature of American strategic thought and policy has been to confuse instrument with desired effect. References to the nuclear deterrent, or the conventional deterrent (much in favor today), provide yet more fuel to the long-standing charge that U.S. respect for Clausewitz's theory of war is fatally deficient in appreciation of the primacy of policy and politics.[44]

Second, it is highly probable that the modern theory of (nuclear) deterrence, the proudest accomplishment of the golden decade of U.S. strategic thought (1955–66),[45] was— and remains—vastly more fragile than two generations of American strategic thinkers believed. It is not the case that we devised a highly reliable theory of deterrence for the political context of the Cold War, a theory that is now of much diminished relevance because security conditions have changed so radically. The problem is that our theory of deterrence has always rested on dubious assumptions. I believe that the American theory, doctrine, and strategy of nuclear deterrence was never severely tested during the Cold War, probably not even during the Cuban Missile Crisis of October 1962, a plausible fact given the weakness at the theory's core.

In the 1960s and 1970s, American defense professionals believed that they had cracked what seemed to be the most challenging strategic problems of the age.[46] Deterrence, limited war, and arms control were subjects that attracted a confident literature. That confidence was extended to self-satisfaction over the belief that crisis management had been mastered, probably with escalation and compellence also in the column of intellectual tools of control. Certainly there was smug self-congratulation over the theory, the doctrine, and sometimes the policy, of strategic stability, namely crisis stability and arms race stability. The latter happy state was deemed to be promoted by behavior that would not fuel the action-reaction cycle, or spiral, that was believed to be the motor for arms race dynamics, as each superpower strove to ensure the security of its ability to inflict unacceptable damage on the other, even after suffering a first strike. Developed to meet the Cold War's policy and strategy needs, this whole body of American strategic thought was remarkable for its near silence on the subject of political context. Perhaps the theorists of the day believed that the established, authoritative fact of Soviet-American hostility disposed of the need for much political analysis. The spirit of the theories was distinctly reminiscent of the didactic and positivist writing of that old American favorite, the Baron Antoine Henri de Jomini, as noted earlier. American theorists appeared to argue that deterrence, limited war, arms control, arms race management, strategic stability, with the exception of counterinsurgency, could become practical skills to be applied successfully by those who had the mastered the right principles and techniques. The inspiration for this attitude is clearly visible in Jomini's writings:

> It is true that theories cannot teach men with mathematical precision what they should do in every possible case, but it is also

certain that they will always point out the errors which should be avoided; and this is a highly important consideration, for these rules thus become, in the hands of skilful generals commanding brave troops, means of almost certain success.[47]

Or, for the Parthian shot in his most accessible work in English, Jomini offers the encouraging and reassuring advice that "[c]orrect theories, founded upon right principles, sustained by actual events of wars, and added to accurate military history, will form a true school of instruction for generals."[48] Through most of the Cold War, the U.S. defense community entertained little doubt that it had discovered the correct theory of deterrence and identified the right principles to shape the strategic force posture in the interest of stability. Indeed, Americans were so confident of the merit in their theory of strategic stability through mutual deterrence with secure second-strike forces that considerable effort was expended in the context of the SALT process to educate Soviet officials in this canon lore of the nuclear age. As Michael Desch has observed:

> The development and deployment of absolute weapons by the United States and the Soviet Union led many to anticipate that this technology would encourage both superpowers to behave roughly similarly. Nuclear weapons were so destructive that they made cultural differences largely irrelevant. Instead, the nuclear revolution ushered in general theories of strategic behavior such as deterrence theory, inspired by the assumptions (homogeneous rational actors) and methodology (rational choice) of economics. Such rational-actor theories of strategic behavior dominated Cold War national security studies in the 1950s and early 1960s.[49]

In other words, those rational-actor theories were forged not in just any period, but rather in the decade when modern American strategic theory was born and grew swiftly to maturity. Those were the golden years for creative theorizing, not least on the crucial, central subject of stable deterrence. Unfortunately, the Soviet Union did not appear to share the dominant American view of stable deterrence. Moreover, it came as a quite startling revelation to many

Americans when they began to realize that their strategic enlightenment, of which they felt perhaps justly proud, was not disregarded in Moscow out of ignorance but was understood and rejected. Rather self-flattering American expectations of strategic intellectual convergence in the early 1970s, naturally with Soviet convergence on the American "correct theory" of stable nuclear deterrence, withered and died during that decade. On the evidence of Soviet behavior in force development, it should have been undeniable that one size in the strategic theory of deterrence did not fit all. The issue is and was not the quality of U.S. theory, doctrine, policy, and strategy for deterrence. Strategy is not a game of solitaire. Approaches to deterrence cannot sensibly be selected for their autarkic intellectual merit, their methodological elegance, or their aesthetic appeal. Strategy, and therefore deterrence, is a duel. A theory of deterrence may score a "perfect ten" for elegance and persuasiveness to us. But, if it rests on false assumptions about intended deterrees, the theory will be worse than useless. Thus, even for the structurally simple, bilateral world of the Cold War, there are serious grounds to doubt whether the adversary shared the dominant American theory of deterrence and strategic stability.[50] Plainly, views could diverge even in the context of a history-terminating scale of nuclear menace, and after decades of a mutual fixation of concern and the experience of talking at, if not often with, each other. How much more serious might the problem be when the targets of deterrent messages have not signed a Faustian pact to keep the peace by a mutual nuclear terror, and indeed may have scant comprehension of the logic and expectations most characteristic of our approach to deterrence?

Third, the American theory and attempted practice of deterrence suffers from a potentially fatal confusion of rationality with reasonableness.[51] There is much popular commentary on whether or not particular foreign leaders are or are not rational. The convenient, but alas fallacious, assumption is that rational foes must share our strategic logic, or at least ought to be readily accessible to its unmistakeable contingent menaces. With some trepidation, I will argue that we can discount the phenomenon of truly irrational political leaders. Such people do exist, of course. To be functionally irrational is to be incapable of purposefully connecting means with ends. There will be political leaders in the future, as there have been frequently in the past, who, because of alcohol, drugs, or illness, either temporarily and erratically, or permanently, will not be able to function rationally. However, this unhappy condition, if severe, is apt to be short-lived, since it is acutely dysfunctional for all concerned and is not long sustainable. More often than not, when the Western media worries about what it labels as irrational enemies or behavior, it is really referring to enemies and behavior that are judged unreasonable. The point that requires wider understanding is that to be rational is not necessarily to be reasonable by our standards. The U.S. problem is not, significantly, one of irrational enemies. Rather the problem is one of enemies, whose entirely rational behavior purposefully connects policy instruments (e.g., suicide bombers) with policy objectives that are an affront to our values, including international legal rules and moral standards. The notion of rational behavior is content-neutral. The idea that such behavior must, or should, be responsive to American strategic logic, as expressed in our theory and attempted practice of deterrence, is simply a proposition; it is not a revealed truth. On the contrary, it is fundamentally in error. In a world marked by great cultural and political diversity, globalization notwithstanding, there can be no solid basis for assuming that our generally rational enemies will rationally pursue goals that we find reasonable. Keith Payne has explained this problem better than anyone and has pointed to what, in principle, must be the attempted solution:

> If rationality alone fostered reasonable behavior, then only in the rare cases of manifestly irrational leaderships would we likely be greatly surprised. Assuming challengers to be pragmatic and rational, and therefore reasonable, facilitates prediction of their behavior simply by reference to what we would consider the most reasonable course under their circumstances; the hard work of attempting to understand the opponent's particular beliefs and thought can be avoided. Such an opponent will behave predictably because by definition, it will view the world in familiar terms and will respond to various pushes and pulls in ways that are

understandable and predictable. Contrary and surprising behavior would be senseless, "irrational."[52]

Payne reminds us that in the 1960s the United States conducted a coercive, if frequently interrupted, air campaign—Rolling Thunder—intended to influence minds in Hanoi, even though it knew nothing about the enemy's policymaking process or how he rank-ordered his values.[53] Hoisted on the petard of the recent apparent triumph for crisis management technique over Cuba, Robert McNamara's Pentagon was not discouraged by its abysmal lack of local knowledge of Southeast Asia. That same Pentagon also advertised, perhaps perpetrated, the grisly metrics of death and damage that it bloodlessly termed assured destruction. Over Vietnam and in conflict with the Soviet Union, the United States acted on the basis of the thoroughly unsound assumption that the adversary could be deterred or compelled fairly reliably, because Americans would pose threats, or inflict pain, that must influence the minds of rational people in predictable ways. In short, the U.S. defense community had invented a Rational Strategic Person who should behave as American strategic theory predicted, which is to say, by definition rationally and as a matter of optimistic assumption, reasonably.[54]

Fourth, because, inconveniently, "[w]ar is nothing but a duel on a larger scale," so success with deterrence must result from a contest of wills and values.[55] Today, it is commonplace for deterrence to be dismissed or marginalized on the apparently plausible grounds that the more ferocious and probably culturally mysterious of our new enemies are allegedly undeterrable. The combination of religious fanaticism, with extra-terrestrial rewards for martyrs and an absence of accessible physical assets for us to threaten, is held to render deterrence largely irrelevant as an effective answer to the new terrorism. A similar conclusion often is reached with regard to the so-called rogue polities who appear to be America's new state-centric foes. The argument is that our new statist enemies are ill understood in Washington. They may be moved to what we would judge irrational behavior by commitment to a hierarchy of values that precludes policymaking on the basis of consequentialist reasoning. If that line of thought is deemed underwhelming, it can be supplemented by the suspicion that there are several reasons why deterrence will not work well enough for the containment of rogue states. We may suspect that the leaders of those unhappy lands either will not believe contingent American threats, or may be in such dire domestic political straits that they dare not comply. To advance the argument yet further, take note of the cautionary point that there may be polities, with particular reference to their acquisition of WMD and the means of delivery, that we judge too dangerous simply to deter, even should we believe deterrence feasible. During the Cold War, preventive or preemptive action against the Soviet Union soon ceased to be a live policy option, on practical grounds for certain.[56] But America's new roguish state enemies, in this period of hiatus between eras of great power struggle, bear no resemblance to the unlamented USSR of yore. We may choose to argue that deterrence would not only be exceptionally unreliable as the point of our policy spear vis-à-vis many rogue states, but also that a strategy of military prevention, not preemption, would be the prudent policy choice.

Fifth, for the magical realm of rational choice by Strategic Persons obedient to a universal consequentialist logic, deterrence will seem a potent strategy.[57] The fifth of my broad points indicating the major reasons for deterrence's loss of popularity is inspired by the timeless wisdom of Carl von Clausewitz and Helmuth von Moltke (the elder). *On War* states that "[e]verything in war is very simple, but the simplest thing is difficult. The difficulties accumulate and end by producing a kind of friction that is inconceivable unless one has experienced war."[58] Clausewitz confides that "[f]riction is the only concept that more or less corresponds to the factors that distinguish real war from war on paper."[59] He argues that "[f]riction, as we choose to call it, is the force that makes the apparently easy so difficult."[60] Unfortunately, friction "is a force that theory can never quite define."[61] Although discipline, training, and actual experience of war are the best counterweights to the friction that can impede tactical military behavior, when we elevate our concern to policy, strategy, and operations, they can no longer be of much assistance. In 1871 Field Marshal Helmuth Graf von Moltke, Prussia's chief of the general staff, wrote that "no plan of operations extends with certainty beyond the first encounter with the enemy's main strength. Only the layman sees in the course of a campaign a consistent execution of a preconceived and highly detailed original concept pursued consistently to the end."[62] If we regard an intended deterrence nexus as a phase in the duel that can become actual war and if we allow Moltke's words to advise us, we might coin the maxim that "no strategic theory survives intact attempts to apply it in the real world." In the pristine world of strategic ideas, as presented in a small library of rigorous texts, the myriad reasons why deterrence may fail are rarely accorded much more than a passing nod. It is easy to be critical of theorists who neglect to grant friction its full dimensional due, but one must admit that it is next to impossible to operationalize the concept.[63] After all, even its original author conceded that it is a "force that theory can never quite define." This fifth broad point means simply that in the real world of deterrence as policy and strategy, many things can go wrong, and even the superiority of ideas and the excellence of the military instrument may not suffice to neutralize friction's grip.[64] It might follow from this logic that military prevention or, if we are desperate, preemption is the prudent path to take, since so much can occur, or fail to occur, which must hinder the prospects for success with deterrence.

CONCLUSION

I have pulled no punches in presenting a shortlist of reasons why the theory and possible practice of deterrence has been marginalized over the past decade and probably can fairly be described today as being in a condition of crisis. To recap, this discussion has pointed out: the inherent unreliability of deterrence; the probable fragility of the theory with which we waged the Cold War; the continuing confusion of rationality with reasonableness; the likelihood that many among our new enemies will not be deterrable; and, finally, that friction lurks to hinder or frustrate our best efforts to deter. Quite deliberately, the analysis thus far has devoted little attention to an effort to provide a more balanced judgment. There are serious difficulties with deterrence as theory, as policy, and in strategy, and they need to be appreciated in full.

Some of the serious problems endemic to a strategy of deterrence happen to be endemic also to deterrence's major rivals. Consider its two principal alternatives: prevention/preemption and reassurance/inducement. At either end of the grand strategy spectrum, both alternatives are undeniably and inherently unreliable. War, as Clausewitz insisted, is "the realm of chance."[65] Even though deterrence may fail, so might military action or attempts to appease and conciliate. While it may be the case that for many years to come the United States will only wage regular wars that it will have difficulty losing, it behooves us to recall Metz and Millen's warning that the age of the stupid enemy is past.[66] They are probably overly pessimistic, but the point is an important one that needs to be taken seriously lest we succumb to a debilitating triumphalism. Moreover, even some of the wars that America wins militarily might be won at a human and political cost that would call into question the meaning of victory (see chapter 2). In addition, since the object of war has to be the attainment of a better condition of peace, the successful conduct of military operations frequently sets the scene for greater difficulties in winning the peace.

To ensure maximum clarity, this conclusion itemizes practical measures likely to enhance American performance with a strategy of deterrence. My purpose here is to answer the question posed implicitly in the title of the chapter: how do we maintain, or achieve, effective deterrence?

General Measures

1. *Do not talk down deterrence.* In some of its more robust language claiming that deterrence is irrelevant to the principal enemies

of today, officials inadvertently and unwisely give the impression that the concept has been abandoned. The official adoption of a preemption strategy logically reinforces the point that little confidence can be placed in deterrence in contemporary conditions. There are several reasons why the official undermining of respect for deterrence is ill advised. First, the United States happens to remain committed to a deterrent strategy, for whatever it can deliver in admittedly difficult circumstances. Also, the main foes may be eminently deterrable states, not elusive terrorists moved by dreams of self-sacrifice. Second, usually the prime victims of an overstated argument are its proponents. U.S. officials stand in danger of over persuading themselves of deterrence's demise. Third, official statements that read like an obituary for deterrence provide evidence for the opinion abroad that the United States is becoming trigger happy and now sees military action as a first, not a last, resort.

2. *Look for deterrable foes.* The inimitable Ralph Peters has drawn a useful distinction between "practical" and "apocalyptic" terrorists.[67] The former are people who have an agenda that might be addressed, if not met, as a result of their criminal deeds. For the latter, in Peters' words, "destruction is an end in itself." He goes on to assert that "[o]ne may be controlled. The other must be killed."[68] However, it risks missing the point that there is much about even apocalyptic terrorism that should be deterrable. To avoid confusing Peters' admirably sharp distinction, al Qaeda—the most potent movement ever committed to apocalyptic goals—has been organized (loosely, for security) and administered by extremely competent and practical people. The facts that many individual members of al Qaeda would welcome martyrdom and that the organization has non-negotiable goals are really beside the point. Al Qaeda cannot be deterred by the prospective death of its troops; the blood of martyrs will attract new recruits. However, the organization itself, in its loose-knit sophisticated network, should be eminently deterrable. While its goals may be apocalyptic, they can only be advanced strategically. Al Qaeda functions strategically and rationally, connecting its hideous means purposefully to its otherworldly

ends. Al Qaeda may be careless of its soldiers' lives, but it protects its key officers. For al Qaeda, death has a purpose. There are several ways in which a strategy of deterrence should be able to help us control this "monster."[69] First, it ought to be deterrable by a growing conviction that it is failing. As the United States and its allies improve their counterterrorist performance, so a sense of futility should discourage both the candidate martyrs and their commanders. It is one thing to die to advance a cause. It is quite another to die in an operation that will both probably fail tactically and serve no obvious strategic, albeit apocalyptic, goal. After a while, the combination of effective counterterrorism and the world's resistance to the impact of martyrdom, including the boredom of overfamiliarity, should be potently deterring. Second, to survive and prosper al Qaeda has to protect its most important members. Were it otherwise, the organization would be out of business in short order. Credible threats to the lives of those people and their ability to function in command can have a deterring effect. Finally, although al Qaeda lacks a central postal address, it has cells in fifty to seventy countries—a distressing piece of intelligence, indeed—and is tolerated, and in some cases assisted, by official bodies for their own distinctly non apocalyptic reasons. Much of al Qaeda's extra-organizational fellow-traveling support structure should be deterrable. What is required on our part, as always, is good intelligence and a willingness to act.

3. *Do not discount general deterrence, or dissuasion.* It is almost a cliché to observe that when deterrence works it is apt to leave a shortage of convincing evidence for the data mills of social scientists. If that is largely the case for instances of immediate deterrence, which is to say crisis-time deterrence, how much more true must it be for the benign functioning of general deterrence, or dissuasion. By general deterrence we mean the effect on behavior and the norms that help shape behavior, of perceptions of U.S. military power, and of the likelihood that it would be employed. Possession of a very powerful military machine, and a solid reputation for being willing to use it, casts a shadow or shines a light—pick your

preferred metaphor—in many corners of the world. That shadow, or light, may have a distinct deterrent effect, even in the absence of explicit American efforts to deter.[70] Regional rogues, ambitious would-be great powers, and perhaps the more prudent terrorists must take into account that they share the planet with a heavily armed superpower with the will to resort to force. The result, quite often, though beyond documentation, will be what is known most accurately as self-deterrence. The United States does not need to issue rafts of deterrence messages, which is not to deny that there will be occasional need for carefully targeted efforts at immediate deterrence. Many of the globe's potential malefactors will judge their potentially profitable misdeeds to be far too risky. Their context is an international order policed by U.S. military power as well as by economic sanctions. By being exceptionally powerful in all dimensions and demonstrating an occasional willingness to intervene militarily, the United States is a factor in the calculations of many rogues, aggressors, adventurers, and patriots. Such folk do not need to receive personalized American messages of discouragement, addressed to them by name, place, and issue. General deterrence, or dissuasion, is at work when a political leader rules out an exciting course of action from serious policy consideration because of the fear that it would trigger an American response. There is probably more successful deterrence "action" of this type than there is in the forms of immediate menaces that appear to succeed in time of crisis. Unfortunately, although common sense, logic, and historical experience all point to the significance of this deterrent phenomenon, it is beyond research.

4. *Develop a more empirical theory of deterrence.* In its immediate form, deterrence is always specific. It is about persuading a particular leader or leaders, at a particular time, not to take particular actions. The details will be all important. A body of non-specific general theory on deterrence is likely to prove not merely unhelpful but positively misleading. It is improbable that broad general precepts from the canon lore of American Cold War deterrence theory could yield useful advice for the guidance of U.S. policy today. What

the United States requires is detailed, culturally empathetic understanding of its new adversaries.[71] That understanding should include a grasp of the psychology of key decision makers, as well as knowledge of how decisions tend to be made. Recall the earlier words of Keith Payne. He said that if we could conveniently assume that "rationality alone fostered reasonable behavior," then we could predict adversary behavior simply by asking ourselves what we would deem to be reasonable were we in their circumstances. If we can predict our enemies' reasoning reliably enough, because of the general authority of our theory of deterrence, "the hard work of attempting to understand the opponent's particular beliefs and thought can be avoided." That the Cold War did not conclude with World War III is not proof that Payne is wrong. It may well be that our strategy of deterrence was not severely tried. There may never have been a moment when the Soviet leadership posed the question: "Are we deterred?"

However, if the United States now aspires to deter the leaders of culturally mysterious and apparently roguish states, the convenient assumption that "one size fits all" with the (American) precepts of deterrence, is likely to fail badly. To improve the prospects for deterrence of polities such as North Korea, Iran, Syria, and the rest, there is no intelligent alternative to undertaking empirical research to understand those whom we strive to influence. It will not suffice either simply to reach for the classics of American strategic thought, or to assume that the posing of a decisive military threat must carry a message that speaks convincingly in all languages. Nonetheless, the general theory of strategy can so educate strategists that they are able to devise the tailored strategies needed in particular cases.[72]

5. *Deterrence should be employed as part of a broad strategy of influence.*[73] Because they do not have history or political science as their root disciplines, many defense analysts are inclined to approach deterrence, or indeed preemption, as it were in a political and historical vacuum. They can find themselves analyzing the possibilities of deterrence in a particular case in what amounts to context-free conditions. What might or might not deter is considered as an

isolated strategic challenge. As a practical matter, deterrence invariably is one strand to a complex political relationship, a relationship that has a history. Furthermore, deterrence cannot be an end in itself; its purpose is to achieve influence over decisions made abroad. Because there are several leading ways in which influence might be secured, it is only sensible to design and execute a strategy of deterrence in company with other approaches. Deterrence should work best when it is backstopped by a credible commitment to preempt, and when it goes hand in hand with a no less credible record of promising, and carrying through on, positive inducements for cooperation. The practical measures required in most instances are those that influence the minds of the adversary's leaders. By and large, and certainly in all except a very late state in a confrontation, the policy challenge is not how to deter, but how to achieve influence: deterrence is only one approach to meeting that challenge.

6. *Take the ideas of others seriously.* To improve performance with deterrence, U.S. officials and theorists would be well advised not to discount the potency of authoritative foreign ideas.[74] As I have indicated already, America's somewhat general theory of strategy, invented to answer the policy and strategic needs of the Cold War, was not eloquent on the subject of possible local variation. The American theories of deterrence, limited war, arms control, and crisis management were assumed to express the objective truth about those subject areas—a truth deemed transcultural. This was nineteenth-century positivism in the modern guise of largely deductive policy science. There could be some difficulty bringing foreigners on board to understand the new American strategy, but the principal task was held to be that of education in the right (American) way of thinking. While there is nothing wrong with being proud of the intellectual guidance for policy that our strategic theorists provide, such pride can lead to a hubris that blinds us to the reality of an international diversity in strategic understanding and preference. For a notably ideological polity, the United States has a defense community perennially inclined to overvalue material metrics. For example, while Soviet analysts tracked what they termed "the

correlation of forces," an inclusive set of measures indeed, their U.S. counterparts studied "the strategic balance." The assessment of that "balance" most typically involved computing the shape of drawdown curves calculated to result from force-on-force strategic nuclear attacks under different conditions of warning. The value of taking a broad and culturally empathetic view of actual and potential foes has not been greatly helped by the neorealist fashion in American international relations scholarship.[75] A core assumption of this austere theory is that all political actors respond in approximately the same ways to similar stimuli. To the rigorous neorealist, one size in strategic theory should fit all cases. However, history and common sense tell us that one size does not fit all and that the beliefs and personalities of local leaders can, and frequently do, serve as the wellspring for their actual behavior. At the very least, authoritative local attitudes and ideas must function as filters that interpret the messages arriving from the culturally alien outside world. So, as a practical measure, the United States would be well advised to study and take seriously the ideas and beliefs of the people it seeks to influence.

7. *Show that terrorism fails.* Like good golfers and tennis players, U.S. strategists should be able to play the percentages as a significant practical measure. The new terrorism contains many undeterrable would-be martyrs, but these foot soldiers for paradise are not usually the decision makers for their movement. What the United States and its functional allies should be able to effect as a practical measure is inoculation of a growing suspicion, leading to a conviction, that the Jihad is futile. Brave people sacrifice their lives for the cause, but what if nothing seems to change in the world? Al Qaeda operates rationally and strategically; it has some terrestrial goals, notwithstanding its apocalyptic ideas. "[T]he support of moderate branches of Islam," as Antulio Echevarria recommends, should level the playing field notably.[76] We can oblige al Qaeda to compete with its own expectations and promises. A patient multinational counterterrorist campaign should show both to practical, as well as to apocalyptic, terrorists, that theirs is a journey doomed

to fail. As Mao Tse-tung wrote, "[t]here is in guerrilla warfare no such thing as a decisive battle."[77] Whether terrorist operations succeed or fail tactically, realization by their perpetrators that such behavior is strategically futile should serve slowly, but inexorably, to reduce enthusiasm and commitment. Few developments have so self-deterring a consequence as the unwelcome recognition that one's efforts are a failure.

8. *Do not encourage the perception that the United States would be easily deterred by WMD.* Unintentionally, though to some extent unavoidably, the United States is raising the political and strategic value of the proliferation of WMD.[78] If the world was in any doubt as to the importance of WMD, U.S. policy, with its strong focus on opposing their proliferation by all means, has resolved the uncertainty. Some observers of the American scene may suspect, even fear, that the acquisition of WMD, especially nuclear weapons, could trigger American preventive military action. But many others will believe that the presence of WMD in a region would have a powerful deterrent effect on the United States. Such a belief is both rational and reasonable. There can be no doubt that American policymakers would think long and hard before they undertook military operations against a nuclear-armed enemy. It may be no exaggeration to say that the United States would undertake such action only if it were absolutely convinced that preventive or preemptive measures would neutralize local nuclear forces entirely. As a practical matter, American officials need to avoid feeding the foreign perception that the most reliable way to ensure nonintervention in regional affairs by the United States is to become a nuclear-weapon state. Some Americans are nervous lest the rhetoric and public policy documents on the subject of WMD inspire excessive, politically damaging anxieties about the prospects of U.S. preventive or preemptive military action. However, those people have more cause for anxiety over the likelihood that the contemporary U.S. fixation on countering WMD proliferation underlines the strategic value of those weapons. The sorry tale of America's dealings with North Korea over the past decade must suggest to many people that

there is much to be said in favor of a modest nuclear-weapon program if one needs to encourage caution on the part of the superpower. Remember the law of unintended consequences. America's sensible and necessary determination to arrest, at least harass and hinder, WMD proliferation can enhance the significance of those much vilified capabilities.

Military Measures

There is no wonder formula that can deliver successful deterrence in all, or even most, circumstances. That said, the better news is that one can identify practical measures, including sensible principles for the guidance of behavior that should maximize the likelihood that America's landpower will help deter what is deterrable.

The guiding question is "what type of military force would best promote deterrence, with particular reference to the role of landpower?" It would make no sense to proceed from preferred force posture to analysis of how that posture might contribute to deterrence. Instead, we must address the question by means of identifying the capabilities it is necessary to develop and sustain in U.S. landpower. Once the missions are well understood, force planning should follow logically. The latter must succeed, not precede, the former.

1. *Force posture must be adaptable and flexible.* Historically, it has been a rarity for defense analysts to predict accurately the character of future war.[79] Similarly, it has probably been unusual for the requirements of effective deterrence to be well identified. One must say "probably," because effective deterrence leaves little trace in the historical record. The U.S. Armed Forces cannot know today to which conflicts they may be committed over the next several decades. As principal guardian of such global order as exists, the American superpower must be largely locked into a reactive policy mode. That political condition might translate into a need to exercise the military operational initiative, but conflicts will happen at times, in places, and over issues not necessarily selected by the U.S. government. An optimist might argue that the United States now enjoys

the luxury of waging only wars of discretion, not compulsion. There is merit in the claim that because U.S. survival, or even vital, interests will rarely be involved in regional quarrels, or even in most potential counterterrorist actions, we should be at liberty to pick and choose when, where, and whether we will fight. Rather than develop a force posture nominally capable of reaching everywhere and accomplishing anything and everything, the United States ought to be able to select its military operations to match its strategic strengths. The United States should have considerable discretion over when, where, and for what reasons it chooses to fight. However, historical experience and a respect for the ability of the course of events to stage surprises, should make us wary of the claim that the United States now inhabits a strategic world wherein its wars will be those strictly of discretion. The U.S. Armed Forces need to be adaptable and flexible, even to cope in wars waged at our discretion. The range of potential conflicts encompasses both traditional interstate hostilities, notwithstanding their currently being largely in remission, as well as what Metz and Millen have described as "protracted, ambiguous, asymmetric, and complex conflicts."[80] Even when the United States elects to enter a conflict from which, strictly, it could stand aside, it does not follow that the terms of engagement can be dictated by American strategy. A smart enemy may find ways to prosecute conflict asymmetrically, grand strategically and not only militarily.

2. *Landpower is essential.* This point is as fundamental, as important, and essentially as impervious to the strategic effect of technological evolution, as it can escape proper understanding. As an enabler of global expeditionary warfare, as well as a source of precise firepower at ever longer ranges, naval power is vital for the effectiveness of joint warfare. Similarly, there is no room for argument over the necessity for air superiority and the influence that aerial bombardment and support, allowed by air superiority, can exercise in combined arms warfare and independently in strategic coercion. However, none of America's recent wars suggests an emerging obsolescence of its landpower, either for deterrence or

warfighting. The two Gulf Wars, even Kosovo and Afghanistan, all had a U.S. landpower story to a greater or lesser extent. Obviously, the mix of forces must vary from case to case. There are several reasons why it is necessary to risk stating what should be blindingly obvious, specifically the continuing importance of landpower. The U.S. defense community has a long-standing love affair with technology. It is inclined to reduce the current process of transformation to the search for more impressive standoff firepower, preferably from altitude. The delivery of firepower for the "servicing of targets" is confused with the whole of war. Some of the claims in the very early twenty-first century for an emerging new American way of war would relegate U.S. landpower to target spotting for the airpower that performs the heavy lifting that supposedly is decisive for victory. The idea of "victory through airpower" is now nearly eighty years old, and although the technology at long last has begun to render the proposition plausible, the sheer complexity of warfare and the variety of wars mean that the quest for decision by bombardment must be a chimera.[81] Whether the focus is on deterrence, warfighting, or—dare one say it—low-level combat in support of peacekeeping operations when the peace is distinctly fragile, there is a unique quality to landpower that cannot be trumped by the technology of aerial bombardment. The heart of the matter has been explained succinctly by a British historian and maritime theorist and by an American rear admiral. Writing in 1911, the British author Julian S. Corbett claimed unarguably that

> [s]ince men live upon the land and not upon the sea, great issues between nations at war have always been decided–except in the rarest cases–either by what your army can do against your enemy's territory and national life, or else by the fear of what the fleet makes it possible for your army to do.[82]

The century of strategic experience and technological advance (with the exception of nuclear possibilities on the larger scale) that has passed since publication of Corbett's most influential work has not dented the essential truth in his claim. The importance of

landpower has never found more eloquent expression than in a brilliant treatise written sixty years after Corbett's work by Rear Adm.
J. C. Wylie. The admiral has a way with words and an enviable
knack of penetrating a subject's core. He argues persuasively that:

> *The ultimate determinant in war is the man on the scene with a
> gun* [emphasis added]. This man is the final power in war. He is
> control. He determines who wins. There are those who would
> dispute this as an absolute, but it is my belief that while other
> means may critically influence war today, after whatever devas-
> tation and destruction may be inflicted on an enemy, if the strat-
> egist is forced to strive for final and ultimate control, he must
> establish, or must present as an inevitable prospect, a man on the
> scene with a gun. This is the soldier.

Wylie proceeds to offer important clarification.

> I do not claim that the soldier actually on the scene is a requisite
> in every case; but I do believe he must be potentially available
> [e.g., Kosovo, 1999: CSG], and clearly seen as potentially avail-
> able, for use as the ultimate arbiter.[83]

3. *No particular military posture is uniquely deterring.* During
the Cold War those of us who worked on strategic nuclear issues
worried incessantly about the details. We were anxious about actual
or potential vulnerabilities, about the design of war plans, about
choices in targeting, and—last but not least—about Soviet approaches to, and choices in, these matters. With respect to deterrence, however, it was probably the case that the details that so consumed our attention were of little or no significance. The Soviet
political minds that we hoped to influence not to sanction dangerous behavior, almost certainly were ignorant of the details of the
U.S. strategic nuclear force posture. The detailed course of a hypothetical bilateral nuclear war was profoundly uncertain. That fact
alone was probably sufficiently reliable and frightening to achieve
all the deterrent effect the United States could desire. This is not to
say that the details of military posture do not matter. But it is to
suggest that political leaders, who are the ones who must decide

whether or not our efforts to deter shall succeed, are not likely to be moved by reports of the details of our military power. The speculative reasoning concerning the strategic nuclear forces in the Cold War should be allowed to speak to us with respect to our military posture today. It is entirely sensible, indeed it is necessary, for the U.S. defense community to worry about the grand design, the favored trends, and the details of the country's military posture. For a host of reasons, our choices in posture, organization, doctrine, equipment, and the rest, really matter to us. However, it is far less certain that our choices among the several somewhat alternative U.S. Armies we might develop over the next decades have any significant implications for the success or failure of deterrence. Militarily, certainly ignorant Soviet leaders appear to have been impressed by the general, but definite, knowledge that nuclear war would be an open-ended catastrophe of historically unprecedented proportions. Today it is probably the general, again definite, knowledge of American military might that secures whatever deterrent effect is achievable. For excellent reasons, the U.S. Army debates alternative approaches to transformation, worries about the extent and pace of demassification, considers how it should employ its Special Forces, and argues over the meaning of combined arms operations in new conditions—all of which are desirable and quite proper. But, compared with the total multidimensional strength of the country, including its global, multi-environmental military muscle, the details of army organization, doctrine, force structure, and equipment can scarcely register at all for deterrence. The point is not that American landpower does not matter for deterrence; nothing could be further from the truth. Rather local, regional, or stateless villains are going to be impressed by their general knowledge of U.S. military power and their perception of America's willingness to use it. They will not know, understand, or care about the kind of military details that so consume our professional military establishment.

If we follow Clausewitz's reasoning on the proper domination of military affairs by policy, it is clear that there can be little sense in expecting military forces of a certain kind to have a particularly deterring effect, outside of the historical and political contexts of the conflict in question.[84] The armed forces may well have vital deterrent value, but that will only be the result of their close fit as a responsive instrument for a policy that carries conviction and engenders fear. Politics and psychology trump military calculations. For example, Saddam Hussein should have found the prospect of being on the receiving end of America's transforming military power hugely deterring, even compelling. However, if as reported, the French repeatedly assured him that international diplomacy would not permit the United States to attack, America's deterrent clout must have all but vanished. Politics rule, which is a persisting historical reality that defense analysts have been known to forget or neglect.

4. *Landpower must be capable of contributing to strategic success in different kinds of conflicts.* Clausewitz insists that "[t]he degree of force that must be used against the enemy depends on the scale of political demands on either side."[85] Determination of the type of military force that might best promote deterrence must in good part be answered with reference to the evolving "grammar" of war, to quote Clausewitz again.[86] However, the grammar of war, which is to say the state of military science, has meaning strictly in relation to the "logic" of policy. If we seek to connect choices in force planning and doctrine to hopefully positive deterrent effects, it is necessary to inquire as to whom we may wish to deter, and from doing what? The actual or potential duties of the sole superpower on behalf of world order, as well as in protection of its own vital interests more narrowly, of course, are so extensive and varied that the U.S. Armed Forces will need to be nothing if not flexible and adaptable. Those armed forces have at least six distinctive missions that derive directly from the global ordering role that is national policy. The weight of the landpower contribution to each of these missions must vary with the nature of the task at issue. Although the focus here is on landpower, it should be understood that the value of the U.S. Armed Forces for deterrence and warfighting is a joint story through and through. If landpower is to help deter it needs to be able to contribute effectively to the following:

- The conduct of raids and brief interventions;

- The taking down of rogue states;

- The holding off or defeat of major regional powers (a requirement that must have nuclear deterrence, and air and missile defenses, as very high priorities);[87]

- The waging of irregular warfare, meaning both war against irregulars and the conduct of war by irregular means (this requirement encompasses all aspects of the global struggle against terrorists);

- Keeping the peace, even making the peace, in stability operations in zones wracked by violence;

- General dissuasion of disordering behavior by states or by stateless movements and organizations.

It is inconvenient that the global domain of America's self-appointed duty as the principal guardian power means that its armed forces need to be competent in the waging of both regular and irregular warfare. American forces must be able to conduct war by decisive maneuver and decisive firepower, as well as by patient efforts to root out and isolate irregular warriors in circumstances where Americans will have to work with local civilians. Metz and Millen are plausible when they identify provision of the capability for strategic victory and proficiency in the waging of "protracted, complex, ambiguous, and asymmetric conflicts" as "the Army's two unique strategic functions."[88] These authors have made the same vital point as Rear Admiral Wylie when he wrote that *"[t]he ultimate determinant in war is the man on the scene with a gun."* Metz and Millen usefully rephrase that view as "strategic victory always requires effective landpower."[89] Just as military victory need not mean strategic victory, so strategic victory need not mean true political victory. If we overly focus on the conduct of war and our immediate war aims, the character of the subsequent peace may suffer from relative neglect.

Landpower continues to extol the virtues of a combined arms approach to warfare.[90] The merit in combined arms, as contrasted with the placing of near exclusive faith in some allegedly and usually novel "dominant weapon," is an ancient principle.[91] It is not likely that the contemporary military transformation—incorporating many "roadmaps," much "planning guidance," and even more high-flying aspirations—will overturn the wisdom of millennia that is expressed in the principle of combined arms. It is possible to identify the kind of American landpower that should prove adequately flexible and adaptable to cope in a strategic context that triggers contrasting demands from policy for military support. What follows is a short list of the more important characteristics and features of an American landpower well suited to deter, if deterrence is practicable, or to fight if necessary. I offer no apologies for the absence of any startling innovations in the list. American landpower needs to be:

- demassified, meaning lighter, more mobile, and therefore more rapidly deployable;

- more truly Joint, in its planning, approach, and ethos (inter-service rivalry continues as a self-inflicted wound of significance);

- more network-centric and better informed by an intelligence function more worthy of its name;

- more competent in the conduct of counterinsurgency (COIN) and counterterrorist (CT) operations;

- capable of waging heavy ground combat—the army needs to be lighter, not comprehensively light;

- better prepared to make effective use of Special Forces; the time is long overdue for their roller-coaster history of political popularity and unpopularity, generally in the context of mainstream service hostility, to be replaced by a settled appreciation of their strengths and limitations;[92]

- more focused on mission accomplishment than on force protection; of course this is a matter of degree, not a stark choice, but potent landpower should be more willing to take risks than was the American norm for many years;[93]

- more skilled at dealing with civilian interface; lack of training or experience in coping with civilian bystanders, in the context of the very high priority accorded force protection, can result in a certain trigger happiness that is as politically damaging as it is physically lethal;

- more patient; U.S. landpower will not always be able to conduct decisive maneuver for the securing of swift military, then hopefully strategic, victory. The future holds protracted and difficult challenges for landpower to meet. The U.S. Army and Marine Corps will need to draw on another major strand in their traditions, the long experience with "small wars;"[94]

- better prepared to work productively with allies, even in an era when allies generally are strictly less important than before. While it is lonely to be the superpower sheriff of world order, it will be both lonelier still and gratuitously perilous if U.S. military power seems to prefer not to have its operations complicated by the need to cooperate with less capable foreign forces.

Deterrence remains essential, notwithstanding its inherent unreliability. However, its theory and contingent practice need to be revisited so that urgent reforms can be effected.

4

TRANSFORMATION AND STRATEGIC SURPRISE

Just when we found the answer, they changed the question.
—Anonymous

We judge the unknown to be unlikely.
—S. Douglas Smith, 2004[1]

It is impossible to predict the future, and all attempts to do so in any detail appear ludicrous within a few years.
—Arthur C. Clarke, 1962[2]

The following discussion seeks to provide what should be a troubling perspective on both defense planning as a whole and the strategic behavior analyzed in chapter 3 under the rubric of deterrence. Strategists seek predictability, especially in the deterrent effect of threats and even just existentially from military capabilities. And yet, surprise happens. Though discounted by Clausewitz in the circumstances of his era, strategic surprise has enjoyed considerable popularity over the past century. The possibility of achieving decisive results from attacks launched on short or zero warning has appeared greatly to improve with advances in technology. It follows that surprise has been recognized as offering golden opportunities and lethal dangers. Since surprise is an ironbound necessity for the tactical success of terrorism, it understandably attracts a major degree of attention today. There is no real novelty about this. After all, for forty years the United States and its NATO allies perpetually worried about surprise attack on the Central Front in Europe, as well as a surprise first strike designed to disarm the United States of the ability to retaliate with its strategic nuclear forces.

This chapter takes a broad view of the problem and the condition of strategic surprise and relates it to the process of military transformation that currently is still in its early stages. Specifically, it argues that in period after period and with few exceptions in war after war, the kind of strategic surprise to which the United States is most at risk is the unexpected depth and pervasiveness of the connection between war and politics. Americans usually are superior in making war, but often they are less than superior in making the peace they want out of the war they wage.

What the global superpower needs is a military establishment it can use in ways conducive to the standards of international order it seeks to uphold, and with the political consequences that U.S. policy intends. Whether that establishment is network-centric or has on-call precision firepower is a matter of less than overwhelming importance. Politics rule. More accurately phrased, perhaps, policy should rule. War is political behavior that should serve policy. Since the conduct of war ought not to be a self-regarding apolitical activity, preparation for it in peacetime as well as its exercise in anger need to be suffused with the sense of purpose that is provided only by the realm of policy.

INTRODUCTION: SURPRISE, A REAL BUT ELUSIVE MENACE

As a highly pragmatic discipline, strategic studies follow events, those that are actual and those that are widely anticipated. The concept of surprise is intellectually fashionable. However, what the practical implications are or ought to be is not self-evident. In common with its conceptual stable-mate, asymmetry, surprise defines a content-free zone. It has no inherent meaning, save with respect to its logical opposite. Surprise and asymmetry must be defined solely with reference to what they are not. This rather unhelpful, seemingly academic point has major real-world implications. The defense community has signed on for yet another big idea that it is ill equipped to pursue purposefully, if indeed such pursuit is feasible at all.

Historically, American strategic theorists and defense analysts have taken their cues from the signals of concern transmitted by officials. Those official signals typically have been triggered by events. For example, the entire conceptual edifice of stable mutual deterrence theory was created in the 1950s, following the first public explanation of a coherent, if highly controversial, nuclear strategy by the Eisenhower administration in 1953–54.[3] The administration was seeking to incorporate nuclear weapons into national strategy in the context of: the lessons of the war just concluded, at least frozen by an armistice, in Korea; the development of fusion weapons; the expansion of the nuclear stockpile; and, of course, the growth of the Soviet nuclear threat in quantity and quality.[4] In the mid-1970s there was a brief flurry of analytical interest in the problems of surprise attack, with specific reference to the possibility of Soviet forces in Europe catching NATO unawares on the Central Front of the inner-German border.[5] Moving to the twenty-first century, a civilian and military defense community that traditionally has been comprehensively uninterested in irregular warfare has rushed predictably to where the policy action is most lively and the money most readily accessible.

Only a few years ago, the writing of books and other studies on terrorism was a distinctly minority pursuit in the intellectual wing of the community. Today, such an endeavor is virtually mandatory if one aspires to be a part of the fashionable, and funded, crowd. Whereas in the 1990s, let alone during the Cold War decades, experts on terrorism and other forms of irregular warfare were exceedingly thin on the ground, now they are truly abundant. Today it is rare to find a defense expert who does not claim counterterrorist (CT) and counterinsurgency (COIN) competency in his or her portfolio of professional skills.

A problem with intellectual fashion is that by its very nature it must change. In the case of national defense it will change as policymakers react to the circumstances that beset them. The official and attendant-dependent worldview moves on, leaving in its wake yesterday's Big Idea. In the field of war and strategy there are no new ideas. Rather there is a storehouse of concepts and theories that are the products of two and a half millennia of intellectual and pragmatic rumination on strategic experience. For the U.S. defense community, "Ideas Persons," intellectual leaders perhaps, go to that storehouse periodically and rediscover the high merit in some long neglected notion. This is how it is with strategic surprise and with its conceptual fellow traveler, the asymmetric threat.[6]

Lest some readers believe that I have strayed into exaggeration with my claim for the contemporary authority of the notion of surprise, former secretary of defense Donald Rumsfeld can be quoted to help settle the issue. Aside from the swipe at the previous administration, Rumsfeld's words expressed a view that became consensual across the political spectrum. In his *Annual Report* for 2002 he advised as follows:

> Well before the events of September [2001], senior Defense Department officials, through the vehicle of the Quadrennial Defense Review, determined that contending with uncertainty must be a central tenet in U.S. defense planning. Too much of the Department's planning over the decade of the 1990s had focused on a few familiar dangers rather than the broad array of potential challenges of consequence to U.S. interests and the nation's inherent vulnerability to asymmetric attacks. They concluded that U.S. defense planning must assume that surprise is the norm, rather than the exception. Adapting to surprise—adapting quickly and decisively—must be a hallmark of 21st century defense planning.[7]

Since terrorism has been identified as the defining threat of this era, and since it can only succeed by surprise, it has to follow syllogistically that surprise is a master strategic concept or principle of our time. Unfortunately, surprise, along with other Big Ideas, such as asymmetry, uncertainty, and friction, is not easy to operationalize outside a narrow band of tactical parameters.[8] The superpowers procured and operated diverse and complex strategic force postures designed to deny success to a would-be surprise attacker. The military challenge was eminently quantifiable, at least it appeared to be so. What though is one to make of, let alone do with, the official advice that surprise is the norm? That sensible sounding declamation is about as useful as the oxymoronic maxim to "expect the unexpected."

This chapter contributes to improving understanding of strategic surprise, especially with reference to the ongoing process of military transformation. I believe that the idea frequently is wrongly conceptualized, that errors in basic understanding can promote undue pessimism, and that the whole subject is overdue for root-and-branch review.

The discussion is organized into subjects that accommodate a total argument with seven points, three serving as conclusions.

BUREAUCRATIC REFORM

1. *Reorganization of intelligence bureaucracies can be useful but is only of marginal importance for reduction in the risks of strategic surprise.* There is always a case for bureaucratic reorganization intended to achieve the kind of reform that should lead to improved performance. However, historical experience and common sense show that the intelligent and praiseworthy urge to reorganize for reform is near certain to disappoint. Whereas better organization should yield a better intelligence product, such improvement is likely to be of marginal value at most. Bureaucratic reforms typically are motivated more by the political necessity to be seen correcting a recent intelligence failure than they are by a serious and sincere determination to make a difference. The truth is that there are systemic reasons why bureaucratic reform, no matter how well designed and executed, is close to irrelevant to the problem of coping with strategic surprise, particularly the kind of political surprise that is the focus of this chapter.

This is not to deny that suitable reforms should treat a few of the endemic pathologies of the intelligence and warning community, at least for a while. Certainly it is possible that a reformed intelligence community could save the country grief on occasion;[9] indeed, the Central Intelligence Agency (CIA) was designed for that purpose. Such a community would be so structured as to encourage both information sharing and competitive assessments, as well as to ensure a proper professional separation between the producer and the user of information. This discussion is not at all hostile to the reform of the intelligence community. I do insist, however, that the preferred pathway to coping with the challenge of surprise does not lead significantly through bureaucratic reform.

Bureaucratic reform simply cannot address the real problems. Those problems, and such solutions and alleviation as one can identify, are beyond the reach of administrative reshuffles. They have to do with the very nature of the subject of surprise and the reasons why it can be so dangerous. Also, they derive from the facts that, for good and ill with regard to intelligence, our analysts must function culturally as Americans within the embrace of a highly decentralized structure of government. It is worth noting the relatively minor importance of those latter potential hindrances when compared with the point registered previously. The major difficulty lies with the nature of the subject of strategic surprise.

For laudable reasons, politicians and officials are always in search of ways to control events. The adoption of stable deterrence as the jewel in the crown of America's Cold War strategic policy is a classic example of this desire made into policy. Today, although deterrence has lost some of its former glitter (see chapter 3),[10] the U.S. government is still very much in the would-be control business. Strategies of prevention and preemption are examples of ideas for the physical control of the military capabilities of polities judged threatening. Alas, preemption, understood correctly as an attack launched first in the last resort, requires a reliable quality of warning that rarely is attainable. Even forcible prevention, which translates as shoot on strong suspicion, could be held to demand an improbable measure of certainty about intelligence information. The uncomfortable fact is that until an enemy actually initiates an attack, a decision to beat him to the punch, by minutes, days, or months and years, unavoidably has to be based on a leap of faith. No scheme to reorganize and reform the intelligence bureaucracies can alter this fundamental reality.

It is orthodox to condemn the intelligence community for relying too heavily on technology in its gathering of information. This criticism is well justified, provided it is not allowed to feed another error. Human intelligence is not a panacea solution to the problem of deficient information. Those who would engineer, or "fix," intelligence and warning difficulties by shifting the balance between machines and people in favor of the latter need to be reminded of some inconvenient facts. To cite a few:

- People take years to train, and many more years to penetrate an alien society and secure positions of trust in which they might learn useful things.

- People, especially if recruited locally, will often be the subject of residual suspicion as to their loyalty.

- The possibility of the U.S., and allied, intelligence community having the right people in the right places at the right time is a long shot.

The U.S. government may later learn that an enemy had the intention of attacking. However, would policymakers in Washington distinguish the "signals" from the "noise," or have sufficient confidence in the "signals" that were recognized as such to take preventive action?[11] Until an attack actually unfolds, one can always hope that the warning signs do not really mean what they appear to indicate. Also, one can choose to "go the extra mile for peace," albeit in the teeth of apparent evidence of malign intent, and hope that something will turn up to divert the would-be attacker from his course. Perhaps he is bluffing.

Critics are right. For at least thirty years the United States has overvalued the technical means of information gathering at the expense of the human. The critics would not be correct, however, to insist that a major rebalancing of effort in favor of human spies would have a significant consequence for the country's ability to avoid, prevent, or preempt strategic surprise.

American culture, including its strategic and military culture(s), has long been highly machine-minded. It is attracted to the definition of conditions as problems that lend themselves to assault by the Yankee know-how that produces the "engineering fix." In many cases, this national self-confidence, determination, and optimism achieves wonders. But, there is a banal sounding, yet profound, maxim before the wisdom of which even a proud superpower is compelled to bow: "The impossible really is impossible." Reform of the intelligence community and its ways of doing business might be of marginal utility though it is well to heed the caveat that such reform has a way of balancing the improvements that it implements with new bureaucratic pathologies. One should never forget the authority of the law of unintended consequences. Purveyors of bright new, or old but refurbished, ideas to improve intelligence as a barrier against strategic surprise, might with profit heed these words by philosopher John Gray:

> The history of ideas obeys a law of irony. Ideas have consequences; but rarely those their authors expect or desire, and never only those. Quite often they are the opposite.[12]

From Carl von Clausewitz to Rear Adm. J. C. Wylie, USN, great strategic theorists have pointed to *control* as being the essence of the practical object in war, the purpose of strategic effect.[13] The subject of this analysis, at root, is how one might better control the dangers that imperil security. Because of its current, partially hegemonic status, as well as for reason of its national, strategic, and military cultures, the United States is especially vulnerable to seduction by unsound ideas. A democratic country burdened with great security tasks will never find itself short of advice. The market for palliatives is open for business. Its global responsibilities, the vulnerabilities that attend them, and its traditional problem-solving optimism mandate caution in approaching the challenge of strategic surprise. Wishful thinking and ethnocentrism conflate potently to mislead. Unfortunately, it is one thing to recognize the unhelpful influence of national culture, it is quite another to identify practical ways to correct that source of pervasive bias. The U.S. government can reorganize itself in any way that the political process will tolerate, but it must continue to be operated by those who are culturally American.

With good fortune, strategic surprise can be controlled in its consequences, as this chapter reveals. However, this control cannot be advanced significantly by the "fix" of bureaucratic reorganization and reform. New organizational structures in the intelligence world are likely to generate new difficulties that would offset much of the benefit anticipated to flow from reform.

The producers and the consumers of intelligence need to keep their distance if the product is not to be contaminated by policymakers' beliefs and concerns. In principle, the intelligence product can be protected from policy bias. However, in practice it is close to impossible to avoid the shaping and coloration of intelligence both by the policy of the moment and, no less significantly, by the assumptions that are current and authoritative within the defense community. And that is to ignore the phenomenon of deliberate attempts by policymakers to encourage the delivery of an intelligence product supportive of their beliefs and intentions. Human nature and the political process usually triumph over organizational reform.

If strategic surprise is defined as a problem in want of "fixing," then the mission is indeed beyond rescue. There are certain to be readers who believe that strategic surprise as a problem really can be hugely alleviated, if not definitively solved, by the right mix of technical and administrative changes. To answer these optimists, I offer an historical observation. A century of cumulatively monumental change in technology and governmental organization has had no appreciable effect on the U.S. ability to eliminate the danger of strategic surprise. 9/11 speaks for itself. The prosecution rests.[14]

UNDERSTANDING THE PROBLEM

2. *Surprise effect, not surprise, is the challenge.* History's nonlinearities, Acts of God, the transmutation of familiar trends into something quite different, the "normal accidents" that afflict all complex systems, and the cunning plans of devious foes can all surprise us. [15] Surprise, though, is not the problem. In point of fact, surprise is not a problem at all, rather it is an insecure condition in which we must live. By analogy, superior intelligence per se is toothless, because there has to be someone at the sharp end to use it to inflict pain on the enemy. Similarly, surprise per se is of little if any value. The question is always: "What are its consequences?" In a brilliant brief analysis, James Wirtz penetrates to the heart of the subject. He explains that

> [s]urprise temporarily suspends the dialectical nature of warfare (or any other strategic contest) by eliminating an active opponent from the battlefield. Surprise turns war into a stochastic exercise in which the probability of some event can be determined with a degree of certainty or, more rarely, an event in which the outcome can be not only known in advance, but determined by one side in the conflict. [16]

Surprise attack has the potential to suspend war's nature as a duel, by eliminating its dialectic. Thus might Clausewitz be confounded. In practice, though, it is rare for a belligerent to be totally eliminated as a consequence of surprise. Ideally, a surprise assault would render its target enemy a helpless victim, unable to recover from the initial disadvantage in which he was placed. In Edward N. Luttwak's telling description, surprise can reduce the enemy to the status of "a nonreacting object." [17] Theoretically, this idea is more than faintly reminiscent of the basic idea behind John Boyd's OODA loop. [18] By surprising speed in our observation, orientation, decision and action cycle, we will begin, and remain, within the action or reaction time of the enemy's like cycle. He will never be able to recover. So much for the theory and high aspiration. Boyd extrapolated from tactical air combat into the far more rarefied zones of strategy and policy. A belligerent may be tactically, even operationally, vulnerable to surprise, yet still be strategically high resilient. Witness the grim experience of the Soviet Union in 1941. A theory sound at the tactical and operational levels is apt to be thwarted by the factors of time, distance, and scale at the strategic.

By definition, the enemy controls surprise. He has the initiative. If this were not so, the events in question would not be surprises. However, we, not the enemy, control the consequences of surprise. Only in rare cases is a strategic- or operational-level surprise so damaging that the defender is rendered incapable of recovery. Whether or not recovery is possible must depend on moral and physical factors. In 1940 and 1941, Britain and the Soviet Union would have fallen along with France, had their national geographies not gifted them the barriers of water or sheer distance that provided time for recovery.

It is understandable and indeed necessary for the intelligence community to strive to prevent malevolent foes from surprising us. After all, if there is no surprise, there can be none of surprise's potentially harmful, even deadly, consequences. However, surprise prevention, though an important goal, is mission impossible, at least it is if we harbor absurd ambitions to inhabit a risk-free security environment. It must follow that the defense community has no practical choice other than to accept that surprise happens; it is a condition of national security. This is not a feature unique to the contemporary world. Surprise has always been an actual or potential characteristic of warfare since "[w]ar is nothing but a duel on a larger scale," in Clausewitz's ageless words.[19] He explains that "[c]ountless duels go to make up war, but a picture of it as a whole can be formed by imagining a pair of wrestlers. Each tries through physical force to compel the other to do his will." Dueling enemies must be motivated to behave in a manner that "eliminates war's dialectic."[20] The feasibility of surprise at the strategic, operational, and tactical levels of conflict will shift with technology, but in theory, at least its attractions remain constant.

In his analysis of the British victory in the Battle of Messines on June 7, 1917, Basil Liddell Hart stated the vital distinction emphasized here. The British assault was anything but a surprise. "The bombardment and 'wire-cutting' began on May 21st, were developed on May 28th, and culminated in a seven days' intense bombardment, mingled with practice barrages to test the arrangements."[21] General Plumer's Second Army had virtually sent the Germans an invitation to the fight. But, as Liddell Hart explains,

> The consequent forfeiture of surprise did not matter in the Messines stroke, a purely limited attack, in contrast to that at Arras, where it had been fatal to the hope of a breakthrough. For although there was no surprise there was surprise effect—produced by the mines [19 of them!] and the overwhelming fire—and this lasted long enough to gain the short-distanced objectives that had been set. *The point, and the distinction between actual surprise and surprise effect, are of significance to the theory of warfare* [emphasis added].[22]

The distinction advertised so clearly by Liddell Hart is indeed of great significance. The technological deficiencies of the day severely limited the effects of surprise. Because they lacked mobility, armies were unable to exploit tactical success rapidly for operational advantage. Also, generals were hampered fatally by the absence of reliable real-time communications. By World War II, technology and doctrine had largely alleviated those inhibitors of 1917.[23]

The problem is not surprise and its frustration. It is more sensible to regard surprise as a condition rather than a problem. The problem is to cope well enough with the effects of those surprises that one is bound to fail to anticipate and prevent. It is important to add that the challenge of surprise effect includes the case addressed in the quotations from Liddell Hart. Even when one is not really surprised by, for example, the failure of an attempt to dissuade, deter, or coerce short of the use of force, still one could be surprised by the actions the enemy takes and, above all else, by their effects.

Conceptually, we have stressed the need to distinguish between surprise and surprise effect. In a more practical vein, we will offer the reminder that prominent among the strategist's analytical weapons should be a skeptical mindset and a readiness to pose the challenging question: "So what?" To be caught by surprise is by and large no disgrace for a superpower that has accepted a global domain for its security interests and responsibilities.[24] Some of the surprises in America's future will be agreeable, many will be of no particular consequence, while a few, inevitably, will bear on issues of significant, even vital, national concern. The challenge to the defense planner and strategist is not to avoid being surprised, but to plan against the more dire potential effects of surprise. The logic of the argument is inexorable. Since surprise cannot be prevented reliably, there is no alternative to our focusing on its potential consequences. Fortunately, though with the noteworthy exception of a nuclear attack on a large scale, it is highly improbable that strategic surprise would achieve useful, let alone conclusive, strategic ends for its perpetrator. It has to follow that our attention should be drawn far more to the possible consequences of surprise than to a forlorn hope to frustrate its achievement.

3. *Some unpleasant surprises should be reliably avoidable.* Clausewitz tells us that "[n]o other human activity [than war] is so continuously and universally bound up with chance. And through the element of chance, guesswork and luck come to play a great part in war."[25] Because "[w]ar is the realm of chance,"[26] meaning that uncertainty is endemic, we must eliminate the risks that lend themselves to anticipation. Most important of all is the need to correct avoidable ignorance. The enemy may well surprise us, with both his initiatives and effects, but if we fail to grasp both the general nature of war, as well as the purpose and character of particular wars, we are guilty of inflicting the severest penalties on our forces. If the character of a war is not understood correctly, then policy, the purpose of it all, is likely to be frustrated and lives and treasure will be sacrificed in vain.

War and warfare have frequently been confused, with the result that Antulio J. Echevarria II highlighted in his study *Toward an*

American Way of War. Building on Russell Weigley's respected work on *The American Way of War,* Echevarria brought the American story up-to-date:

> Their [the Americans in Weigley's book] concept of war rarely extended beyond the winning of battles and campaigns to the gritty work of turning military victory into strategic success, and hence was more a way of *battle* than an actual way of war [emphasis in the original]. Unfortunately, the American way of battle has not yet matured into a way of war.[27]

There is, of course, another and contrasting American way of war, as Echevarria correctly notes. In its extensive historical experience of irregular warfare, which is to say of warfare against irregulars, the U.S. Armed Forces were rarely able to defeat their enemies by decisive maneuver and conclusive battle.[28] There is no doubt, though, that the Napoleonic ideal of successful warmaking has been iconic. By analogy, it is uncontentious to claim that in the twentieth century Germany proved exceptionally competent in the bloody trade of fighting, yet, fortunately, outstandingly incompetent at making war. To lose one world war in a thirty-year period might be attributed to bad luck, but to lose two requires a more systemic explanation.[29] The United States betrays disturbing elements of the weaknesses that Germany failed to recognize and correct.

I will go further than did Echevarria in his persuasive critique. He charged the dominant American way of war, past *and present*, with resting on a concept of war that fails to make the necessary connection between military and strategic success. While that charge is well made, it does not go far enough. The purpose of war is not strategic, rather it is political, success. Moreover, the object of war, as Liddell Hart insisted, should be "a better peace."[30] He was expressing the core rationale of the long traditional religious concepts of *Jus ad bellum* and *Jus in bello*. War is about the peace that follows. Necessarily in this perspective, warfare must be waged with a mind to the character of the postwar settlement that is sought.

This section levels one charge and poses one question. The

charge, that war and warfare are apt to be confused by the U.S. Armed Forces and the civilians who oversee and direct them is somewhat controversial. By contrast, my question may attract an answer that is controversial in the extreme. Stated bluntly: "Is the U.S. defense establishment insufficiently committed to effecting the right transformation?" Is there cause to worry lest a more agile and adaptable army will be employed in such a way that it commits old sins against the political-military lore of war in more effective ways? What the American sheriff requires most is a transformation in its ability to threaten or employ force for its political goals. It is difficult to avoid noticing that the various "roadmaps" to transformation, not excluding the claimed *Strategic Approach* of the Department of Defense's erstwhile Office of Force Transformation, have provided no convincing linkage between military excellence and ultimate political benefit—or even just recognition that such linkage is of the utmost importance.[31] It is precisely and strictly that linkage that legitimizes and gives meaning to military behavior. A cynic, perhaps a skeptic, might be excused observing that the U.S. military is in the process of improving its ability to do that which it already does well. That military is unsurpassed in decisive maneuver and the delivery of precise firepower, two important abilities. Moreover, it is probable that a transforming army will be more capable of waging warfare both against irregular enemies, as well as against regular foes who are obliged by America's material strengths to behave in an irregular mode. However, fighting is not the issue here, it is not what war is all about. Historian Peter Browning provides useful clarification when he explains that "warfare is the act of making war. War is a relationship between two states or, if a civil war, two groups. Warfare is only a part of war, although the essential part."[32]

The United States has a history of being unpleasantly surprised: in minor key by its difficulty in translating military success into strategic success; and in major key by the problem of turning strategic success or advantage into a political victory that can be expressed in a desirable and sustainable postwar settlement. The United States has been surprised in war after war, and in imbroglios great and small, to discover that somehow, somewhere, it had misplaced the glue that should connect its military prowess with its anticipated political reward. This surprise, notwithstanding its magnitude, in theory at least is eminently avoidable. All that is required is a sound strategic education. Unfortunately, though, the principal source of the problem lies not with particular officials, who can be easily replaced, but rather with national strategic and military cultures that approach warfare and politics as unduly distinctive behaviors.

There have been politically effective exercises of U.S. military power. By far the most impressive example was the Civil War. But, alas, we cannot count on having an Abraham Lincoln on hand when the country needs one. There have been too many cases, great and small, when American military effort was not directed, or exploited, effectively for the political and other (e.g., humanitarian) purposes of the enterprise. Those cases include World War I, World War II in Europe, the worst phases of the Korean War, Vietnam, Lebanon, Iraq 1991, Somalia 1993, Kosovo 1999, Afghanistan 2001, and then Iraq again in 2003. Military victory is always important, nay vital. However, it is no guarantor of policy triumph. It is not clear that the momentum of military transformation is going to feed usefully into the transformation that the United States needs most urgently. Above all else, the United States needs a transformation in its ability to wield the sword with political skill. There is a word, a concept, for this function—strategy.

In its more technological variants, the contemporary American process of military transformation rests heavily on and indeed requires "information dominance."[33] The army's vision is more sophisticated, as one would expect, given its focus on the warriors rather than their tools.[34] But it has yet to be demonstrated that an American transforming force will strive as seriously to understand the enemy, and neutral bystanders, as it will to locate him for his obliteration, though current indications, admittedly, are unusually promising.[35] There has been and probably still is inadequate appreciation of the apolitical bias in American strategic thought and action. The information dominance that is the ambition of some "transformers" is apt to be too narrowly military in conception. The U.S. way in warfare is inclined to have the consequence of prejudicing the country's policy goals. The revolution in approach that is needed may prove beyond attainment by a non-permissive American culture. Although Americans are justly proud of their adaptability, that useful cultural virtue itself paradoxically is constrained by culture.

LEVELS OF ANALYSIS

4. *The geopolitical context is the most important.* Most analyses of surprise distinguish strategic, operational, and tactical levels of concern, while some extend their reach to encompass the technological also. Those studies are drawn inevitably into the ongoing and long-running debate over intelligence and how to improve it. That literature is mature and useful in its way, but nonetheless, it typically misses the level of analysis that should be accorded logical and practical priority. Namely, the literature on surprise, strategic and other, is not rich in its treatment of geopolitical context. Since all our strategic concerns, including anxieties over surprise attack, flow ultimately from the character of their historical context, this neglect, even omission, is as strange as it is unfortunate.

Context, from the Latin *contextere*, has two meanings. It may refer to "that which surrounds," which now is its everyday meaning, or "that which weaves together."[36] When one worries about strategic surprise, especially in connection with a long-term program of military transformation, the inquiry should begin with geopolitical contextual, rather than strategic, operational, or tactical uncertainties. Problems at those levels derive basically from the political context that gives them meaning. It is of the utmost importance to address the question of the character of the global environment for which we are transforming the armed forces. Surprise at this level of concern has a way of triggering traumatic consequences. The familiar kinds of analyses that treat strategic, operational, and tactical surprise do not usually raise their sights to consider the context for it all. To fit what kind of a world are the armed forces transforming themselves? What range, quantity, and intensity of duties will, or plausibly might, U.S. foreign policy lay upon them?

It would be wholly reasonable to argue that the questions just posed are neither researchable nor answerable. After all, the future has not happened and the planned transformation, even with its constant course adjustments, does not carry any promise of time travel. Unfortunately, my questions are neither merely rhetorical nor academic in a pejorative sense. The Department of Defense is committed to a long-term process of transformation that must shape military capability, and hence its utility as an instrument of policy, for decades ahead. What do the armed forces know about the future of the world for which they are now in the process of transforming themselves? There is a great chain of reasoning that connects the army's transformation plans to working assumptions about the contexts for which those plans will need to be well enough suited. That great chain comprises the latest *National Security Strategy*, *Quadrennial Defense Review*, and *National Military Strategy* documents that provide guidance for the *Army Campaign Plan,* which specifies the assumptions on which it is based. Fortunately, we are far from blind when peering into the future, even without the benefit of crystal balls or time travel. As a practical matter, whether one is optimistic or pessimistic about defense planners' abilities to "get it right enough" for the medium-term future, those responsible officials must do their best from a situation of irreducible fundamental uncertainty.

The context for U.S. national security truly is a unity. Each relevant dimension impinges on and interweaves with the others. However, it is convenient and useful to identify three contexts, never forgetting that this trinity is compatible with the essential unity referred to above. The contexts that fuel strategic surprise are the geopolitical, the cultural, and the technological. These are not neatly distinctive, fenced-off realms. Furthermore, the geopolitical is by far the most important of the three.

Politics is about power. War is about politics. If organized violence is not politically motivated, it is not war. It has to follow that war, strategy, and defense preparation, including military transformation, also are about power. But what is the power, really the relative power, story for which the armed forces are transforming themselves? What should today's transformers understand and assume about the relevant geopolitical future? Errors committed at this most elevated level of analysis could lose us the country. We might choose to recall a comment by one of Hitler's intimates shortly before the Nuremberg Trials. Field Marshall Keitel, not a man generally respected for his wisdom, observed that errors in tactics and operations could be corrected in a current war, while mistakes in strategy could be corrected only in the next. German behavior failed to abide by the advice implicit in this principle. The higher the level of concern, the more serious the stakes. The level of concern for the contemporary transformer does not come any more elevated than the geopolitical context.

Tectonic, apparently nonlinear, shifts in the geopolitical context happen; in fact, they happen frequently. Consider the differences in the U.S. geopolitical context between the 1900s and the late 1910s, the 1930s and the early 1940s, the mid-1940s and the Cold War decades, the 1980s and the 1990s, and the 1990s and the 2000s. In the 1980s the U.S. Armed Forces prepared for a geopolitical context that was to vanish in only a few years. The preparation was not wholly unconnected with the geopolitical revolution in question.[37] The 1990s, the post-Cold War era, was a no-name decade that had no dominant organizing geopolitical feature. American primacy was recognized, but not really articulated or productively exercised. 9/11 changed that.

Are the armed forces transforming themselves for a geopolitical context in which the United States will long, indeed indefinitely, remain the unchallenged military hegemon? Do they need to adjust to a world in which they will not require the ability to wage "heavy" combat against major states, and perhaps not against states at all? Should they "lighten up," or perhaps "down," and become

Special Operations capable to fit suitably into a geopolitical context wherein America's enemies variably, but emphatically, must conduct only irregular warfare? The answers to questions such as these are of the highest importance for the shape and direction of the long process of military transformation. Fortunately, it is possible to provide answers in which some confidence can be placed. On the evidence available, the army, for example, is adapting itself quite prudently for a future that may well include combat against both regular and irregular enemies. Also, the army recognizes that regular adversaries are likely to rely heavily on "asymmetric means" so as "to mitigate their relative disadvantage."[38]

Strategic surprise on the greatest of scales occurs as a result of changes in the contexts for national security. Although this analysis has identified a contextual trinity of politics, culture, and technology as the prime sources of strategic upheaval, it has also insisted that politics, tuned as the geopolitical for its relevance to war and strategy, is the driver among them. For example, the most significant systemic shock to U.S. national security over the past twenty years was the abrupt, albeit temporary, retirement of the Russian enemy from the geopolitical field of honor. This was one of history's rarities, a benign great strategic surprise. The information revolution and the consequent debate about RMA and military transformation appear to many people to register high on the Richter scale of strategic importance. Nonetheless, the issues in that debate pale into near insignificance compared with the impact of the alteration to the geopolitical landscape caused by the reduction of the superpower column from two to one.

Although one could attempt to consider the contexts—geopolitical, cultural, and technological—as independent variables, indeed many studies do so, that approach is not favored here. Turning first to the cultural context for national security as a possible source of strategic surprise, I am not persuaded that it is a context superior to, or greatly influential over, the geopolitical dimension.[39] And I say that as a long time advocate of the necessity for cultural study in strategy.[40] At least, that is what I believe about the United

States. Insofar as it bears on attitudes toward national defense and war itself, American culture is more shaped by, than shaping, the geopolitical context.[41] This is not claimed as an eternal, let alone universal, truth. It is, however, a claim with a powerful reach. For example, for a variety of historical reasons Donald Rumsfeld's "Old Europe" has appeared to have entered into a post-modern, post-military era. Many of the societies of "Old Europe" have become thoroughly debellicized.[42] This commonly noted phenomenon expresses: reactions to Europe's bloody history in the twentieth century; the strategic fact that those societies have been security wards of the U.S. superpower for sixty years; and a perilous assumption that good security times are here to stay, irreversibly and indefinitely. The anti-military culture of "Old Europe" is primarily the product of its currently permissive geopolitical context. Europeans have discerned no need to take their own defense seriously. It is a logical next step to convert a necessity into a virtue. Until recently they appeared not to notice, or perhaps chose to ignore, the several signals from Moscow indicating an intention to restore some of its global status and influence, possibly in loose strategic and economic association with a rising China.

In the American case, culture is not plausible as a potential source of strategic surprise. Although by definition culture must reflect deep-seated attitudes and habits, it is also very much a living context, subject to influence by unfolding events. This claim presumes that American culture is permissive of a range of foreign- and defense-policy behaviors, depending on circumstances. For example, it is always possible that a populist politician might appeal successfully to the isolationist strain in American society. If this were to happen, the strategic surprise effect on the national military posture could be profound. However, this inquiry is not persuaded that such an event is at all likely. It is judged improbable even when the country, performing as global sheriff, suffers much pain and disappointment and, as a consequence, becomes resentful at the ingratitude of what, not without irony, is referred to as the international community.[43] The cultural context for U.S. national security is clearly a variable dependent on perceptions of the country's geo-political context. In the 1990s, American society did not care much about the Balkans or the Horn of Africa, hence the spate of writings on the need for a "post-heroic" American style in war.[44] There are, of course, demographic and other sociological explanations for a potentially policy- and strategy-enervating societal aversion to the suffering, or even infliction, of casualties. However, careful study and experience tell us that the claim for an extreme U.S. casualty aversion is a myth, provided Americans care about the mission in question.[45] What American society will not tolerate is the conduct of hostilities in a half-hearted manner by an administration that seems to have no notion of, or serious commitment to, victory. American society is not likely to provide the kind of unpleasant strategic surprise that would inhibit or prohibit perilous geopoliti-cal behavior. Culture follows politics, at least it usually does.

The third potentially important context for strategic surprise is the technological. I declare boldly, perhaps rashly, that technologi-cal surprise is not a probable strategic problem for the U.S. military. The depth, breadth, and consistency of the U.S. commitment to military technological excellence, backed by a civilian sector tech-nologically of the first rank, guarantee against the surprise emer-gence of a technological shortfall potentially lethal to national se-curity. In fact, so many and various are the possible ways in joint warfare, so diverse and complex are today's tools of the military trade, that it would be highly implausible to anticipate strategic disaster for reason of a particular technological failing. However, the prudent focus for concern is not so much on new technologies, but rather on how other countries' or groups' ways of war might choose to employ them. Reasonably, but alas incorrectly, some American commentators believe that, in its information-led RMA/ transformation, the U.S. defense establishment is simply leading the way in the modern style in warfare.[46] Given the global diffusion of IT and a presumed universal military meaning to common tech-nological knowledge, it should follow that to know the American way is to know the future for all who aspire to master the state of the art in military affairs. Unfortunately, the world does not work like that. The reasons why it does not are both geopolitical and cultural.

Geopolitically, America's rivals will pick and choose from the technological menu so as to privilege their unique strategic advantages and hopefully to compensate for their deficiencies. Also, there has never been a truly common "grammar" of war.[47] Different belligerents will have their own views on how a basically common technology should be exploited. An outstanding collection of essays, titled *The Diffusion of Military Technology and Ideas*, offers some cautionary words among its findings on local culture's impact on the consequences of such diffusion:

> One of the central contributions of this volume is to alert practitioners to be cautious in their expectations that the spread of new military knowledge is easy or straightforward. It cannot be easily controlled, nor held back indefinitely. This is so for several key reasons. First, culture will *continue to shape the development and diffusion of military knowledge, producing indigenous adaptations that will be difficult to predict* [emphasis added]. True emulation is rare, implying that others will probably not leverage the IT-RMA the same way as the United States.[48]

In *War and Power in the 21st Century: The State, Military Conflict and the International System*, Paul Hirst made much the same point, only more broadly. He advised that "war is driven by ideas about how to use weapons and military systems almost as much as it is by technical and organizational changes themselves. Ideas are thus crucial."[49]

To summarize the argument of this section: technology does not pose a significant threat of strategic surprise, rather the challenge lies in the unexpected uses that other strategic cultures may choose to make of it. Overall, such uses would constitute grave threats to U.S. national security only because of a geopolitical context characterized by notable rivalries. Technology and culture and the strategic surprises to which they might be crucial are strictly dependent variables. They are dependent on the political context for their strategic meaning.

CONCLUSION

Thus far the study has taken the problem, actually the condition, of future strategic surprise exceedingly seriously. That attitude is, of course, mandated by the subject's nature; the stakes may be high. However, we are far from helpless in the face of strategic history's potential to ambush us. At least, we are far from helpless if we keep our balance, respect what history can teach us if we so allow, and take sensible precautions.

5. *Do not exaggerate the dangers from surprise.* The now distant, but still culturally potent, examples of Pearl Harbor, the trauma of 9/11, and the rediscovery of the ancient attractions of preemption have served to elevate awareness of surprise attack in official and public consciousness. There is no denying that attacks apparently "out of the blue" can wreak severe damage. Generally, the tactical success of such attacks is attributable to the facts that ample signals of intention were lost amid the noise, or that policymakers chose not to believe what their intelligence arms were trying to tell them. The pathologies of intelligence gathering, assessment, and use for policy have been well explored by scholars, as well as revealed by retired officials, and need no further comment here. But, how important is strategic surprise? More precisely, how significant might be its effects? During the Cold War, no briefing team in either capital stood much of a chance of persuading political leaders that a massive surprise nuclear attack could succeed in disarming the enemy, or otherwise render him incapable of retaliation. This is not to deny, however, that a cool appraisal of the possible danger did not always triumph over a predisposition to believe the worst.[50] Obviously, surprise nuclear attack or attack on very short warning was possible, and its effects must have been close to, if not actually, history-ending for both parties as well as many others. From at least the mid-1960s, it was never plausible to anticipate comprehensive success from a would-be disarming first strike. In principle, the peril of large-scale nuclear attack remains today. For now, though, the geopolitical context renders the danger strictly notional, since the

only possible candidate for the role of villain-disarmer, the Russian Federation, lacks the necessary political motivation.[51] As we keep insisting, the condition of potential strategic surprise is driven by the geopolitical context, not by technology, culture, or briefers.

History is our only guide to the future.[52] It never repeats itself in detail, but the problems and opportunities it reveals from the past do not alter generically. That is the basic reason why the writings of Thucydides, Sun Tzu, and Clausewitz still speak to us meaningfully. The feasibility of strategic surprise assuredly has increased with the advent of air power, ballistic missiles, and the exploitation of computers in war. History, though, alerts us to the fact that surprise is no panacea solution to war's imponderables. As a matter of record, surprise attacks rarely have the effects that lead their perpetrators to gain decisive victory. The law of unintended consequences strikes ruthlessly. If anything, the surprise attacker, trusting in deception and cunning to offset real weaknesses, is wont to begin a conflict that it cannot finish.[53] When great faith is placed in the presumed potency of strategic surprise, the failure, or only partial success, of that "Plan A" is likely to leave the aggressor unprepared with a suitable "Plan B." Indeed, most likely it is the infeasibility of any attritional "Plan B" that drives the choice for a "Plan A" designed to paralyze the foe's power of resistance and thereby register instant conclusive success.

The peril of strategic surprise is a condition of international and national security. The danger is real, particularly for a militarily hegemonic superpower acting in the self-appointed role of sheriff of world order. America's enemies are obliged to seek to suspend the dialectic of war, to quote Wirtz again. Materially weak enemies can only aspire to win by seizing and keeping the initiative, and by paralyzing America's ability to act effectively. Exactly what would be won and for how long are, of course, highly salient questions. One must again ask the most characteristic of strategists' questions: "So what?" So what that the United States might be surprised strategically? A superpower with a global security remit cannot anticipate or prevent surprise attacks of all kinds, in all places, at all times. But what really would be at risk? What would be the effect of surprise, not only on the victim, but also on the policy, strategy, and behavior of the assaulted superpower?

Strategic surprise is not a metaphorical "silver bullet." Its attempt is more likely to prove ultimately self-defeating than to be the high road to victory. Competent or better armed forces are alert to the perils of surprise attack, just as they themselves must be ready to undertake such a task if policy so directs. The problem is not surprise per se, it is the effect of surprise. And that effect is easy to exaggerate. Since strategic surprises do happen, as 9/11 reminded us, and their effects can be extremely damaging, governments and their armed forces are obliged to concede the reality of potential peril. The fact that the risks and even the prospective effects of strategic surprise are readily exaggerated does not remove the official obligation to be prepared. How does one, though, prepare for surprise and its effects? It is to this practical matter that we now must turn.

6. *Minimum regrets must be a guiding principle.* The armed forces cannot transform themselves by targeting the particulars of future strategic surprise. Respect the sense in the mantras "The unknown is unknown" and "The impossible is impossible." These truisms duly granted, the strategic future is fortunately far from a closed book. Thanks primarily to Clausewitz, we are blessed with an excellent, empirically founded, if incomplete, theory of war.[54] That theory is of universal and permanent validity. Clausewitz argued persuasively that "all wars are things of the *same* nature [emphasis in original]."[55] Although military transformation will change some of the equipment, organization, doctrine, and generally perhaps the culture as a whole, though that has to be less certain, it will not change the nature of war, at least not the "objective" nature.[56] Certainly, military transformation may well alter the character of the warfare we wage, war's "subjective" nature as Clausewitz expressed it, though we dare not forget the inconvenient fact that enemies will contribute to that character.

The proud contemporary American military establishment has to be careful lest its commitment to a strategically somewhat unfocused process of transformation obscures the prospect of fighting on terms it will not prefer. The army recognizes this problem and is sensible about adaptive adversaries who will seek and "discover niche conventional and unconventional capabilities."[57] However, to have the mindset able to cope with the unexpected is entirely different. That is a matter of military culture. We have emphasized the inevitability of strategic surprise, the need to recognize that the problem lies mainly with surprise effect, and the overwhelming importance of the geopolitical context. That context is literally unknown and unknowable, but prudent guesswork is both necessary and feasible.

Uncertainty over the timing and character of future policy demands for their services compels the U.S. Armed Forces to adopt an approach to their transformation best understood as one of minimum regrets. Defense planners must aim to make only minor errors in their planning. For example, one might well come to regret having fewer batteries deployed for the purpose of national missile defense than events demonstrate to be desirable. However, such regret would likely be as nothing compared with the regret one might have were the country to deploy no such missile defence at all, and were an unsporting enemy to notice and exploit that strategic vacancy. The great challenge in defense planning is to design and execute a surprise effect-tolerant military posture. The surprise in question could take the form of an unanticipated demand by U.S. foreign policy for strategic support, in addition to unexpected unpleasantness initiated from abroad.

Success for defense planners, including those currently driving the process of transformation, can be explained in the vernacular as getting the big things right enough. Phrased as a blessing for such people, we would say, "may our future regrets over your decisions be only minor." As a pervasive attitude, a determination to strive for a military condition of minimum regrets helps counter undue enthusiasm for a focus on the threat of this month or year.

7. The operational level is not the whole of war. Are the armed forces pursuing the most appropriate vision in their transformation? In war after war, the U.S. military has been surprised to learn, actually relearn, that there is far more to war than warfare. In addition, it is apt to forget that war is about peace; it is not a sporting event wherein performance is measured by its own endogenous rules and metrics. American's professional military culture has been deeply hostile to any blurring of the line between politician and soldier. Peace is the business of civilians, while the waging of war is the business of military professionals.[58] There is much to commend this Jominian view. Unfortunately, though, the way in which the soldier approaches and performs his expert military duty can, indeed almost invariably must, have profound political implications. In practice the realms of policy and warfare influence each other continuously, even in areas that appear to be strictly political or strictly military. The outcome to World War I, and the manner of its termination by an armistice (contrary to General Pershing's preference, one must add), taught a valuable lesson about the connection between the waging and conclusion of war, and especially about the provision of political fuel for a follow-on event.[59] The U.S. part in the defeat of Germany in World War II revealed to many people the tie between the conduct of war and the character of the succeeding peace and international order. For at least the last eighteen months of the war, Stalin was fighting more for the peace settlement that he wanted than for the most efficient demise of German military power. The United States, in contrast, was fighting almost strictly with reference to the course of the war. Moreover, America's impatience to transfer all its military effort to the war in the Pacific was decidedly unhelpful in its conduct of the closing phases of the war in Europe. Over Korea, the United States learned that its enemies were conducting grand strategy, not military strategy. The Chinese fought and negotiated seamlessly. Mao Tse-tung, we know, was an admiring student of Clausewitz.[60] The core of my residual uneasiness about the current process of U.S. military transformation, despite the admirable sentiments expressed in its guiding documents, lies in

Clausewitz's words:

> Once again: war is an instrument of policy. It must necessarily bear the character of policy and measure by its standards. The conduct of war, in its great outline, is therefore policy itself, which takes up the sword in place of the pen, but does not on that account cease to think according to its own laws.[61]

To continue the history lesson, in Vietnam Military Advisory Command Vietnam (MACV), though admittedly not the Marines, waged the war ineffectively in at least two major respects. The nature of the conflict was misunderstood, with the result that a military solution was sought to what, fundamentally, was a political challenge that could be met effectively only by local indigenous effort. As if that were not damaging enough, even the military dimension of the war was conducted in good part inappropriately, because MACV did not comprehend, let alone favor, counterinsurgency. In particular it failed to give first priority to the provision of security to the bulk of the population.[62]

More recently, the two wars against Iraq again revealed repeatedly that American military prowess was not cashed at close to its full value in political returns. This was unfortunate because those anticipated returns were, after all, what the fighting was all about. It may seem that these critical observations are unfair. One might object on the grounds that I exaggerate the extent of the divorce between U.S. military strategy and operations and U.S. policy; and that I lay fault on the armed forces, when, if fault there be, it lies principally with civilian policymakers. In reply, I would deny exaggeration, but agree that the ultimate responsibility for the American way of war and its performance as an instrument of policy certainly rests with civilians rather than soldiers.[63]

The concluding argument of this chapter, the one that binds together all that has gone before, is that the American approach to war and peace fails to regard and employ force as political behavior for political purposes, which is to say for policy. Time after time the American problem with the permanent condition of possible strategic

surprise has stemmed from unpreparedness for the political consequences of military action. The American practical divorce of military and political behaviors creates a vulnerability to being surprised
by the actions of enemies and allies who do not maintain that separation. In addition, the political consequences of American military action frequently have been unanticipated.

The evidence provided by U.S. experience in and after recent
wars suggests strongly that the process of military transformation,
though desirable in itself, focuses attention on a relatively minor
problem, while leaving the major challenge unaddressed and perhaps even unrecognized. Through transformation, the army, for
example, should improve its ability to defeat both regular and, hopefully, irregular enemies.[64] Those who believe that much of the army
can become Special Forces–like in response to a changing strategic
context are, alas, fooling themselves. The army must not only remain capable of defeating any and every regular foe in heavy combat, in addition it has growing need of Special Forces (SF) worthy
of the name. Immature young soldiers are not appropriate SF material. At least they are not for so long as the SF are not so expanded,
co-opted, and eventually melded into the rest of the army that they
lose much of what ought to be their distinctive quality.[65]

By all means let the armed forces innovate and improve their
fighting power. That is not at issue. I am in full agreement with the
Economist writer who observed that "success in battle, according to
one military maxim, may not, on its own, assure the achievement
of national security goals, but defeat will guarantee failure."[66] What
is at issue is whether the process of transformation is in danger of
fostering a military culture that values military skills, especially combat skills, almost for their own sake. For once, history reveals a clear
lesson to those among us willing to learn. It tries to tell us that by
far the most serious inhibitor of U.S. strategic effectiveness is a seemingly systemic difficulty in employing military force in ways that
promote the chosen political goals. The strategic surprises that have
ambushed U.S. national security performance overwhelmingly have
been political, not military, in kind. Military transformation is close

to irrelevant to the real problem that persistently constrains the value of U.S. strategic prowess.

◆ ◆ ◆

War is about peace. Peacetime preparation is about being able to conduct the wars that might erupt in a manner that serves political ends, or more valuable still, it is about deterrence. To repeat the familiar refrain, there is more to war than warfare. Above all else, war is about the kind of peace that should follow. As a consequence, war needs to be waged in a way that does not compromise political interests. Recognition of the importance of these elements of the lore of war and peace is the high road to achieving a marked reduction in the incidence and severity of strategic surprise.

5

RECOGNIZING AND UNDER-STANDING REVOLUTIONARY CHANGE IN WARFARE: THE SOVEREIGNTY OF CONTEXT

War is more than a true chameleon that slightly adapts its characteristics to the given case. As a total phenomenon its dominant tendencies always make war a remarkable trinity—composed of primordial violence, hatred, and enmity, which are to be regarded as a blind natural force; of the play of chance and probability within which the creative spirit is free to roam; and of its element of subordination, as an instrument of policy, which makes it subject to reason alone.
—Clausewitz, 1832[1]

All wars are things of the same *nature [emphasis added].*
—Clausewitz, 1832[2]

The only empirical data we have about how people conduct war and behave under its stresses is our experience with it in the past, however much we have to make adjustments for subsequent changes in conditions.
—Bernard Brodie, 1976[3]

Set in the context of long-standing Islamic insecurities, the consequences of the politics and culture of resistance to Soviet occupation of Afghanistan (1979–88) ultimately produced the true strategic surprise of 9/11. The U.S. defense community in the 1990s and the new Bush administration in the eight months prior to 9/11 were focused on a technology-led putative Revolution in Military Affairs (RMA). History, however, was preparing to demonstrate its capacity to astound and proceed apparently in a non-linear mode. Could it be that the revolutionary change in warfare that defense experts had debated so vigorously, a revolution that was technological

121

to its core, would not be the master narrative of future strategic affairs?

Since Andrew W. Marshall and his Office of Net Assessment in the Office of the Secretary of Defense (OSD) introduced into public debate the concept of an RMA, the idea of revolutionary change in warfare has gripped the official U.S. strategic imagination. All such master notions, or metanarratives, have lengthy antecedents.[4] The provenance of RMA can be traced in the use of laser-guided bombs in Vietnam; in the 1970s "Assault Breaker" project to develop rocket-delivered smart bomblets to target Soviet armor far behind the front; in Soviet speculation about a Military-Technical Revolution (MTR) and the feasibility of "reconnaissance-strike complexes"; in the *Discriminate Deterrence* reports of the late 1980s (sponsored by then–undersecretary of defense for policy Fred Iklé and inspired by Albert Wohlstetter); by the dramatic appearance and effects of stealth and precision in the 1991 Gulf War; and by a rising argument among academic historians of warfare in early-modern Europe.

In the United States, debate evolved into official commitment. RMA was to be realized as transformation or, for a less ambitious expression, as revolutionary change in the way American forces would fight. The fascination with revolutionary change persisted through the 1990s, survived—indeed was given "gravity assists" by the newly mandated Quadrennial Defense Reviews (QDRs)—because of a change in administration in 2001, and was scarcely dented as the dominant defense concept by 9/11. Truly it seemed, and remains for many people, to be an idea with longevity: initially for the no-name post–Cold War decade, now for the Age of Terror, and prospectively for whatever the decades ahead will bring.

This discussion provides an audit, a not wholly unfriendly critical assessment, of the concept of revolutionary military change. It offers a review of what those who theorize about, and those who are committed by policy to execute, such a revolution ought to know about their subject. As the subtitle of the analysis announces, the argument's leading edge is the potency, indeed the sovereign importance, of warfare's contexts.

The chapter strives to avoid confusion over definitions. It points out that the concept of RMA is eminently and irreducibly contestable. The RMA debate has provided a happy hunting ground for academic historians to wage protracted internecine combat. All definitions of RMA present problems, a fact that is of practical consequence for a U.S. military now taking what is intended to be a revolutionary path. I prefer a truly minimalist definition: an RMA is a radical change in the conduct and character of war. The more detail added to the definition, the more hostages are offered to reasonable objection.

The first of the study's three major sections poses and answers basic, yet highly important, questions about revolutionary change in warfare. Does the RMA concept make sense? Is it useful? Does it matter? Is military change more a product of evolution than revolution? Are continuities as important as changes in their relative contribution to military effectiveness? And, is revolutionary change the high road to victory? By and large, though not without rough handling, the RMA concept, the notion of transformation, or simply the descriptive idea of revolutionary change, survives the ordeal of question and answer.

The core purpose of this enterprise, the second major section seeks to recognize and understand revolutionary change in warfare by explaining that war and its conduct in warfare is dominated by its contexts. To date, no other study has taken such a holistic view of warfare's contexts with reference to RMA. The argument is presented through six contexts: the political, the strategic, the social-cultural, the economic, the technological, and the geographical. While each context is vitally significant, the occurrence of war—as well as its course in warfare, its outcome, and its consequences—derive its meaning only from politics. As I argued in chapter 4, American strategic performance is apt to disappoint on occasions, because the strategic bridge between military behavior and the political context is not always in good enough repair.

INTRODUCTION: A USEFUL IDEA?

The history of the "great RMA debate" of the 1990s and beyond remains to be written, though hopefully not until many more years have elapsed. At present the story is unduly incomplete, and too many commentator-historians would employ their versions of recent history in the service of contemporary argument.[5] That granted, national security policy, grand strategy, military strategy, doctrine, and force structure cannot be put on hold pending properly scholarly assay. As war is conducted in a climate of uncertainty, so those who aspire to offer strategic advice must do their best with imperfect information and the unavoidable biases bequeathed by the time and place of their writing.

For every fashionable concept there is a season, and inevitably so it has proved for RMA. However, the RMA concept has demonstrated an exceptional potency and longevity, facts plainly attributable to the attractions of the promise in the idea as well as to its strong appeal in American culture. Revolutionary change in warfare is a notion that cannot be dismissed. Unlike network-centricity or effects-based operations, revolutionary change is not a cliché that conceals rediscovery of the long familiar and well appreciated.[6] Whatever one's thoughts about the RMA hypothesis, there can be no denying, on the one hand, the appeal of riding the wave of revolutionary change, or on the other, the fear of being victimized by another polity riding that wave. Now that the RMA debate of the 1990s has matured into argument about the realization of RMA in a lengthy process of "transformation," and also has been overtaken, even taken over, what do we think we know about recognizing and understanding revolutionary change in warfare? No less to the point, what are the practical implications of that knowledge for national security, strategy, and defense planning?

While the use of history, or should one say the past, is controversial, it is the only potential evidence available.[7] If we deny the past any relevance, then analysis and prognosis will rest entirely on current concerns and nostrums. Though that might be good enough, it would seem to this theorist to be a gratuitously reckless self-impoverishment.

REVOLUTIONARY CHANGE IN WARFARE: WHAT ARE WE TALKING ABOUT?

Often only a fine line separates necessary precision in language from the malady of scholarly pedantry. Probably most readers of this chapter already are comfortable with the idea of revolutionary change in warfare. After all, it is an idea blessed by the authority of seemingly endless repetition over the past fifteen years, while it also carries a self-evident meaning. Revolutionary change is not exactly an obscure, arcane idea. It is not unreasonable to believe that we can recognize such change when it looms or occurs. To meet the test of common sense, revolutionary change must be change that overturns an existing order. But, is the subject strictly change in warfare, or must it extend to change in war itself? War and warfare are not synonymous despite being commonly used interchangeably, an error that has great potential to promote misunderstanding. Warfare is dominated by its several major contexts, not the least among them being the institution of war. Lest there be any uncertainty on the matter, this study holds that warfare is the actual conduct of war, principally in its strategic and military dimensions, with regard to the threat or use of force. In contrast, war is a political and sometimes legal relationship between belligerents. War also is a social institution. Just as a transformation of war can trigger revolutionary change in warfare, so can the broader transformation drive the implications of such change, possibly to the point where they are substantially offset by extra-military developments. Should anyone harbor any residual uncertainty on the matter, war is a relationship wherein organized violence is carried on by political units against each other for political motives.

The concept of revolutionary change in warfare is typically not given enough detailed explanation. However, given this analysis' mission to help in the recognition and understanding of RMA, we cannot afford to be relaxed about our subject's content. The scholarly pedant in this theorist will explore what is meant by revolutionary change, or, if that is a demand too far, what is the depth and scope of the uncertainty.

Though RMA as a professional term of art has long gone out of fashion, its meaning effectively is identical to the concept of revolutionary change in warfare. There is a subtle distinction between the two, with RMA possibly carrying theoretical baggage that the simple seeming concept of revolutionary change does not, but truly it is a distinction without a significant difference. Notwithstanding its longevity in defense and academic historical discourse, RMA remains a deeply contested concept. Its historical reality is contested, as is everything else about it: for example, its content, utility, and significance. Before too many readers abandon this chapter in irritation at the scholastic trend in the discussion, I must insist that this rather abstract analysis has profound practical implications. What we are discussing is nothing less than the prospects for and the meaning and probable consequences of the military transformation to which the American defense establishment has committed itself. The armed forces have signed on for a revolutionary change in warfare. It is vital that they recognize and understand what it is that transformation implies.

As already noted, I prefer minimal definitions that avoid arguable descriptive attributes. Readers may find more elaborate definitions attractive. My basic definition holds that an RMA is a radical change in the character or conduct of war.

In 2001's *The Dynamics of Military Revolution, 1300–2050*, historians Williamson Murray and MacGregor Knox drew attention to a significant distinction between Military Revolutions (MRs) and RMAs. Whereas the latter are chosen happenings pursued purposefully by states to produce "new ways of destroying their opponents," MRs "brought systemic changes in politics and society. They were uncontrollable, unpredictable, and unforeseeable. And their impact continues."[8] Murray and Knox identified five MRs: the creation of the modern state and its military institutions in the seventeenth century; the French Revolution; the Industrial Revolution; World War I, which combined the effects of the previous three; and the Nuclear Revolution. To this list we may wish to add the Information Revolution. The key difference between an MR and its antecedent and subsequent RMAs is that it forecloses on choice. Polities must cope with the contexts it creates as best they can. The MR/RMA distinction has significance for this discussion; if the contemporary process of transformation is best understood as a response to an MR, it is not a matter of policy or strategic choice, at least not overall. Of course in detail it is eminently challengeable.

Andrew F. Krepinevich provided the most widely used and accepted detailed definition of RMA in an influential article published in 1994. As a close associate of Andrew W. Marshall, the American godfather of the RMA concept, Krepinevich's definition carried unusual weight. He explained it thus:

> What is a military revolution? It is what occurs when the application of new technologies into a significant number of military systems combines with innovative operational concepts and organizational adaptation in a way that fundamentally alters the character and conduct of conflict. It does so by producing a dramatic increase—often an order of magnitude or greater—in the combat potential and military effectiveness of armed forces.[9]

By way of a final offering, a 1999 RAND study by Richard O. Hundley tells us that

> [a]n RMA involves a paradigm shift in the nature and conduct of military operations
>
> • which either *renders obsolete or irrelevant* one or more *core competencies* of a dominant player [emphasis added],
>
> • or creates one or more new core competencies, in some new dimension of warfare
>
> • or both[10]

Hundley defines his key term, "core competency," as "[a]

fundamental ability that provides the foundation for a set of military capabilities."[11] By way of a contemporary example, Hundley cites the "the ability to detect vehicular targets from the air and attack them with precision weapons is today a core competency of the U.S. Air Force."[12]

Although Hundley's brave and innovative specification of the passing grade for an RMA provides a test that has merit, it is one that, perhaps ungenerously, I judge unduly restrictive and debatable. Jeremy Black's cautionary words in 1995 continue to warrant respect. Professor Black emphasized the subjective nature of RMA as an historical descriptor. He argued that "there are no agreed-upon criteria by which military change, especially qualitative developments, can be measured or, more significantly, revolution discerned."[13] Whether or not one shares Black's skepticism about the historical sense in the RMA concept, he performs a useful service by reminding us of the contestability of historians and defense analysts' claims for the presence of RMAs.[14] Scholarly debate about RMA has a real-world resonance. After all, the armed forces currently are proceeding through the early stages of a long process designed to achieve transformation, a dynamic condition that we can translate fairly as a revolutionary change in how warfare is waged. The conceptual RMA horse has already left the theory stable and, indeed, has progressed beyond starter's orders into the race itself. Still, though, it is prudent for officials and soldiers to check on the state of the conceptual runners in the scholarly debate. Albeit in modified form, strategic ideas fuel policy, plans, and military behavior. What is the state of the contemporary debate over RMA?

All strategic debates flourish, then wane, and die as the issue in question is intellectually exhausted, or as policy concerns move on, or both. The RMA concept, if not the term and initialism, has been atypical, because it continues to attract interesting commentary, even after a decade and a half of high exposure. This fact is best explained with reference to: its inherent potency; its appeal in American strategic and military culture; its official adoption by Democratic and Republican administrations as the master concept inspiring, and in a sense licensing, the transformation of the country's armed forces; and, last but not least, to the U.S. experience of armed combat from Kosovo in 1999, through Afghanistan in 2001–8, to Iraq since 2003. The Department of Defense is endeavoring to effect an RMA, a revolutionary change in the way U.S. military forces conduct warfare. For an approximate historical analogy, one must look back to the 1950s, when the newly minted theory of stable nuclear deterrence gradually was accepted and then was embalmed as the intellectual architecture that dominated U.S. defense policy for nearly forty years. There was, however, at least one vital difference between the theories of deterrence and RMA. Unlike the latter, the former was driven by the pressing needs of a political context of acute interstate hostility. Nonetheless, deterrence and RMA share the character of responding to technological challenge, even though the former was shaped by the needs of a definite political context of threats, while the latter was not. The theory of nuclear deterrence was developed to make sense of and guide policy, strategy, and plans for the nuclear RMA. RMA is an imperial concept, or a metatheory.

The now long-running debate over the RMA idea in its evolving variants has proceeded predictably through several stages. It moved from intellectual discovery (with thanks to Soviet theorists), to conceptual elaboration and counterattack by skeptics, through empirical investigation, to second and third thoughts, which is the condition today. Some positions have hardened, perhaps matured, over the years, as often happens in debate. For example, Jeremy Black, who has written extensively on the subject of military revolutions, sought to bring down the curtain on the RMA concept once and for all. He has written that "[m]ilitary realities, however, are both too complex and too dependent on previous experiences to make the search for military revolutions helpful."[15] As usual, his argument is cogent and plausible, though I do not endorse the full measure of his skepticism. In the historians' debate about RMA, the rival poles have been represented not only by people who are friendly or unfriendly to metanarrative, but also by those who attribute greater or lesser significance to technological change. If we recall Andrew Krepinevich's definition of RMA, he specified "innovative operational concepts and organizational adaptation" to exploit new technologies in "a significant number of military systems."

Despite the sophisticated and originally fairly tentative, essentially speculative, view of Andrew Marshall and OSD Net Assessment, once the RMA idea became general property it was captured by a profoundly technological view of the revolution that seemed to beckon the armed forces into a new golden age of enhanced effectiveness.[16] This technophilia was to be expected, given America's technological strengths, its military culture, and its preferred way of war, and given the particular character of the RMA that seemed to be inviting adoption and exploitation. After all, the contemporary revolutionary change in warfare quintessentially is about the uses of the computer. Unfortunately, though again predictably, the counterblasts against the technophiles who promised to disperse "the fog of war" and like improbable, not to say impossible, achievements were taken too far. Scholars and analysts made the telling points that many, perhaps most, historical RMAs were led by political and social, not technological, change.[17] Also, they argued persuasively that organization, doctrine, and force employment mattered more than technology. Hundley made that point with exceptional clarity when he wrote, "Without an operational concept, the best weapon systems in the world will never revolutionize anything."[18] He cited the machine gun's early history in support of the point, to which one could add French and Soviet experience with the tank in 1940 and 1941, respectively.

As was bound to happen, the assault on the paradigm of technology-led RMA was overdone. Skepticism about the relative importance of technological innovation slipped inadvertently into what began to approach a technophobic perspective. The balance needs to be restored. While those of us who have written skeptically about the significance of technology for military and strategic excellence, and I count myself guilty on this count,[19] have slayed the technological dragon of such technophiles as Adm. Bill Owens, we have proceeded intellectually beyond "the culminating point of victory."[20]

Although we have drawn attention to the high importance of culture—public, strategic, and military—and have scored historically well-attested points on the vital significance of organization and operational concepts, we need to reconsider the role and relative potency of technological change. The technophiles have lost the debate, though whether they lose in the shaping of U.S. military transformation is, of course, another matter entirely. There is general agreement that how weapons are used is more important than the quality of the weapons themselves. Similarly, it is not especially controversial to maintain that morale is the most vital factor contributing to military effectiveness. However, the quality of weapons does matter. Moreover, morale, no matter how high initially, cannot be relied on to survive lethal close encounters with a better armed enemy. So many and complex are the dimensions of warfare that there will be ways to compensate for a technical shortfall. However, such compensation can be insufficient, and its desperate necessity should be avoided.[21] Technology matters, even though it does not matter most.

This largely conceptual section of the study concludes with the posing and brisk direct answering of the most salient questions on RMA, the notion of revolutionary change in warfare.

1. *Does the RMA concept make sense?* On balance, it does, though it can only be accepted with some reservation. Constant repetition of the RMA initialism deadens critical faculties. It is sensible to recognize that the character and conduct of war are always changing, and that the rate of change periodically, if irregularly, accelerates and manifests itself in non-linear outcomes in a new way in warfare. While it is no more than common sense to appreciate the historical reality of occasional bursts of revolutionary change in warfare, transcending such a mundane understanding and postulating RMAs is perilous. We are in danger of captivation by our own grandiose concept. After all, as a metanarrative, the RMA thesis holds that strategic history effectively has been organized and moved on

by periodic revolutionary discontinuities in military affairs. There is merit in that view, but only some. It is rather too monocausal for comfort. We should not forget that there is a subtle, but important, difference between the concept of RMA and the rather less definite notion of revolutionary or radical change in warfare. As we have noted already, there is no acid test for how revolutionary or radical change needs to be before it becomes RMA. Recall the Krepinevich definition that holds that an RMA "alters the character and conduct of conflict . . . by producing a dramatic increase—often an order of magnitude or greater—in the combat potential and military effectiveness of armed forces." What appears to have occurred is that a large fraction of the defense community succumbed to the reification fallacy. It forgot, if it ever realized, that RMA is an intellectual invention by theorists, including historians, the latter being members of a profession usually hostile to far-reaching ideas. As a consequence, there is an expectation that dramatic benefit will surely accrue, if only the United States can implement an information-led RMA. Without the reified idea of an RMA, it is probable that more modest and measured expectations would attend the pursuit of a revolutionary change in warfare.

2. *Is the RMA concept useful?* The obvious answer is that surely it must be, since it has dominated American defense discourse for many years. Even 9/11 and the consequent attention to countering terrorism and strengthening homeland security generally failed to deflect the march toward execution of an information-led revolution in the conduct of war. However, popularity and merit are not always the same. It may be worthwhile to consider the opportunity costs of the RMA thesis. While American defense professionals were earnestly and prolifically exploring and debating RMA, even in its less grandiose form as radical change, what were they not investigating? For one suggestion, they were not usefully debating the strategic purposes of the mooted revolutionary change in warfare. Historically, revolutionary military changes have been task-driven. What were, and are, the tasks that foreign policy could lay on the country's armed forces? It is difficult to resist the conclusion that in the minds

of many the quest for revolutionary change, RMA, then transformation, comes perilously close to being an end in itself. As I argued in chapter 4, the United States has a persistent strategy deficit rather than any dangerous incapacity to exploit the revolutionary military possibilities of information technology.

3. *Does the RMA thesis matter?* Despite these skeptical, even negative, comments, the answer to this question has to be "yes." The RMA thesis holds that revolutions in warfare happen and that they render an existing way in combat obsolete. It would be hard to exaggerate the importance of that proposition. Whether or not it is true, or true enough to warrant respect as a general verity, is another matter. A problem with the RMA thesis is that it encourages its devotees to overreach with their expectations of consequent advantage; this is because of two principal reasons. First, even a genuinely revolutionary change in the conduct of warfare simply may not deliver the "dramatic increase" in military effectiveness that the Krepinevich definition promises. Moreover, even if it does deliver, the military and strategic output may fall far short of ensuring success. To repeat the mantra, there is, after all, more to war than warfare. Second, if we recall the first of the Clausewitzian epigraphs to this chapter, it is a persistent fact that warfare manifests itself in many varieties, often even within the same war. One size of revolutionary military change is unlikely to fit all cases of American strategic need.

4. *Is change in warfare evolutionary rather than revolutionary?* An important reason why it can be difficult to recognize and understand revolutionary change in warfare is that it is a process that must mature over time. We cannot be certain that a revolution worthy of that description has been achieved until it has been demonstrated in battle, and possibly not even then. For example, the initial German gains in their great Michael Offensive launched on March 21, 1918, were indeed secured by means of new—at least relatively so—infantry tactics; those tactics, however, were flattered by the frailties in the British defense as well as by the meteorological fog that compounded the usual fog of war to confuse and panic

the defenders.[22] Similarly, the iconic RMA success of German arms in France in May 1940 may be the exemplar of the benefit to be reaped from revolutionary change. As in the previous example, though, the potency of the German offensive depended significantly on an extraordinary measure of operational incompetence on the part of the French High Command, as well as on exemplary old-fashioned performance by infantry units.[23] It would seem that the effectiveness of revolutionary change in warfare lies not, at least not only, in the new style of combat itself, as the RMA thesis claims (see the Krepinevich definition), but very much in the military and strategic contexts of its application. Changes in warfare cannot be effected overnight. They have to be the product of an evolution. There is an obvious circularity of argument threatening here. We can only be certain that an RMA has occurred when a revolutionary style of warfare is demonstrated successfully in battle. However, new styles of warfare do not always succeed. Once the enemy has assimilated that he faces an unfamiliar style, he may be able to defeat it by a mixture of emulation and calculated evasion, always provided he has the space and time to do so. Recall that the standard RMA definition (see Krepinevich again) preemptively resolves the issue of desirability by specifying that military revolution produces a dramatic increase in combat potential and effectiveness. It follows from this discussion that two major difficulties impede recognition of the reality of revolutionary change. First, military capability of necessity evolves and the state of its evolution cannot be assessed with high confidence without the test of battle. Second, because war is a complex phenomenon and warfare has many dimensions, it will not always be self-evident why victory or defeat was the outcome. In the conventional Gulf Wars of 1991 and 2003, the U.S.-led coalition victories were hugely overdetermined.

5. *Are continuities as important as changes as contributors to military effectiveness?* Naturally, a focus on revolutionary change must privilege discontinuity. Indeed, by definition, the revolutionary is expecting to secure "an order of magnitude or greater" improvement in military potential and effectiveness. Without challenging

that view directly, I find it is necessary to point out that the conduct of war is a complex undertaking, and even a revolutionary change in method will have only a limited domain of competence. To resort to a controversial phrase, history shows that even an apparently superior new method of war cannot compensate for errors in policy and strategy. Tactical, and even operational, excellence is meaningless, save with respect to its political and strategic contextual significance. Moreover, the revolutionized military force needs to be available in decisive quantity, as well as quality, if it is to fulfill its tasks. In addition, history also seems to suggest that even armies unable or unwilling to follow the RMA leader all the way to and through a revolution sometimes are able to blunt the cutting edge of the forces of the revolutionary leader. Morale, discipline, leadership, attention to the much maligned "principles of war," an imaginative search for the distinctive vulnerabilities in a new way of war, and a devoted effort to find offsetting advantages are all candidate contributors to counterrevolutionary effectiveness. The potency of a revolutionary change in warfare must depend critically on the contexts within which it is applied. Because warfare has many variants, it is improbable that a single, albeit revolutionary, change in style will be effective in all cases of potential need. The generic continuities in military activities from period to period are many and strong. Indeed, it is probably sound to believe that often there is less to gain from a new way of fighting than there is from the reliable recovery of past skills. Counterinsurgency springs to mind as a skill set that has an uneven record in status as an episodically much needed core competency of the U.S. Army.[24]

6. *Is revolutionary change in warfare the high road to victory?* The answer plainly is "no." Viewed politically and strategically, superior conduct of what is sensibly judged to be the wrong war will, indeed must, produce well-merited defeat. The two finest armies of the twentieth century, those of Germany in the two world wars, lost and lost catastrophically in the second instance. It is easy to be misunderstood. This study is not skeptical about, let alone hostile to, revolutionary change in warfare. What is at issue is not revolution,

but what is asked and expected of it. The target here is neither revolutionary change nor transformation, but rather the assumption that investment in such a venture must guarantee future military and strategic success. It may be an exaggeration when posed this way, but as such it helps make a vital point. One has to beware of talismanic faith in a favored vision of military revolution. Why? First, because war is multidimensional, and the dimensions that we succeed in revolutionizing are likely to be outnumbered and to be substantially offset in their effects by behavior in the dimensions that we either have not, or cannot, change.[25] Second, it is a persisting weakness of prophets for new ways in war not to pay the enemy due respect. Thus far in this analysis, little has been said on the all-important subject that war is a duel. Enemies, current and potential, could not fail to notice the emergence of a revolutionary change in the U.S. way in warfare, especially since we have spent fifteen years debating its character and promise and have offered demonstrations in warfare itself. There is a danger that the armed forces will be so committed to their own network-centric transformation that they fail to recognize the true character of potentially effective offsetting revolutionary change elsewhere. As a simple matter of historical record, RMA leadership has not always led to ultimate victory in war. Hundley argues, "*RMAs frequently bestow an enormous and immediate military advantage on the first nation to exploit them in combat* [emphasis in the original]." Although that is true enough, the nation that wins the final combat in a conflict, not the opening round, secures the victory.

THE CONTEXTS OF WARFARE

Warfare is about context. It is not self-referential, autonomous behavior. Instead, it is about relative power, which is to say it is about politics. The political context is the source of, and provides the meaning for, war and its conduct in warfare. The analysis in this section does not discount the importance of military science, or of what Clausewitz called the "grammar" of war.[26] This section rather intends to help correct an imbalance in analysis, contribute to the recognition and understanding of revolutionary change in warfare, and address a subject that typically is discussed literally and, therefore, narrowly. Of course, it is important to recognize and understand changing ways in warfare in their military dimension. However, it is scarcely less important to gain the insight into the prospect of occurrence of those changing ways, as well as into the likely character of the changes, that can come only from the study of warfare's contexts.

When defense professionals strive to recognize and understand revolutionary change they need to: leap the ethnocentric barrier and consider the strategic context from an adversary's point of view; pay full respect to the authority of the political context; recognize that revolutionary change does not necessarily deliver a step-level jump in effectiveness, only because it is new; and, finally, appreciate that warfare, as Clausewitz reminds us, can assume many forms.[27]

Happy is the defense planner who must devise ways to contend with a single kind of foe in combat of known and predictable character conducted by familiar methods with a stable arsenal over issues and in geography that are thoroughly familiar.[28] Poor leadership, bad luck, normal friction, and so forth, may deny one victory, but at least there should be little danger of preparing for the wrong war. Alas, the U.S. situation today is maximally uncertain, in the sharpest of contrasts to the hypothetical condition outlined above. The American superpower is committed explicitly to global strategic preeminence.[29] This commitment is logical and indeed necessary, given the country's role as the principal armed agent of world order, the global "sheriff," as I have argued elsewhere.[30] The trouble is that the global guardian of order's role attracts hostile attention from those who would deny the United States influence in their neighborhoods.[31] The role carries obligations to intervene selectively, at least to accept responsibilities, for maintaining or restoring order in deadly quarrels among alien societies and polities. It follows that the U.S. defense community faces two tasks of extraordinary difficulty. First, because the United States may have to dissuade, deter, and if need be defeat a wide range of regular and irregular enemies, the scope of needed effectiveness placed on the country's ongoing RMA, or transformation, is exceptionally wide by any historical standard. Second, it will be challenging in the extreme for the armed forces to anticipate and recognize emergent alien ways in warfare that are, to a degree, purposefully asymmetrical to the new U.S. model of excellence.

While changing defense planning so that the principal driver is capability rather than threat is permissible, for several reasons such an address-free generic approach is apt to leave the planner short-changed on policy guidance. Capabilities are not always self-explanatory, especially in an age of "unrestricted warfare."[32] Also, defense planners must realize that the effort to recognize and understand revolutionary change in warfare is best approached in its respective contexts. These contexts explain why war occurs and how it is waged. It may be a revelation to many in the technology-focused U.S. defense community to realize that, historically, military method and capability have by no means been revolutionized by technological innovations alone, or even at all in some cases.[33]

This section's purpose is to explore the roles of the principal contexts of warfare, the ones that drive and shape the activity. If we are to improve our ability to recognize and understand revolutionary change, we must look beyond military science, which is to say beyond Clausewitz's grammar of war, to the impact of change in and affecting these contexts. The contexts discussed are the political, the strategic, the social-cultural, the economic, the technological, and the geographical. Although these contexts are separately identifiable, naturally they influence each other.

1. *The political context*: This is the breeding ground of war, and hence warfare. If there is no political context, there can be no war. Although organized violence may be criminal, or recreational-sporting, if it is not about the relative power of political entities, not only states, it is not warfare. RMA theory can seduce the unwary into finding favor in a grand historical master narrative that at least implies near autarky for military developments. One can

compose a military history of the past two centuries that tells the military story almost wholly in military terms. In this study, we suggest that such a partial perspective, though in its limited way essential, is certain to promote misunderstanding. It neglects the most important engines of change. The state of the art in military prowess is not divorced from political and social influence. Revolutionary change in methods of war does not comprise a first-order problem. Wars do not occur because of military change, revolutionary, or other. The German way of war in the victory years of 1939–41 was, of course, significant, but it was of secondary importance. In the 1930s, it would have been useful for French, British, and American observers to have secured a better grasp than they did of the military meaning of Germany's innovative *Panzer* divisions and obsession with dive bombing.[34] Even more profit, though, would have flowed from an intelligent understanding of the changing political context. The problem was not the *Panzer* division, or even the so-called Blitzkrieg strategy—rather it was Adolf Hitler. The Third Reich was determined to wage war, virtually regardless of the military method it would be obliged to pursue.[35]

As the international political context alters, so do the incentives to pursue military innovation. The end of the Cold War is of far greater significance for national and international security than is the information-led RMA. The demise of the USSR upset the global geopolitical game board. The United States debated and, at a modest pace, proceeded to exploit the information revolution, even though it remains uncertain what tasks will dominate the future of the military establishment. However, to recognize and understand the revolutionary military change that should be of most concern to Americans, there is an acute need to comprehend movement in the threat environment. It is not sufficient, indeed it would be foolish, to seek to recognize and understand revolutionary military change if one did not first recognize and understand the character and location of those who one may have to deter or fight.

2. *The strategic context:* As the ever-changing political context fuels demands for military preparation and occasional action, so

the strategic context expresses the relationship between political demand and military supply, keyed to the particular tasks specific to a conflict. The concept of strategic context is infrequently defined. It tends to be a familiar and rather grandiose term that is rhetorically useful mainly for its vagueness. Bearing in mind that strategy is the bridge between political purpose, or policy, and the military instrument, we will define strategic context as the tasks or missions assigned to armed forces by policy in the light of expected difficulties and opportunities, especially those created by enemies.

Geopolitics has much to say about strategic context. For example, beneath, and derivative from, the political context of superpower antagonism in the Cold War was a strategic context dominated by a central geopolitical reality. Although the Soviet-American rivalry was in a sense global, ideological, and ultimately territorially non-specific, the respective spheres of interest met around, generally onshore, the Rimlands of Eurasia.[36] For forty years the principal challenge for U.S. strategy was the need to extend a credible, or not incredible, nuclear deterrence over allies and friends an ocean away from North America and in the bloated Soviet imperium. This distinctive strategic context drove the United States constantly to revise its nuclear strategy in the hope that its credibility of contingent employment might be enhanced in the service of deterrence.

It may be sensible to conflate the political and strategic contexts, in recognition that "[t]he conduct of war, in its great outlines, is therefore policy itself."[37] Nonetheless, in this study, we prefer to keep strategy in clear focus, while appreciating its vital bridging function.[38] It is not too much of a challenge to explain the significance of strategic context for the mission of this study. If we ask the direct questions, "where might revolutionary change in warfare come from?" and "where should we look?" the leading answers must lie, first, in the political context as the *sine qua non*, and second, in the strategic context that derives from the political. What are the strategic relations, the problems and opportunities, implicit in a particular political context?

3. *The social-cultural context:* Warfare has many dimensions and

the most potent are included in this conflated "super category." We must emphasize the fact of complex interpretation. Although we isolate six contexts here for convenience, history does not work along neatly separate grooves. They are all variably significant and influence each other simultaneously. As I have argued for many years, strategic study has to be conducted holistically. On a cognate matter, of "[t]he strategic elements that affect the use of engagements," Clausewitz identified only five types: "the moral, the physical, the mathematical, the geographical, and the statistical."[39] However, he issued a stern and grim warning:

> It would however be disastrous to try to develop an understanding of strategy by analyzing these factors in isolation, since they are usually interconnected in each military action in manifold and intricate ways. A dreary analytical labyrinth would result.[40]

Social-cultural trends are likely to prove more revealing at an early stage of the prospect for revolutionary change in warfare than missile tests, defense contracts, military maneuvers, or even possibly limited demonstration of a novel prowess in combat. Consider the information-led RMA that is the heart and soul of some people's vision of transformation. It is true that the US Army understands that transformation is about soldiers, people, as armies always have been.[41] However, that ancient truth is not universally accepted, except nominally.

The current policy on transformation, which, at Defense Department level at least, is very much a high technology story, is a direct reflection of the trends in American society.[42] There is merit in the Tofflers' deterministic claim that societies fight in approximately the same manner that they produce wealth.[43] In World War II, when America was preponderantly an industrial society, it waged industrial-age war on a scale that confounded foes and astonished allies. Now that America is evolving into a post-industrial society, wherein the manipulation of information is the key to prosperity, so, naturally enough, the armed forces must reflect that emerging reality.

Consider another example of the social-cultural roots of revolutionary change in warfare. The comparatively recent contemporary phenomenon of religiously motivated irregular warfare, including terrorism, was plainly detectable in the course and outcome of the war waged in Afghanistan against the Soviet atheists in the 1980s. With the uplifting example of the 1979 Iranian Revolution, followed by the demonstrated potency of holy warriors in defeating a superpower, albeit with some vital arms provided by other unbelievers, it should not have come as a great surprise to find that military revolution might follow.[44] In the 1990s, most American defense professionals were eagerly debating what is and is not an RMA. In the Middle East, though, a revolutionary change in warfare was brewing as an Islamic revival of an extreme fundamentalist kind met up with and exploited the tools of the information age.

The social-cultural engine for revolutionary change in warfare works in two ways. On the one hand, it can, and typically does, shape the character of the revolution attainable. On the other hand, society and its dominant beliefs provide the fuel for the political decisions, the policy, that actually produce the military revolution as well as the exercise of that revolution in war. It is worth considering the possible implications of the point that, by definition, revolutionary change in methods of war are extraordinary events. They are undertaken only for serious reasons. RMAs are certain to be hugely disruptive, they are probably very expensive, and being revolutionary, they are bound to be fraught with uncertainty over effectiveness. This discussion leads inexorably to the argument that, as with arms race analysis, the political and the social-cultural always have pride of place in causation over the grammar of war. In the 1930s, the democracies would have been well advised to study the bizarre ideology of the curious new German führer and the steps by which he and his gang of opportunists eventually secured a total grip on society and its common assumptions.[45] Of course, while the evolution of German military method mattered, that was only because of an official public culture—as made manifest in what passed for policy—that would send it into open-ended battle.

Many people have noticed that in the defense community's understandable fascination with the potential for revolutionary change in warfare, and now its commitment to the long-term execution of such change in a process of military transformation, it has paid too little attention to what amounts to a social and cultural transformation in Western public attitudes toward war and warfare. In his articles published in the mid-1990s, Edward Luttwak rang this bell loudly on the dawning of an age of what he called, evocatively, "post-heroic warfare."[46] Cultural assumptions about war, its legitimacy, its proper conduct, and its utility play a crucial role in strategic history. Not only do states and other polities wage war, but societies as well. Additionally, there is much more to war than warfare itself, which is to say war's grammar. When we scan the strategic landscape for evidence of revolutionary change, we must not neglect the domestic and foreign social context.[47] The attitude of our society to war and warfare, and especially to casualties, can have major implications for the range of acceptable military methods available to our generals. It is a matter of notable significance that other societies, with different cultures, will not share all, or even many, of America's cultural assumptions.

4. *The economic context:* Wars are rarely waged because of economic reasons, popular beliefs to the contrary notwithstanding, and with the granting of some colonial exceptions. However, warfare is economic behavior, inter alia, as it also has to be logistical behavior. Revolutionary change in warfare does not require an enabling economic revolution, because the change in question may not critically depend on a radical alteration in the use of material resources. However, societies that "take off" industrially and then are locked into a temporally indefinite process of scientific, industrial, and agricultural progress typically will develop foreign interests, responsibilities, and a sense of relative self-importance that is near certain to require military expression. There are no laws of political and strategic behavior comparable to the laws of the natural sciences. We can, though, hazard as a quasi-law the axiom that newfound economic strength breeds political ambition, which must have a strategic

context and implications for military posture. This is not to deny that revolutionary change in warfare can be attempted, even effected, by the economically challenged. Such revolutionaries must seek in desperation to find ways to fight smarter and certainly more cheaply than their richer enemies. All that we claim here is that ways in warfare, revolutionary and other, have an economic context. Although not as significant as the political, strategic, or social-cultural, the economic context can still provide a valuable source of warning of possible, or even probable, future strategic problems. For example, the Chinese rate of economic growth has the country well on the road to true super-statehood. There are a number of reasons why the fragility of China's exhaustible export-led prosperity should discourage her powerfully from staging a serious challenge to American military hegemony. However, the strategic history of the past two centuries attests conclusively to the unreliability of economic rationality as a predictor of state behavior. All that we claim is that political and military greatness requires the underpinning of economic greatness.[48] A polity rising economically very rapidly cannot help but acquire the means to afford a significant jump in its military capabilities. Since it will be coming up from behind in the competitive stakes, it is certain to be motivated to identify short cuts to military effectiveness. In other words, China is an ideal customer for new ways in warfare.

5. *The technological context:* While warfare always has a technological context, that context is not always the principal fuel for revolutionary change. Scholars have highlighted this lesson of experience by distinguishing between a Military Technical Revolution (MTR) and an RMA.[49] The MTR is simply a technology-led RMA. This was the idea that so exercised Soviet analysts in the 1970s and early 1980s, especially in the truly prescient form of the "reconnaissance-strike complex." That particular Soviet high-technology vision of future warfare was indistinguishable from the cutting edge of the technological dimension to the American military transformation of the twenty-first century. What did the regular warfare in Afghanistan and Iraq in 2001 and 2003 showcase if not

an excellence in command, control, communications, computing, intelligence, targeting, and reconnaissance (C⁴ISTAR)? To which, in recognition of Stephen Biddle's careful review of military events, one must add the perennial favorite, combined arms.[50] Although Andrew Marshall and his Office of Net Assessment in OSD broadened the Soviet-sourced concept of MTR to RMA and recognized the importance of organization, operational concepts, and numbers, contemporary American awareness of and interest in the possibility of revolutionary military change has always had a powerful technological motor. This has been inevitable and, up to a point, desirable. After all, the exponential growth in computing capacity has sparked the current rash of technological fires. Moreover, technological seers advise that there is no plausible scientific or engineering reason why Moore's Law should be falsified in this century.[51]

There are obvious and profound differences among the services in their relative dependence on and attitude toward technology. Whereas sailors man ships and airmen fly aircraft, soldiers *use* equipment. The quality of technology can be a matter of life and death to sailors and airmen. Operating in a more complex geography, soldiers often have more choices to help them compensate for technological shortfalls.

Appreciation of war's changing technological context is an essential intelligence function, as well as a vital source of inspiration for change. However, a common material context across societies does not necessarily equate to a common understanding of the scale or character of the change that may be on offer.[52] Given their unique contexts, different public, strategic, and military cultures exploit and pick and choose among new technologies according to their own criteria of utility—not in obedience to a universal military logic. For example, if we consider the mechanization RMA(s) of the period 1930–45, it is clear that, notwithstanding a tolerably common technological base, each of the principal combatants in World War II developed air and mechanized ground forces along nationally distinctive lines, for reasons that appeared to make sense for each polity's strategic and military situation.[53] Many military technologies lend themselves to varied employment, depending on the local military tasks and strategic context, and the preferences in operational concepts and organization. Identifying technological trends, no matter how accurately, is no guarantee of a grasp of their meaning. One could make much the same point by observing that superb overhead reconnaissance will provide formidable detail on people and their movement. Unfortunately, that intelligence can tell one nothing at all about what is in their hearts and minds.

Paradoxically, the more firmly an RMA leader, such as the United States with information technology, becomes wedded to a distinctive and arguably revolutionary paradigm of future warfare, the more likely it is to misread the character of military change abroad. It is difficult for a proud and self-confidently dominant military power to accept the notion that there can be more than one contemporary military enlightenment.[54] The strategic sin of ethnocentricity is readily revealed. First, other military cultures may not agree with the dominant power's military logic. Second, even if they appreciate the sense in the RMA leader's choices, those cultures will be bound to make their own decisions on investment in innovation, based on such local circumstances as distinctive military tasking, affordability, and the need to offset the RMA leader's putative advantages.[55]

Despite the contrary claims and implications of dozens of television series, the technological dimension to warfare is only rarely decisive. War and its conduct in warfare are complex. Just as its outbreak typically is the product of redundant causation, so its course and outcome, no less typically, is not attributable to technological advantage. It is easy to see why this should be so. Given war's complexity, the large number of dimensions that are always in play, of which the technological is only one, there are simply too many factors other than the technological that must influence events. This is a long familiar truth. For example, a study of Alexander the Great and his way of war concludes that although his army was "a well-armed force . . . not too much should be made of the technological edge it enjoyed over most of its enemies."[56] The author, David Lonsdale, explains:

> In the close-order combat of this period [fourth century BC], the tactical prowess and morale of the forces was more important to the outcome of battles. Technology does not win wars. Even on those occasions when technology was clearly very significant, for example in the use of siege engines, breaches in the enemy's defences still had to be exploited by Alexander's men in face-to-face combat with the enemy. However good Alexander's instrument was, this outstanding army still had to be led and handled effectively. [57]

Though the book's subject is Alexander, the analysis has contemporary relevance.

6. *The geographical context:* No study of warfare can afford to neglect the geographical context. Time after time over the past century, military revolution keyed to the emerging exploitation of a new geographical environment has beckoned the visionary theorist and the bold military professional. Since 1900, RMA anticipators and spotters, had there been such in the early twentieth century, would have been obliged to recognize and understand the meaning of: *submarines*, for a potential revolution in sea warfare; *aircraft* for a potential revolution (a) in warfare as a whole, (b) in warfare on land, (c) in warfare to, at, and from the sea; *spacecraft* for a potential revolution with aircraft in warfare as a whole as well as in each of the terrestrial geographies; finally, the computer as *cyberpower*. Undoubtedly, there has been no historical precedent for the scale and diversity of the challenges posed by the geographical expansion of warfare since 1900. Over the past hundred years, defense analysts, strategic theorists, and the soldiers and sailors, who would be at most immediate risk, have had to contend with the promise and peril of no fewer than four new environments (including the undersea). We are so familiar with the concept of airpower, even spacepower, and now—just about—cyberpower, that we are apt to forget how novel the modern geographical challenges to the

comprehension of military and strategic affairs are and have been. From a time before recorded history, humans had waged war in only two dimensions, on land and on the surface of the sea. For us to have added no fewer than four geographical environments to those traditional two in less than a century one may register as progress or, less optimistically, at least as monumental cumulative change. How revolutionary, though, would the submarine, the aircraft, the earth satellite, and the computer prove to be? It is sobering to realize that even today, a century since the first flight of a heavier-than-air vehicle, the potency of the airpower RMA remains controversial.

Thus far this discussion has stressed the challenge in the novelty of the expansion of warfare's geography. It is necessary, however, to balance that analysis with recognition of the geographical context's more permanent features. Because this inquiry's subject privileges radical change, it threatens to drive into the shadows the more significant contextual elements that slowly change, if at all. While it is necessary to recognize and understand revolutionary change in warfare, it is scarcely less important to recognize and understand the constants or slow-to-change variables. The latter concern can be controversial. The history of the advocates of military revolution claims that its favored new method of war, exploiting a new geography, would certainly render obsolescent, then obsolete, older concerns tied to the other geographies. This has been the pattern of claims from the submarine, to the aircraft, to the satellite, and now to the computer. Cyberspace, we have been told, not only shrinks space, and therefore time, it is effectively beyond geography, it exists everywhere and in a sense, therefore, nowhere.[58] If "command of the nets" is the decisive enabler of victory in future warfare, as Bruce Bekowitz maintains, physical geography cannot fail to suffer a marked demotion in strategic significance.[59]

Through the several RMAs of the past century, up to and including the current exploitation of the computer, the geographical context has retained features whose importance has scarcely been scratched by revolution. Notwithstanding the marvels of submarines, aircraft, spacecraft, and computers, humans are land animals, and functionally viewed, war is about the control of their will. In the timeless and priceless words of Rear Admiral Wylie, "*the ultimate determinant in war is the man on the scene with the gun* [emphasis in the original]. This man is the final power in war. He is control."[60] Whether they dream of decisive mechanized maneuver, bombardment from altitude, or electronically triggered mass disruption, military revolutionaries should never forget Wylie's maxim. It is perhaps strange to record that in our enthusiasm for novelty, especially for that of a technical kind, we can forget what war is about as well as who wages it. War is about politics, warfare always is about people, and people inhabit and relate to a particular territorial context.

Another more controversial aspect to the salience of physical geography is what we call the geopolitical. The arrangement of continents, ocean, and islands is what it is. Undeniably, changes in warfare, especially in the technologies of communication, have altered the meaning of geographical distance and, hence, time. However, there is much, indeed there is very much, of a geopolitical character in warfare's geographical context that alters hardly at all.[61] National geographical location continues to matter greatly. Location dictates the necessary balance among a polity's military instruments. It determines the identity of neighbors. It translates into a distinctive history and culture, and it provides strategic opportunity and carries implicit strategic perils. Despite the wonders of network-centric warfare (NCW) and effect-based operations (EBO), significant differences between combat in the jungle, the desert, the mountains, and the city will long remain. Exploiting its cyberpower, an information-leveraging military establishment may well improve its performance in all environments. However, a prudent process of transformation must be flexible, adaptable, and ever mindful of the eternal fact that war is not about the enemy's military defeat, necessary though that usually will be. Instead, war is about persuading the enemy that he is defeated; to repeat, it is about influencing his will. Warfare is about human behavior, ours and the enemy's. Every RMA, actual or mooted, is no more than a means to affect the minds of the people in our gunsights. Those people live in physical geography, and whether we traverse that geography hypersonically or at marching pace is really only a detail.

REVOLUTIONARY CHANGE IN WARFARE: FINDINGS AND IMPLICATIONS

The information-led revolution has been advancing, initially slowly, for more than thirty years. We can argue over whether the Gulf War of 1991 was the last war of the industrial age or the first one of the information era. However, it is a matter of public record that that conflict alerted the world that regular conventional warfare was changing in potentially radical ways.[62] The RMA concept emerged from the brew consisting of several ingredients: monitored Soviet analyses, mentioned already; a decade-plus of research and development effort to find technological offsets to Soviet mechanized strength, tactics, and inferred operational designs in Europe, hence the quest for long-range precision strike and stealthy delivery; the dramatic evidence of a new precise way in war that was much advertised in briefings on the 1991 victory; and the historians' debate, with their somewhat arcane, not to say parochial, controversies over what were and were not historical RMAs. Understanding of revolutionary change in warfare is sufficiently mature today for it to be feasible to attempt an overall critical assessment.

    1. *Contexts rule.* The chapter's central message is that war's contexts impart most of the story. The political context is what war, warfare, and revolutionary change in either or both are about. The strategic context derives strictly from the political, while the social-cultural, economic, technological, and geographical define the bounds of feasibility. After all, strategy for the conduct of war is "the art of the possible," inter alia.[63] The future of the armed forces will be propelled not so much by the strength of the drive to transform, but more by the political and strategic contexts that will shape its missions and tasks. That future is not in the hands of a reified Science of War, no matter how expertly determined by our more scientifically inclined theorists and analysts. The armed forces'

future is rather at the mercy of the answers to such questions as: "Will China assemble an anti-American coalition to contest global leadership?" and "Will America's enemies principally be non-state in character for decades to come?" These questions come with the implication that the U.S. military establishment should transform itself in such a way as to privilege COIN as the most core of its competencies.

2. *Revolutionary change in warfare may be less important than revolutionary change in attitudes toward war and the military.* While the U.S. military establishment has been planning and beginning to implement a revolutionary change in its capabilities for warfare, it has been behind the curve in understanding revolutionary change in the social-cultural context of the institution of war. Too much can be made of this argument. However, two revolutions are plausibly underway: one in warfare, the subject of the protracted debate over RMA and then transformation; and the second in the social-cultural context of war.[64] Although war has a constant nature, attitudes toward its legitimacy and appropriate conduct have been highly variable. The pilots of U.S. P-47 Thunderbolt fighter-bombers massacred German forces desperately striving to escape from Normandy through the Falaise Gap in August 1944. By contrast, in 1991, the United States wielded an air arm that it felt obliged to rein in because of the historical replay of Falaise that was unfolding on the so-called highway of death leading north from Kuwait City. Standards of acceptable military behavior vary over time, from conflict to conflict, and sometimes within the same war against different enemies. The reasons are in part political-pragmatic, as the conduct of war is scrutinized by the media with an immediacy and in a detail that is historically unprecedented.[65] This process began as long ago as the 1850s in the Crimean War. It was the result of greater public literacy, and hence the demand for more news; the creation of the new profession of war correspondent; the invention of the electric telegraph; and, of course, the slow growth of democratic politics, which engendered a sense of public involvement in the country's strategic ventures and adventures.[66]

Some theorists today believe that the RMA, which is the responsibility of the U.S. defense establishment to effect, is of less significance than a Revolution in Attitudes toward the Military (RAM) is. The future American way(s) of war, singular or plural, will be shaped by the social-cultural context that defines the bounds of acceptable military behavior, as well as by the military-technical opportunities that beckon as a consequence of the exploitation of information technology.

By way of an extreme, but telling, example of the potency of this second finding, consider the character of the Soviet–German War (within a war) of 1941–45. While one must explain the scale of the struggle in terms of the combatants' extraordinary strength, the breathtaking brutality of what was truly a total war owed less to the military methods of the belligerents than to the rival ideologies and the finality of the stakes; it was either victory or death. It is plausible to argue that Germany might well have won its war in the East had the social-cultural context of that conflict not been defined by the Nazi leadership as a struggle for racial survival; but then, of course, the Nazi leaders would not have been Nazis.

Revolutionary change in warfare is always much more than a narrowly military matter. What is more, social-cultural contexts differ among societies. It is not safe to assume that strategic behavior deemed morally unacceptable by our society would meet with identical prohibition abroad. Although this chapter registers approval of the newfound official significance attached to war's social-cultural dimension, two caveats need to be noted. It is all too easy to seize on a fashionable, and basically prudent, idea and agree without considering the implications. First, in the current discourse on defense policy, recognition of the relevance of "culture" has noticeably become a part of the necessary canon of right beliefs. As such, it is in danger of evolving rapidly, if it has not already done so, from an excellent idea into little more than a panacea.[67] In the latter case, it is being touted as *the answer* to America's military and strategic difficulties when intervening in alien societies. However, it is not the answer—only a part. The second caveat is to remind the army that it commands warriors, not cultural anthropologists. Of course, while understanding the enemy, and one's friends as well, is important, armies are, at root, about fighting. Given the global domain of America's ordering interests, it is thoroughly impractical to expect more than a small number of military specialists to acquire a deep knowledge of the relevant local societies with their values, beliefs, languages, and histories.

3. *There are vital conditions for success in carrying through revolutionary changes in warfare.* Primarily based on the authority of eight case studies, focusing on the 14th century up to 1940,[68] historians MacGregor Knox and Williamson Murray advanced four historically founded claims about RMAs. First, they argue that "technology alone has rarely driven them; it has functioned above all as a catalyst"; second, that "revolutions in military affairs have emerged from evolutionary problem-solving directed at specific operational and tactical issues in a specific theatre of war against a specific enemy. Successful innovators have always thought in terms of fighting wars against *actual* rather than *hypothetical* opponents, with *actual* capabilities, in pursuit of *actual* strategic and political objectives"; third, that "such revolutions require coherent frameworks of doctrine and concepts built on service cultures that are deeply *realistic*. Innovation, to be successful, must rest upon thorough understanding of the fundamentally chaotic nature of war"; and fourth, that "revolutions in military affairs remain rooted in and limited by strategic givens and by the nature of war. *They are not a substitute for strategy*—as so often assumed by utopians—but merely an operational or tactical means [emphasis in the original]."[69]

I quote Knox and Murray so extensively because theirs is the most mature, authoritatively researched, and persuasive collective statement from the historians' realm about revolutionary change in warfare to have appeared. Their edited book is especially impressive, because it is authored by scholars who are friendly to the RMA thesis, while being prudently skeptical of extravagant claims for the revolutionary impact of innovative technologies. In addition, the book appeared ten years into the long-running debate. By that time,

the authors, the editors in particular, had had ample time to out-
grow any early opinions that may have leaned unduly in praise or
criticism of the RMA postulate.

At this juncture it is necessary to refer to a conceptual and contextual point registered earlier. Specifically, the conclusions to Knox
and Murray, just quoted, need to be seen in the context of the key
distinction that they highlighted between RMAs and the much rarer,
but vastly more traumatic, indeed unavoidable, MRs. The course
and dynamic objectives of the current process of transformation are
arguable. But to the extent to which this process is broadly a response to the global information revolution, effected by the leading
information-using society, the American, it is inevitable, unstop-
pable, and in a sense, beyond criticism. It simply reflects the way of
the world in the twenty-first century.

Knox and Murray have shown that history can be accessible to
and useful for policymakers and soldiers.[70] This is an important
claim, if true. If untrue, it is still important, but a danger. There is
no law that requires one to learn only correct and appropriate things
from historical experience. However, it is the view of this analysis
that historical study, notwithstanding the biases and other fallibilities
of historians, can make an essential contribution to the recognition
and understanding of revolutionary change in warfare.

4. *While recognition of change in warfare is one thing, understanding the character, relevance, and implications of change is something else entirely, given the sovereignty of the political and strategic
contexts.* Historically, recognizing and understanding revolutionary
change has been far more a matter of consequences than of existential recognition. Would-be belligerents tend to be tolerably well-
informed about the capabilities of their intended foes, though there
have been many notable, and notably catastrophic, exceptions.

A belligerent power is not usually as ignorant of the enemy's
military strengths as was Germany in 1941 when it invaded the
USSR. German military intelligence, the Foreign Armies East of
the Army General Staff, confidently undercounted Soviet divisions
initially by a wide margin and, for the future, by a margin so great

as to beggar the imagination. Naturally, there is difficulty in comparing divisions, let alone division-equivalents. German divisions typically were more substantial than Soviet, but wartime attrition, Germany's disastrous and progressively more desperate combat manpower shortage after the 1941 Moscow campaign, as well as the lower fighting quality of Axis allied divisions, heavily increased the German numerical shortfalls. When Barbarossa was unleashed on June 22, 1941, the Foreign Armies East estimated a total Red Army strength, in all theaters (i.e., including Asia), of approximately 240 divisions and their equivalents. They made no allowance for the quasi-army of the NKVD (the Secret Police), the regime's private army, which fielded no fewer than 53 divisions, 20 brigades, several hundred regiments of various types, as well as hundreds of smaller units with special assignments. The main fact on which the Foreign Armies East erred was that the Red Army on July 1, 1941, nominally had 281 division equivalents, not 240 or so, a figure which grew to the incredible figure of 581 by February 1, 1943, when Stalingrad fell, and which expanded to 603 by December 1 of that year. Those figures do not include NKVD forces. The Foreign Armies East was not only highly unreliable on the strength of the Red Army, but it also had no notion of the scale of the USSR's relocation of its armaments factories to the Urals and beyond. Also, it knew nothing about those factories' production capacity. That is what happens when there is no aerial reconnaissance deep over the intended victim's territory (it was forbidden by high policy and the Luftwaffe lacked planes with the necessary range), and when the Abwehr literally had no agents in that country (again, this was forbidden by policy when Hitler was wooing Stalin and later did not want to risk fueling his suspicions).[71] It is more common for belligerents to be as well-informed on the salient facts as they are apt to be ignorant of their true meaning. Whether a process of transformation is best regarded as an MR or an MRA is beside the vital point that no measure of military revolutionary change can alter the sovereignty of warfare's political and strategic contexts. Of course, military effectiveness matters crucially. However, that effectiveness has no value in and of itself. It can only be a means to political ends, via the transmission belt, the bridge, of strategy.

Logically, revolutionary change in warfare can turn the political context into a dependent variable. However, do policymakers shape decisions favoring war because they believe that they have available a reliable military tool? Perhaps this occurs occasionally. But, far more often than not the will and the decision to fight precede confidence in the promise in a new military instrument. If historians are prone to believe the evidence that suits them, so too are policymakers. Some excellent recent studies by historians cast doubt on the popular long-standing image of the military professionals of the mid- to late-nineteenth century and the first half of the twentieth as ignorant buffoons, men as baffled by new technology as they were careless of their men's lives.

It should be instructive for us to note that most senior military leaders of the principal belligerents of 1914 did not share the myth of the "short war illusion." They were not convinced that a great-power war could be so contained that it would not expand to be a general conflict. Rather they believed that a future war among the great powers would engage the efforts of the whole of society; it would be a people's war, as the Franco-Prussian War became after the defeat of the regular French Army. As for the style in warfare appropriate for the conditions of the 1910s, as Antulio Echevarria has shown beyond reasonable challenge, the German Army had attained a good understanding of modern civilian and military technologies' meaning and had proceeded to write excellent tactical doctrine that expressed that understanding. The trouble was that, notwithstanding the legendary superiority of German training methods, many commanders in 1914 ignored the official drills, with lethal consequences for their poorly prepared citizen-soldiers.[72]

At long last, culture is recognized as a dimension known to be important to the success of transformed forces in action or for deterrence. However, to recognize that culture matters is not the same as knowing how it matters or what one should do with the cultural knowledge acquired—and acquired by whom? Theater military planners and soldiers on the ground need cultural enlightenment, not only policymakers in Washington. The effectiveness of a revolutionary American way of war will not be wholly within America's competence to ensure. Americans may wage the wrong war the wrong way, or the right war the wrong way, because they failed to recognize and understand the character of the political and cultural contexts of the conflict at issue.

Public, strategic, and military cultures contribute mightily to the strategic and military choices one makes. Also, they constitute an ideational and normative prism through which we regard the behavior of other cultures.[73] To see foreign strategic behavior as its foreign authors see it can readily overstretch a particularly encultured strategic imagination. An important study of U.S. intelligence performance in spotting foreign military innovation in the interwar years offers conclusions highly relevant to this discussion. Thomas G. Mahnken finds that U.S. intelligence was substantially the victim of its preconceptions.[74] He discovered, perhaps unsurprisingly, that foreign military innovation was most likely to be identified when: it fitted what Americans were predisposed to expect; it had already been demonstrated in battle; or when it was a development that was also of interest to the armed forces. Overall, Mahnken's study warns that it is difficult to spot military innovations, or to assess them realistically, if they are unfamiliar, if they are familiar but not favored by us, or if they are generally despised as unpromising or worse.[75] A cognate idea is Jeremy Black's deployment and use of the notion of cultural assumptions.[76] Predispositions and cultural assumptions clearly can comprise a formidable barrier to understanding. Unlike eighteenth- and nineteenth-century European warfare, American warfare in the twenty-first century will engage notably asymmetrical foes who will fight in unfamiliar ways.

5. *When we make a revolutionary change in the way we fight, we must be adaptable and flexible. If we fail the adaptability test, we are begging to be defeated by the diversity and complexity of future warfare. If we lock ourselves into a way of warfare that is highly potent only across a narrow range of operational taskings, we will wound our ability*

to recognize and understand other varieties of radical change in war-fare. Moreover, we will be slow to respond to them. Clausewitz states that "war is more than a true chameleon that slightly adapts its characteristics to the given case."[77] He proceeds to comment that we need a theory able to accommodate the rich diversity of war's variable character. Clausewitz reposes the heart of his theory of war in his primary trinity, a theory that has to maintain a balance among: violence, hatred, and enmity; chance and probability; and the reason that should be behind policy. He offers a potent simile when he likens the relations among his three tendencies to "an object suspended between three magnets." In other words, although "all wars are things of the same nature," that nature is exceedingly permissive of variety and innovation.

First, while "contexts rule" is the most important of our general findings, its military complement has to meet global strategic responsibilities of the United States to ensure that the radical change it intends in its way of war is sufficiently adaptable and flexible. Historically, successful executors of RMAs have effected change that could be exploited in different ways against different enemies in different geographical conditions. No matter how wonderful the promise of a particular RMA, airpower for a classic example, if it is developed to deliver major advantage only in warfare across a narrow, albeit vitally important, range, it is going to fail the critical strategy test.[78] It will provide means inadequate to support policy. In my book *Strategy for Chaos*, I argued that the implementation of revolutionary change in warfare is strategic behavior.[79]

The necessity for the U.S. Armed Forces to plan, organize, train, equip, and write doctrine for an adaptable transformation can cite no clearer precedent than the experience of "the greatest military strategist of all time."[80] Alexander the Great was never defeated in battle. He carried through an RMA, building on the changes already implemented by his gifted, if notably rough-hewn, father, Philip II. Alexander enjoyed twelve years in supreme command, including the ten-year long series of campaigns to bring down and supplant the superpower of the era, Persia. His army waged war victoriously against regular and irregular enemies, against Greeks and a substantial fraction of the warrior races of Asia, over all manner of terrain, including the worst in the world, and in all weathers. He fought limited wars to coerce, as well as wars of conquest. When feasible, he was pleased to allow diplomacy to secure for him by grand strategy what otherwise would have to be bought by the blood of his soldiers. It is true that the key to Alexander's success was not his RMA, rather it was the personal and national loyalties that sustained morale and his own irreplaceable genius. Nonetheless, despite its highly individual human centerpiece, this tale of distant strategic and military excellence has major implications for today.

Alexander inherited and improved a flexible combined-arms force that proved itself adaptable to the challenges posed by enemies of all kinds, with styles of war utterly strange to the Greeks— for example, the Indian—as well as cunningly contrived to offset Greek strengths. His army functioned well enough in all climes and combats great and small. Alexander's army is an exemplar, perhaps the exemplar, of what armed forces should aim to be, if they need to transform to meet the demands of an ambitious national security strategy. Over the next several decades, U.S. strategic needs will be at least as stressful as those that the Macedonians were obliged to overcome from 334 to 323 BC.

Second, to implement a revolutionary change in warfare is not necessarily to command warfare's future character. To venture a contestable phrase, history appears to show that the combat effectiveness of revolutionary change depends critically on the inadvertent cooperation of a poorly prepared enemy. The initial German assaults in late March 1918, the Blitzkrieg victories of 1939–41, and even the follies of hapless Iraqis in 1991 and 2003, and Talibans in 2001, all illustrate this fact. More distantly, the armies of the French Revolution and Empire depended more on superiority of numbers, on the Emperor's operational, not so much tactical, skill, on their high reputation and morale, and on the prior demoralization of the enemy than they did on a new way in warfare. Rather like the North's Union armies in 1862–63, prior to Gettysburg at least,[81] France's enemies were half-defeated before a shot was fired. However, what if the enemy declines to cooperate physically, morally, operationally, or strategically in his own defeat? What if he seeks, and sometimes finds, a style or form of warfare that does not privilege the "way" of the revolutionary innovator? This is not to suggest that an RMA leader always can be thwarted by a materially disadvantaged foe who needs to fight smarter. It is rather to maintain that in many cases warfare, especially when approached in the broad contexts of the pertinent war, can be prosecuted in a number of alternative ways. The U.S. military competencies magnified by intended revolutionary change should yield vital advantage in warfare of all kinds, but this is a truth with limitations. Intelligent enemies should be able to blunt the U.S. sword by attacking not necessarily American soldiers but rather the American style in warfare. For example, casualty creation will have obvious grand strategic, hence political, attraction. Cunning and capable enemies fight grand strategically, not only military strategically. Wars are waged at every level.

The second implication derives not so much from the diversity of warfare but rather from its complexity. If one asks, "what is war made of?" and "how does it all work?" the answer is depressingly complex.[82] I shall content myself here simply by citing as a fact the many dimensions of warfare and strategy. To maintain focus, I challenge readers to ask themselves in what ways an ongoing military transformation should enable the entire effort to achieve that "dramatic increase—often an order of magnitude or greater—in the combat potential and military effectiveness of armed forces," of which Krepinevich wrote in 1994. Warfare may seem to be a straightforward enterprise. It entails killing people and breaking things for the purposes of high policy. However, to achieve competence in those violent arts a vastly complex institution has to function well enough, though mercifully not perfectly. The point of importance is not to spot the correct number of war's dimensions, an absurdly misconceived task, or to argue about their precise identity.[83] Instead, what matters is to recognize just how complex is the institution of war and its conduct in warfare, and therefore just how vulnerable its course can be to ambush from a wide variety of sources. Folly, incompetence, bad luck, or plain ineffectiveness on almost any of war's dimensions has the potential to make a mockery of that aspiration for a "dramatic increase" in military effectiveness to which Krepinevich pointed.

The third implication of the diversity and complexity of warfare is that even the new way of war may not deliver decisive victory if the political and social-cultural contexts are not permissive. This is not an argument against innovation, revolutionary or other. It is, though, a reminder that few, if any, military establishments are equally competent in the conduct of warfare of every kind. Similarly, RMAs, no matter how well conceived and executed as prudent strategic behavior, always have their distinctive limitations. It is perhaps true to claim that the contemporary American revolution in warfare is more of a grand military revolution (MR) than a humble RMA or MTR. If that is the case, generic limitations should be less damaging. Nonetheless, the traditional American way of war, one which favors firepower and machines over the human touch, is likely to exploit the information revolution militarily in a way that does not yield equivalent benefit in all forms of conflict.[84]

The fourth implication of the diversity and complexity of warfare is that there will often be opportunity for traditional military virtues to triumph over, or at the least embarrass, innovative virtuosity. Military revolution could fail to deliver victory if it is executed in action in a non-permissive political, social, or indeed strategic context. Even if revolutionary change is effected and applied as force in permissive looking contexts, still it may not succeed. Such old fashioned virtues as command efficiencies, discipline, training, morale, and leadership, for key examples, may suffice to blunt the cutting edge of a new way of war. Historically speaking, it is not the case that investment in revolutionary military change yields a ticket to guaranteed victory.

6. *Revolutionary change in warfare always triggers a search for antidotes. Eventually, the antidotes triumph. They can take any or all of tactical, operational, strategic, or political forms. To maximize its*

benefits and duration, an RMA needs to be adaptable, flexible, and dynamic, as recommended above. One cannot understand revolutionary change in warfare without taking full account of warfare's adversarial dimension. As Clausewitz insists on the first page of *On War*:

> War is nothing but a duel on a larger scale. Countless duels go to make up war, but a picture of it as a whole can be formed by imagining a pair of wrestlers. Each tries through physical force to compel the other to do his will; his *immediate* aim is to *throw* his opponent in order to make him incapable of further resistance [emphasis in the original]. War is thus an act of force to compel our enemy to do our will.[85]

War is a struggle against an adversary with an independent will. Sound analysis of war can neither ignore the enemy nor treat him merely as a helpless victim. Because of war's adversarial nature, enemies must always be motivated to seek antidotes somewhere amid war's rich complexity to the threat posed by a rival's revolutionary enhancement in military effectiveness. The historical life cycle of RMAs includes adversary response and then the counter-response, and so on in a process of interaction. There can be no final move.[86] Every revolutionary change in warfare has met, if not its Waterloo, at least an effective enough answer. Even the MR of the nuclear revolution has been neutralized politically and strategically, though assuredly not militarily, by the potency of emulation that creates a condition of variably stable mutual deterrence. At least this was true enough during the First Nuclear Age of the Cold War. It is no longer so in the Second Nuclear Age, with its trickle of new regional nuclear weapon states.[87]

No polity ever is permitted to enjoy for long, unchallenged, the benefits of a successful revolutionary way in warfare. This claim rests on the rock-solid basis of the anarchic structure of international politics, past, present, and one can assert with confidence, future. America's rivals cannot afford to concede military and strategic superiority, if that is what revolution appears to yield. The idea that they can be dissuaded indefinitely from competing by the scale of the task America poses, is, alas, a fantasy. I am reminded of the old saying that "the difficult we do immediately; the impossible takes a little longer." By common discovery, imitation, theft, or purchase, especially if revolutionary change is demonstrated in war, the RMA of the day will be recognized and eventually comprehended. When feasible and judged desirable it will be copied in parts. When borrowed it will be domesticated to fit local cultural preferences and strategic circumstances.[88] If it cannot or should not be imitated, then the challenge will be to find ways of warfare that negate much of its potential. Common sense tells us that this must be so, but happily we need not rely solely on such unreliable authority. In the conclusions to their edited work on RMAs, Murray and Knox deliver the unqualified verdict that "every RMA summons up, whether soon or late, a panoply of direct countermeasures and 'asymmetrical responses'."[89] We are warned.

CONCLUSION

Revolutionary change in warfare is only revealed by the "audit of war," and not necessarily reliably even then. If it is to be conducted competently, review of that audit must take full account of war's complex nature: the core competency of a military force is the ability to apply sufficient tailored violence so that the polity's enemies lose the will and, if need be, the ability to resist further. In a long period of peace, when they cannot test their prowess, military establishments tend to forget that war is their business and fighting is their distinctive contribution to that institution. There is something to be said in favor of Murray and Knox's claim that "only the audit of war, a war conducted against a significantly backward opponent, will demonstrate that an RMA has occurred."[90] However, the experience of trouncing hopeless adversaries is as likely to mislead as to enlighten. After all, we are not interested in revolutionary change as an end in itself, in the mere fact of its unilateral achievement. Rather must we always, and solely, be concerned with understanding the consequences of change, the distinctive domain of strategy. Enemies who are significantly backward probably can be defeated by any moderately competent way of war. In that event, who needs an RMA?

There may be some inadvertent confusion between a revolutionary change in methods of war and an order of magnitude increase in military effectiveness. Andrew Krepinevich links the two in the definition I have quoted several times. There is no doubt that the intent of revolutionaries is a "dramatic increase" in effectiveness. However, to change one's method of warfare is not necessarily to change one's military performance very much for the better. One might, indeed one should. Not all revolutions, though, have revolutionary consequences. Particularly is this likely to be so in the contexts of war wherein there must be an active opponent and the nature of the activity is vastly complex. That complexity, to repeat, allows opportunities for offsetting tactics, operations, strategies, and policies.

The RMA concept, the notion of revolutionary change in means and methods, is perilously short of firepower for coping with the rich diversity and complexity of war. It is probable that revolutionary change, of any character, will yield dramatic advantages only along a narrow stretch of the warfare spectrum, although the Alexandrian example showed what can be achieved when true genius is in charge. It is a certainty that such change eventually will trigger a quest for offsetting means, methods, and policies on the part of enemies. These negative observations do not amount to a condemnation of the concept of revolutionary change. Instead, they suggest that a military establishment committed to a particular vision of its modernization would be well advised to assess the integrity of its vision in the light cast by appreciation of the contexts of war and warfare.

6

IRREGULAR ENEMIES AND THE ESSENCE OF STRATEGY: CAN THE AMERICAN WAY OF WAR ADAPT?

There are only wars.
—Stuart Kinross, 2004[1]

Without some sense of historical continuity, Americans are likely to relearn the lessons of history each time they are faced with a low-intensity conflict. But what is more dangerous is the fact that during the relearning process Americans may suffer casualties and develop policy directions that can only lead to defeat.
—Sam C. Sarkesian, 1984[2]

The conduct of small wars is in fact in certain respects an art by itself, diverging widely from what is adapted to the conditions of regular warfare, but not so widely that there are not in all its branches points which permit comparisons to be established.
—Charles E. Callwell, 1906[3]

Can the traditional American way of war adapt so as to be effective against irregular enemies? This question shapes and drives what follows here. As has been already noted, Carl von Clausewitz offered his theory of war in terms of a "remarkable trinity composed of primordial violence, hatred, and enmity[,] . . . the play of chance and probability[,] . . . and subordination, as an instrument of policy, which makes it subject to reason alone." He defined his task as a need "to develop a theory that maintains a balance between these three tendencies, like an object suspended between three magnets."[4] While the theoretical analogy may be imperfect, still it is useful. Just as Clausewitz sought to explain war as the product of inherently unstable relations among passion, chance, and reason, so this analysis has at its core the unstable interactions among strategy, irregular enemies, and the American way of war. It defines and explains the essence of strategy; it identifies what is distinctive about irregular enemies and the kinds of warfare that they wage; and then it proceeds to outline the traditional American way of war. We critically consider the fit between the separate elements of that "way" and the requirements of sound practice in the conduct of warfare against irregulars.

Unlike Clausewitz, however, our purpose is not to develop or improve on general theory. Instead, the intention is to confront and answer the specific question with which this paragraph began. To this end, strategic theory is deployed pragmatically, as an aid to soldiers and officials who face pressing and serious challenges. Further, beyond the commitment to offer useful education, the purpose of these pages includes the desire to better explain to the defense community how the separate pieces of the trinitarian puzzle relate to one another. Readers could ask themselves how this chapter's subject relates to the concept and practice of revolutionary change in warfare, the topic of chapter 5. The information-led Revolution in Military Affairs (RMA), or Military-Technical Revolution (MTR) if one prefers, is a mainstream activity for the U.S. defense community. It is technology oriented and is geared to the better achievement of decisive military victory over enemies willing and able to commit to a regular style in warfare. However, if the warfare of the era should prove to be predominantly irregular, is the transformation of the U.S. Armed Forces into a more maneuverable and precisely deadly military force all that important? What way of war best serves American strategy when the enemy declines to offer itself up for destruction by decisive maneuver and precision bombardment? This chapter's dominant themes and the previous chapter's are all too intimately connected.

INTRODUCTION: THE RETURN OF IRREGULAR WARFARE

Today the armed forces are struggling to contain and defeat insurgencies on the continent of Asia. Strategic history is truly cyclical, a judgment resisted weakly and unsuccessfully by those who believe in linear progress in strategic affairs.[5] This chapter considers irregular warfare in the light of strategy and—no less important—examines the strengths and weaknesses of the historically dominant American way in warfare with reference to its consequences for the conduct of war against irregular enemies. The less challenging and controversial part of the analysis explains the relationships among irregular enemies and warfare and the essence of strategy. This essence is as certain and enduring a composite of ingredients as irregular enemies are disparate and, to a degree, unpredictable. By far the most difficult task undertaken here is the effort to answer the question in the chapter's secondary title: "Can the American Way of War Adapt?" Is the United States, not only its military tool kit, capable of performing effectively, which is to say (grand) strategically, against irregular enemies? Although Clausewitz is essential for our education, as he insisted, his general theory can only help prepare us for the specific challenges we face.[6]

After a decade wandering in the policy and strategy wilderness, we strategists, as well as politicians, have returned to a security context marked by a clear definition of era-defining threat. Strategists thrive on bad news. When it does not exist, we do our best to invent it. For a decade, though, from 1991 to 2001, few people believed our professional pessimism. In January 1994 I gave an inaugural lecture at the University of Hull, England, in which I described the 1990s as an interwar period.[7] Some people found this news to be shockingly pessimistic. Surely, peace had broken out, and despite the host of irregular wars underway at the time, large-scale war between states was now obsolete or at least obsolescent. To talk of the 1990s as an interwar period seemed to be almost criminally backward looking.

In 2005 the Department of Defense issued a document with the imposing title, *National Defense Strategy of the United States of America.* The first sentence of this august offering stated, without qualification, "America is a nation at war."[8] Bad times always return in world politics. I do not know how many Americans feel as if they are at war, since most people do not suffer many of war's characteristic hardships. America's allies in Europe certainly do not feel themselves to be countries at war. One of the burdens of greatness is that the sheriff of world order is obliged to undertake a disproportionate share of the heavy lifting for security on behalf of what is termed, ironically, the international community.[9]

The no-name post-Cold War era is well and truly over: it detonated on September 11, 2001. For a decade the threat board was confusingly naked of major strategic menace. Without the True North of the Soviet threat to provide reliable guidance, the American defense community did not know what it was about or, more important, why it might be about it. As was discussed in chapter 5, for the better part of ten years we debated the idea and meaning of RMA. This exciting concept appealed to some historians and to the many technophiles among us. However, the debate was not overburdened with strategic argument. Historically viewed, strategic thought, as a practical subject, tends to slumber between episodes of security alarm. Bookshop shelves today are groaning under the burden of good, bad, and ugly works on terrorism and insurgency. In the 1990s it was a struggle to find anything on irregular unpleasantness. Those of us with gray hair will recall that Nikita Khrushchev's general declaration of support for wars of national liberation and the enthusiastic response of the Kennedy Administration to that challenge sparked a flurry of studies of guerrilla warfare and related topics. No doubt thirty or forty years from now, in best or worst cyclical fashion, a new wave of irregular strategic happenings will trigger yet another burst of writing on "small wars" (wars between regulars and irregulars).[10] Another generation of strategic thinkers will rediscover the obvious, at least they will rediscover what we know today. They will invent an impressive sounding concept, some equivalent to Fourth Generation Warfare, and give dazzling briefings to credulous officials in need of an icon of assurance of understanding.[11]

The idea that strategy has an essence is deeply attractive. Strategy sounds incredibly rare and valuable, like something that could be bottled and sold. Unfortunately, American understanding of and sound practice in strategy is desperately rare. Strategic thinking and behavior are endangered activities in the United States. This is hardly a stunningly original insight. However, familiar though the criticism should be, it loses none of its bite for reason of longevity. Much as the U.S. defense community periodically is prodded by irregularist anxiety to worry about insurgency and terrorism, so from time to time it remembers the value of strategy. Though many American defense professionals do not know what strategy is or how it works,[12] they know that it is a matter of grave importance. The pattern has been one wherein a politician or a senior official with a personal interest has lit the fire of genuinely strategic discussion. The fire briefly flares brightly but then dies away for want of fuel. The fire is not fed, because there is not much demand for the heat and light of truly strategic argument in the United States. Although America is not quite a strategy-free environment, such a characterization would err in the right direction.

THE PLOT, WITH CAVEATS

I shall make an argument with three intimately connected points. In addition to the three points that carry the main burden of the argument, I offer seven important caveats that bear particularly on the debate over how to respond to irregular enemies. First is the triadic plot.

1. *War is war and strategy is strategy.* Forget qualifying adjectives: irregular war, guerrilla war, nuclear war, naval strategy, and counterinsurgent strategy. The many modes of warfare and tools of strategy are of no significance for the nature of war and strategy. General theories of war and of strategy, such as those offered by

Clausewitz, Sun Tzu, and Thucydides, are theories with universal applicability.[13] Because war and strategy are imperially authoritative concepts that accommodate all relevant modalities, a single general theory of war and another of strategy explain both regular and irregular warfare. While irregular warfare is, of course, different from regular, it is not different with reference to the general theory of strategy. If one can think strategically, one has the basic intellectual equipment needed to perform competently in either regular or irregular conflict.[14] Needless to add, understanding and performance are not synonymous.

2. *The United States has shown a persisting strategy deficit,* which reflects and feeds a political deficit in its way of war. No matter one's competence at regular or irregular warfare, if one does not function strategically, which is to say by intelligent design, one will not reap the political rewards that American blood and money have paid for. American military power has been as awesome tactically as it has rarely been impressive operationally or strategically. Fighting should be guided by a theory of victory, otherwise the result tends to be "a strategy of tactics," as Andrew F. Krepinevich Jr. observed of the United States in Vietnam.[15] The German Armed Forces in both world wars suffered from the same malady. Clausewitz did his best to educate his readers so that they could not be confused about the night and day difference between strategy and tactics, but his wisdom has not always dropped onto fertile soil. One would think that the following definition and explanation must defy even determined efforts at misunderstanding:

> Strategy is the use of the engagement for the purpose of the war. The strategist must therefore define an aim for the entire operational side of the war that will be in accordance with its purpose. In other words, he will draft the plan of the war, and the aim will determine the series of actions intended to achieve it: he will, in fact, shape the individual campaigns and, within these, decide on the individual engagements.[16]

3. *American public, strategic, and military culture is not friendly*

to the waging of irregular warfare, which is to say to the conduct of the only kind of warfare that can be effective against irregular enemies. There is a traditional American way of war, and its features do not privilege the strengths required to succeed against irregulars.[17] In the 1960s, and more recently, American military culture has proved resistant to radically adjusting its style of warfare to meet the distinctive challenges posed by an irregular enemy. New technology has been harnessed to "the American way" in the expectation, or hope, that the confining rules for effectiveness in irregular combat could be broken. While Sun Tzu's insistence on the need for self-knowledge in war is so familiar as to be a cliché,[18] it is essential here to emphasize his argument. There is no little danger that the American military transformation now underway may disappoint in the benefits it confers. The principal problems will be neither cunning asymmetrical enemies nor even a shortage of funds to carry it along. Instead the prospective gains from America's military transformation will be limited, if not frustrated, by the working of American public, strategic, and military culture. If one does not "do strategy," it will not much matter whether one's armed forces are transformed or not. The issue is not only, or not primarily, how good will U.S. forces be tactically and operationally? Rather, how will they be used? And to achieve what ends will they be committed? Will those ends be selected and exploited by a coherent theory of victory so as to promote a desirable postwar political context?

In sum, the U.S. Armed Forces face two different challenges to their effectiveness. First, their efforts are liable to be poorly rewarded, because the country has a persisting difficulty using force in strategically purposeful ways. Second, whether or not America can raise its game and function more strategically, U.S. forces have a long preferred style in warfare that is not well suited to conflict with irregular enemies. These remain major challenges today.

The three elements that constitute the core of the argument here do not make agreeable reading for those concerned with improving America's effectiveness as the main guardian of the current world order. I stress the potency of culture, because it is a concept that is easily misused. Today it is popular to point to the need for greater cultural awareness of enemies and allies. Thirty years ago, even twenty, it was not.[19] Major General Scales has called for a new culture-centric American approach to warfare.[20] While he is largely correct, the real problem is with us and our culture, and this problem is more of a condition with which to cope than a challenge to be overcome. We may transform the U.S. Armed Forces in some respects, but it may not be possible to transform a preferred way of war that expresses enduring cultural realities. To risk banality, America is what it is and its strategic culture faithfully reflects American historical, social, ideological, and material realities.[21]

As benefits the narrative of strategy and war, strategic history is hugely complex. This complexity is a happy hunting ground for the professional historians who thrive on the rich uniqueness and contingency of events. However, for strategic theorists, defense analysts, and policy advocates and policymakers, complexity usually is anathema. After all, strategy is a practical business and the aim is not perfect knowledge or elegant theory, but rather solutions to real world problems that work well enough. The U.S. defense community is more than amply populated with theorist-advocates who offer patent strategic medicines of variable plausibility as the answer to current woes. What the medicines have in common is that they tend to contain a single Big Idea, and as powerful theories are wont to do, they reduce the complexity of which we have just discussed. Generally speaking, the Big Idea has merit, sometimes even great merit. Nonetheless, each Big Idea, each patent solution to America's contemporary strategic dilemmas, needs to be accompanied by a health warning. What follows are seven caveats to the triadic argument presented earlier. They do not invalidate or contradict that argument, but they do combine to shout caveat emptor. These reservations have a direct bearing on judgment as to whether or not the American way of war is likely to prove sufficiently adaptable to be effective in combating irregular enemies.

The first caveat warns of the danger of imposing an undue clarity of strategic distinction between regular and irregular warfare. It is a highly expedient and easily defensible distinction. Moreover, it points to an important difference. As with all of these caveats, the fault lies not with the idea but rather with its exploitation in an oversimplified manner. Bear in mind the ambiguity about the notion of "irregular enemies." That can mean enemies of any genus who choose to fight in an irregular mode; or it may refer to foes deemed irregular by definition, because they are not the licensed sword arms of officially recognized polities. In practice, many wars have been waged regularly and irregularly, sometimes simultaneously, and often with shifting emphases. The Vietnam War (1965–1975) is a classic example of a war characterized by all modes of combat. Prior to Tet 1968, the war was primarily unconventional and irregular on the part of the Viet Cong, but there was that complicating, growing presence of People's Army of Vietnam (PAVN) units. After Tet, for reason of the debilitating attrition suffered by the irregulars and the failure of a general rising to occur, the war became ever more regular. Since 2003 Iraq has witnessed irregular violence, but occasionally that violence has been manifested as highly organized insurgent action in defense of symbolic or important urban terrain. The beginning of wisdom probably is to be achieved by means of reacquainting oneself with Mao Tse-tung's three-stage theory of protracted revolutionary war.[22] Although political agitation, guerrilla warfare, and regular conventional combat may be distinct phases in a struggle, they can be undertaken in parallel, and if need be, one can step back from a phase if one has overreached. This caveat against undue neatness in the categorization of conflict carries the warning that one size of military response probably will not fit the whole of the conflict in question, let alone the whole of the military context of an apparently emerging era.

The second caveat is the brutal point that to understand how insurgency works, and therefore how counterinsurgency (COIN) should be pursued, is not necessarily able to succeed at COIN. To those whose military education has been overwhelmingly regular and conventional, the secrets of COIN may appear exotic, not to say counterintuitive. Indeed, the requirements of COIN pose what amounts to a full frontal challenge to the dominant traditional American way of war. However, the international experience of COIN, successful and otherwise, has yielded a tactical and operational lore that is beyond intelligent challenge. To state the matter directly, we know how to do COIN. It is not a dark art capable of mastery only by a relatively few elite soldiers with distinctively colored berets. Nonetheless, in conflict after conflict, the most elementary, yet vitally important, rules for behavior in COIN tend to be flouted. The results are typically and predictably unfortunate.

It would be agreeable to claim that the requirements of COIN are so well understood that the problem must lie in the realm of the impediments to implementation. However, that may be too generous a view. It is at least plausible to argue that missionary work remains to be done before insurgency and COIN are comprehended as well as their regular counterparts.[23] It would be more difficult to excuse incompetence in COIN if the military and its political masters understand the distinctive challenge but elect to behave in the manner they prefer, regardless.

Caveat three is a reminder of what we are apt to forget when we turn conviction into capability and behavior. By behavior I refer to action at all levels from the tactical, through the grand strategic, to the political. Irregular enemies and irregular forms of warfare do not present a single challenge that calls for a single master doctrinal response. Analyses by Steven Metz and Raymond Millen, as well as by Michael F. Morris, have pointed out that insurgencies can be of a liberation or a national variety, while even that binary distinction lends itself to much further fine tuning.[24] Morris's fascinating essay on al Qaeda speaks all too eloquently and persuasively to the variety of contexts for irregular conflict, the complexity of the connections between terrorism and insurgency, the ability of organizations to shape-shift radically, and the wide range of tactics that irregulars can employ in different circumstances. In Iraq the motive force of ethno-religious opportunism in a context of political chaos misled insurgent-terrorists into the error of neglecting hearts and minds in rival communities in favor of sheer brutality. This kind of enemy has to be defeated in a manner of which Ralph Peters would approve unreservedly.[25] The clear message is that the U.S. Armed Forces should transform themselves so as to be more adaptable. They cannot apply a simple template or rely on power-point wisdom that promises victory over irregulars in "five easy steps." Each historical case is different. Only at the level of the general theory of strategy does one size fit all.[26]

Caveat four is the warning that the theory and practice of COIN does not comprise a magical solution to irregular violence. COIN doctrine and capabilities may become fashionable, in reaction against the slim rewards from aggressively pursued attritional or victory-by-maneuver strategies. When doctrine for a mode of warfare is officially blessed and attracts widespread favorable notice, the critical faculties of new devotees often take a leave of absence. Classic COIN methods are not always feasible, no matter how expert the military practitioners and their civilian partners. COIN takes time, usually a great deal of it. Also, it requires a locally plausible political story and framework to support and advance. The necessary political underpinning for COIN may not be available. Moreover, the historical slate may not be sufficiently clean. The would-be COINers might well have prejudiced their mission fatally through the manner of their previous conduct of warfare, which is to say conduct prior to their serious resort to the COIN option. In short, COIN expertise and capabilities are essential and will frequently bear fruit. However, they need permissive conditions, not the least among which is the political tolerance of the American public with respect to strategy to counter an enemy who uses time as a weapon of war.[27] There is danger that having rediscovered the obvious merits of COIN doctrine, the American defense community will proceed as if it is the all-purpose solution to many irregular enemies.

Still on the COIN theme, caveat five is the intentionally subversive thought that it may not be politically sensible, or strategically profitable, for American forces to be extensively engaged in counterinsurgency operations. There is no question that the U.S. Armed Forces, especially the army, need to be adept at COIN.

Similarly, there is no doubt that COIN competence, in common with the Special Forces, was not held in high official regard for many years.[28] There has been a serious capability and doctrinal deficit to make up. However, recognition that COIN prowess is at a premium in today's global strategic context does not mean that Americans should practice COIN often. Because America's traditional way of war, privileging firepower, mobility, and an aggressive hunt for the main body of the foe is ineffective against elusive irregular foes, it does not necessarily follow that COIN, by Americans, is the superior alternative. As a general rule, local forces, regular and irregular, military and civil, should perform the heavy lifting in COIN. It would be inappropriate for the U.S. superpower to commit a large fraction of its armed forces, particularly its army, to COIN duties. This activity can be performed successfully only by those who have the benefit of local knowledge and intend not merely "to stay the course" but to stay. While Americans can help (as well as hinder), history and common sense reveal that the more active American soldiers are in providing security for local clients, the more they undermine the political legitimacy of those whom they try to assist.

The sixth caveat is the reminder that war and warfare are different concepts, and the difference is a matter of great importance. War is a total relationship—political, legal, social, and military. Warfare is the conduct of war, by and large, by military means. A focus on warfare, which is natural enough for armed forces, can obscure the need to function grand strategically. In this all-encompassing domain, military behavior is only one dimension to the effort, albeit a vital one. In war with irregular enemies, warfare is unlikely to be the dominant mode of fruitful engagement. Since irregular foes will rarely concentrate and present themselves for open battle, the COIN struggle must take the form largely of political, intelligence, economic, social, and police activity. Additionally, in wars of all kinds, warfare occurs in the context of the whole war and needs to be conducted in such a way that it fits the character of the war and thereby yields the needed strategic effectiveness. When this key distinction and relationship between war and warfare is not understood, the inevitable result is misdirected warfare, virtually no matter whether or not the activity is prosecuted efficiently. Clausewitz insists that

> everything in strategy is very simple, but that does not mean that everything is very easy. Once it has been determined, from the political conditions, what a war is meant to achieve and what it can achieve, it is easy to chart the course.[29]

Though his final judgment quoted is an exaggeration, he lays proper emphasis on the nesting of military action, and the direction of that action by strategy, within the political context of the whole war.

My final caveat to this study's grand argument is a warning parallel to the COIN theory and technique. Recognition of the significance of culture—public, strategic, and military—in war, warfare, and strategy inadvertently is encouraging its elevation to the status, or role, of panacea. Appreciating the disadvantages of local ignorance, American soldiers wisely endorse cultural awareness, if not expertise, as a key, perhaps the key, to the achievement of enhanced effectiveness. Obviously, for COIN to be successful, cultural education is not merely desirable, it is essential. The problem lies with the iconic adoption of culture as the answer. It is not. Recognition of culture's importance is a part of the answer of how to be effective in war against irregular (and regular) enemies. But culture is a difficult concept to define and grasp.[30] It is even more difficult to work with or around in alien environments, and it does not encompass all that matters in the waging of war. For example, no measure of cultural empathy would suffice to compensate for a missing political framework or for military incompetence.

The United States has two distinct problems in coping with the subject of this chapter, problems flagged with scant subtlety in the title. The first problem is strategy deficit. The United States often has difficulty with strategy, because the "normal" theory of American civil-military relations barricades or blows up the strategy bridge so as to prevent the traffic flows that should lock politicians and soldiers into an unequal, but never-ending, dialogue over means and ends.[31] The second problem is the challenge of coping with irregular enemies. As we will discuss, there is difficulty in adapting the traditional American way of war to render it effective against asymmetrical enemies.

It is perhaps arguable which of the two problems is the more serious, the strategy deficit or the hindrances to adaptation to meet irregular foes. Debatably, a new excellence in COIN, resting in part on a military performance enhanced by education in cultural awareness, will resolve most of America's recent dilemmas in dealing with irregular enemies. I do not believe this claim, valuable though such a development would be. Unless America "does strategy," which is to say relates military and other means to its political ends in a purposeful, realistic, and adaptable way, improvements in military prowess ultimately must yield disappointing results.

THE ESSENCE OF STRATEGY

The key to strategy, certainly to thinking strategically, is recognition of its most vital intellectual tool, the simple and rather offensive question: "So what?" Strategists are not interested in the actual conduct of regular or irregular war; instead their concern is what this conduct means for the course and consequences of a conflict. Tactical and operational excellence is always desirable, even if not always strictly necessary. Since, inter alia, warfare is a competition in learning between imperfect military machines, fortunately one need only be good enough. Tactical excellence is quality wasted if it is not employed purposefully to advance political goals. Of course, this is much easier to advocate than to do. Recall the old saying that "nothing is impossible to the person who does not have to do it." So, what is strategy and how should one characterize its invaluable essence? What should be poured into bottles of "Essence of Strategy"? I suggest three ingredients.

First, following Clausewitz, I insist that strategy is about the use made of force and the threat of force for the goals of policy.[32] "Strategic" does not mean very important, nuclear, independently decisive, or long range. No weapon or mode of warfare, including terrorism, can be inherently strategic. All have strategic effect. This is not to deny that the vital concept of strategic effect is hard to assess.

Second, strategy is about the relationship between means and ends. Again, this is easy to specify, but fiendishly difficult to direct competently. It is tempting to adopt the attitude that we will win the fights and let the politics take care of itself. Or, for a cognate approach, if we keep winning tactically, our strategy will flow agreeably from the cumulative verdicts of the battlefield. In practice, a war may be waged innocent of political guidance beyond an injunction to win. If the politicians focus on the ends, as they should, and soldiers are consumed with matters of means, it is probable that no one will be keeping open the "strategy bridge" that should be linking military means with political goals. There needs to be a continuous, albeit "unequal," dialogue between civilian and soldier. War and warfare are permeated with political meaning and consequences. A competent supreme command knows this and behaves accordingly. However, this relationship carries implications for civilian participation in military decisions in wartime that run contrary to the traditional American way in civil-military relations.[33] If the strict instrumentality of force is not to be neglected, there has to be a constant dialogue between policymaker and soldier. Policy is a nonsense if the troops cannot perform "in the field," while the troops may be so effective in action that policy is left gasping far behind unexpected opportunities opened by events. *On War* states that "the conduct of war, in its great outlines, is therefore policy itself." The reader has already been informed that "at the highest level the art of war turns into policy—but a policy conducted by fighting battles rather than by sending diplomatic notes."[34]

Finally, in case the point should fade from view under the pressure of military events, politics must rule. To quote a famous dictum: "War is simply a continuation of political intercourse, with the addition of other means."[35] The most essential of the ingredients that when mixed become the essence of strategy is the instrumentality of the threat or use of force. In practice, the pressures and demands of the waging of war have a way of relegating policy purpose into the background. All too often, policy may seem to serve war rather than war serving policy.

If the essence of strategy is so simple, then why is it that it is so difficult to "do strategy" well? I will offer a few suggested answers.

First, strategy by its very nature, in its essence, is extraordinarily difficult to do.[36] Strategy is the bridge connecting the military instrument with the guidance of political purpose. Strategic expertise is neither military skill nor policy wisdom. It is the use of the military for political ends. Who is expert in strategy? Neither soldiers nor politicians are trained strategists. Indeed, excellence as a soldier and excellence as a politician are both off the mark as proof of strategic expertise. Moreover, it is not entirely self-evident that competence in strategy can be taught. After all, by definition it requires the exercise of judgment about the value of military effort in terms of political effect. Since war, at its core, is a contest of wills, the judgment required of the strategist strictly requires knowledge and skills unlikely to be widely available, if available at all.

The second difficulty worth highlighting is the cultural- and skill-bias contrast between soldier and civilian politician. This problem area is especially relevant to the American context and its dominant traditional way of war. Theory insists that policy and military means must march together—indeed truly they are one and the same—though with policy in the lead. However, policy goals, war and peace aims, should only be chosen and periodically revised in the light of military probabilities. All too obviously, the professional soldier and the no less professional politician, though culturally both American, in fact inhabit distinctive cultural universes. In practice, true two-way communication of often unwelcome news can be difficult. Clausewitz does not address this problem, beyond offering the sage advice that "a certain grasp of military affairs is vital for those in charge of general policy."[37] What, though, if it were missing?

Or, what if the politicians and generals do not respect, like, or trust one another? What if they do not share certain key values? How much influence should America's commander in chief be willing to exert over the direction and course of military events in time of war?[38] Should he or she leave military decisions to the military, even though he or she knows from Clausewitz and historical experience that warfare is inalienably political in its consequences?

Third, although the concept of strategic effect is crystal clear as an abstraction, how is it to be measured? What is the exchange rate between military success and desired political consequence? Especially in the conduct of warfare against irregulars, what is the legal currency for the measurement of this effect? Understandably, albeit unfortunately, the mystery of strategic effect is apt to be solved by soldiers and officials who seize on whatever can be counted as they take the default choice of favoring attrition. Again, one must cite the strategist's essential question: "So what?" The strategist must know what military behavior means for the political purpose of the enterprise. Body counts need to be interpreted for their strategic value. They cannot be declared triumphantly as tactical achievements with self-evident strategic meaning.

Fourth, strategy is difficult to do as an orderly and well-integrated exercise in the matching of means to ends, because of the high inconvenience of an intelligent enemy's semi-independent behavior. Under the exigencies of actual war against a live and somewhat unpredictable foe, regular or irregular—it does not matter which—military necessity may compel military behavior that is undesirable in its political consequences. Remember the grim irony from Vietnam that "we had to destroy the village in order to save it."[39] It is amazing how often supposed defense experts and strategic thinkers neglect to take proper account of the enemy on his own terms.

Finally, friction and the other elements of the war's climate, such as "danger, exertion, uncertainty, and chance," are entirely capable of thwarting the best-laid strategic plans.[40] Also, the weather, human error, and other frailties are not to be despised or discounted.

Things always go wrong. That is to be expected. A sound strategy is tolerant of history's unpleasant surprises. Adaptability must be regarded as a cardinal military virtue.

IRREGULAR WARFARE

While strategy is strategy regardless of circumstance, the military and related behavior that it guides and exploits differ radically from case to case.

The U.S. Armed Forces excel at high- and mid-intensity regular warfare. Regular and irregular modes of warfare often coexist. Also, elite units of regular forces are trained to wage war irregularly.[41] However, irregular soldiers do not always confine their combat to guerrilla style. They will stand and fight in a regular manner either when they have no choice, or more likely, when they believe they have a crushing tactical advantage over an isolated element of the regular enemy's forces. Following the destruction of most of the Vietcong's fighting power in the Tet Offensive and the subsequent attacks, the Vietnam war became ever more regular in style. Paradoxically, in March 1968, with the change in command at Military Advisory Command Vietnam (MACV) from Gen. William C. Westmoreland to Gen. Creighton Abrams (formerly a Patton protégé of armored maneuver), the American effort spearheaded by the intelligent and already existing Civil Operations and Revolutionary Development Support (CORDS) program reaped major dividends from its proper conduct of COIN.[42] Meanwhile, the enemy was condemned to expose himself to repeated regular defeat. None of which really mattered, of course, because the political center of gravity of the war in America was well on the path to collapse.

As the armed forces proceed with their long-haul transformation, they must never forget that in the future they may well have to face competent regular enemies as well as a crowd of irregular foes. However, there is relatively little risk of them finding themselves improperly prepared with ideas, doctrine, trained people, organization, and equipment for regular warfare. Of course, it could happen.

Nonetheless, this chapter deals with trouble in the high realms of strategy and, at this juncture and later, with irregular warfare. We elect not to venture here into the woods of controversy over the future of regular, conventional combat.[43] Instead, the focus is on insurgency and terrorism. The irregular enemies are assumed to be insurgents and terrorists. The two categories of undesirables overlap, although in principle there is a distinction between the two. Terrorism, in common with guerrilla war, is simply a mode of warfare; it carries no particular political baggage. Anyone can do it, and for any set of motives. Insurgency, however, is a concept that has considerable political content and constitutes by far the more serious menace to order and stability. Although none of the popular definitions are beyond challenge, that offered by Andrew F. Krepinevich Jr. captures the heart of the matter well enough.

> An insurgency is a *protracted struggle* conducted methodically, step by step, in order to obtain specific intermediate objectives leading finally to the overthrow of the existing order [emphasis in the original].[44]

While Krepinevich is unduly specific as to method, he highlights the point that an insurgency is an armed effort to effect revolutionary, at least radical and decisive, change. Certainly, terrorism will be one of the tactics employed by insurgents. But, if an irregular enemy confines himself, or is compelled to be limited, to acts of terrorism, the threat that he poses to political stability is an order of magnitude less severe than is the menace from insurgency. Terrorism is an expensive and occasionally tragic nuisance for a society. However, an organization that expresses its frustration, anger, and ambition solely by committing isolated outrages is an organization that is going nowhere and can pose no real danger to a basically stable society. Needless to add, perhaps, if terrorists are to become insurgents, they usually need considerable assistance from what should be the forces of order. The struggle between terrorists and counterterrorists is a contest over legitimacy in the eyes of the public. It is useful and appropriate to treat insurgency and terrorism as comprising a single class of behavior, here termed irregular warfare.[46]

Insurgency is not a simple phenomenon. It has to follow that COIN, similarly, must adapt to the specific character of irregular challenge in question. An insurgency may move and breed among the people, the rural population in the Maoist model or urban dwellers as society changes. Alternatively, especially if they favor terrorist tactics, irregulars may devote little attention to political efforts at proselytization and place their faith instead on the violent deed's anticipated power. By military action they intend to demonstrate the impotence of the government to provide protection. This "foco" theory of revolutionary warfare has a decidedly mixed record of success, as Che Guevara demonstrated in Bolivia in October 1967. Despite the range of terrorist-insurgent challenges, a single working theory of irregular warfare and how best to oppose it has sufficient integrity to deserve our confidence.

What do we know about the irregular warfare of insurgency and terrorism?

1. *Protect the people.* In COIN the center of gravity is the people and their protection. The battlespace of most significance is the mind of the public. If people can be protected and believe they are protected, then COIN is well on the way to success, if not outright victory. However, to accord first priority to direct population protection is not a tactic that has wide appeal to a military establishment imbued with an aggressive spirit and understandable reluctance to appear to surrender the initiative to the enemy.

2. *Intelligence is king.* The key to operational advantage in COIN is timely, reliable intelligence. If COIN is to root out an insurgent-terrorist infrastructure, then it must have information that can come only from the local public or defecting insurgents. Again, if the people feel that they are protected, that they have a good enough future with the established authorities, and that the authorities are going to win, then the intelligence problem should solve itself. If insurgents lose in the minds of the people, then they will lose the actual battle. With superior intelligence, COIN wins. Insurgents or

terrorists survive only by remaining elusive, by hiding in the sea of the people or in remote areas where they are ineffective. If the people can no longer be trusted to protect their identities and safe houses, they cannot function safely. A hostile, even unsympathetic, public translates as a social context non-permissive for irregular warriors.

3. *Ideology matters.* Every insurgency mobilizes around a political cause. Although there are apparent exceptions, insurgents typically rally to a potent idea, political or religious, or both. Much of the complex insurgent action in Iraq of recent years appeared to violate this principle. In many cases, it seemed to be driven more by a determination to foment chaos than to advance any particular creed or vision of the just society. The history of insurgency and COIN is unambiguous in its thoroughgoing endorsement of Clausewitz's insistence on the political character of all military behavior.[46] Because COIN is, and can be explained as, a set of rules and techniques and a method for winning an irregular conflict, the technique lends itself to being mistaken for the "victory kit." For example, the French Colonial army learned in Indochina what to do and what not to do against a revolutionary insurgent enemy. Educated by defeat in Southeast Asia and in the POW camps of the Viet Minh, thoughtful French paratroopers, legionnaires, and light infantrymen were ready to wage *la guerre moderne* in Algeria.[47] They effectively waged modern, which is to say irregular, warfare. Unfortunately for them, they failed to secure a firm intellectual grasp on the truth that war is a political act and that people are political animals. Tactical competence does not enable the counterinsurgent to manufacture an adequate political story. French-style modern war could work tactically and operationally in Algeria but never strategically. Despite its tactical excellence and intellectual sophistication, the military effort was always politically hollow. The French effort carried no political promise with a potent appeal to the Muslim populace. The COIN force must work in support of a publicly attractive political vision. That vision cannot be imposed from outside the society. More to the point, Western politicians, soldiers, and administrators cannot "build nations" as the arrogant and

absurd, but familiar, concept suggests. As always, there will be an exception or two. If a country is utterly defeated and is occupied by the victor, then political reconstruction may possibly be effected, even in the face of an alien culture. One thinks of Japan after World War II. However, even in that case, much that is uniquely Japanese survived cultural assault from abroad.

4. *The irregular enemy is not usually the target.* Since the battlespace in COIN is in people's minds and the protection of the people is the overriding priority, it follows that military plans for COIN should be radically different from those adopted for regular warfare. It would be a gross exaggeration to argue that insurgent forces are irrelevant, but that assertion, shocking to many conventional military minds, contains a vital verity. When success is possible, which is not always the case, COIN wins over a public that the COIN forces have persuaded will be protected and provided a better future. Victory will not be the product of engagements, even successful engagements, with insurgents, though military defeats will be damaging because they undermine the crucial protection story. If the irregular enemy is so foolish as to present himself in the open for destruction, so much the better, always provided the COIN elements do not lay waste to whole neighborhoods in a ruthless quest to maximize the body count of suspected enemies. However, while an irregular war can be lost militarily, generally it cannot be won in that mode. If an insurgency is allowed to mature from Mao's second phase of guerrilla action into the third and final phase of open conventional combat, then indeed military events can prove conclusive. Nonetheless, from the COIN's point of view, the irregular enemy is as much a distraction as a focus for aggressive attention.

Insurgents and counterinsurgents are competing for the public's allegiance, though more often their acquiescence. Combat between regular and irregular warriors has no strategic significance, save with respect to the protection of the people and the relative reputations of the belligerents in the eyes of the public. Contrary to traditional military practice, the COIN's objectives are neither the irregular enemy's forces nor, with a necessary reservation, the territory they occupy and use. Insurgents' sanctuaries are essential targets, because an irregular foe can be defeated logistically if it is forcibly deprived of reliable supply and intelligence. As a result, it will be compelled to operate in closer proximity to the more heavily populated areas where most of the COIN forces should be deployed. Writing a century ago about the lessons to be drawn from the colonial "small war" experiences of several imperial powers, giant theorist of irregular warfare Col. Charles E. Callwell identified a central problem that we need to treat with great reserve in today's different conditions. Callwell noted the near truism that "[i]t is the difficulty of bringing the foe to action which, as a rule, forms the most unpleasant characteristic of these wars [regulars against irregulars]."[48] Contrary to Callwell's message, this chapter maintains that determination to bring an elusive irregular enemy to battle more often than not proves to be a snare and a delusion. Typically, victory is not won in COIN over the bodies of dead insurgents, probably not even if one imposes attrition on a Homeric scale.

5. *Unity of effort.* Irregular warfare is, at least should be, waged on both sides grand strategically. All of the instruments of persuasion, coercion, and influence need to be employed. The conflict will be political, ideological, economic, diplomatic, and military in several modes. The irregular enemy will not aspire to defeat the U.S. Armed Forces in battle and does not need to. If those forces strive to win a military victory, then they will only exhaust themselves, frustrate their domestic supporters, and dissipate their strengths chasing a chimera. To beat an insurgency, when that is feasible, the COIN forces must organize and direct a strict unity of civilian and military effort, with a single chain of command and a political authority unambiguously in supreme command. While all warfare is political, irregular warfare is the most political of all, if I may be forgiven for qualifying an absolute. Military action has to be subordinated to political priorities. And, as continually noted, the top priority must be the security of the majority of the population. Though it may sound attractive, the argument that does not

effectively work is that to protect the people one needs to chase after their irregular tormentors wherever they happen to be. An analogy with piracy is false. Undoubtedly the superior solution to piracy is to take the initiative and attack the pirates at home. Unfortunately, few insurgencies provide the functional equivalents of pirates' lairs. For a better maritime analogy, the introduction of convoying compels the pirate, the submarine, to seek out civilian targets where they are protected. The experience of two world wars demonstrated conclusively that the conduct of aggressive hunting parties sweeping the seas looking for raiders was a waste of effort. Parallel logic holds for the conduct of irregular warfare on land. The focus must not shift from the true center of gravity of the struggle, the minds of the people. COIN can only succeed when the military instrument is employed as part of a team that is led by political judgment and privileges real-time intelligence gathering from the public and solid police work.

6. *Culture is crucial.* In regular warfare between regular armies, the terms of engagement and character of military behavior will be so substantially similar as almost to warrant description as transcultural, notwithstanding asymmetries in capabilities and methods. The belligerents will share strengths and weaknesses in a fairly common contemporary "grammar" of war.[49] Cultural differences will weigh in the balance, as each side adapts ideas and equipment to suit its own circumstances, traditions, preferences, and service politics.[50] However, one can imagine a decisive military outcome to regular warfare achieved virtually regardless of the cultural differences between the protagonists. This category of hostilities usefully contrasts with a condition of irregular warfare, insurgency, or pure terrorism. In the latter case, underappreciated cultural differences by a well-meaning but foreign COIN effort are near certain to prove fatal to the prospects for success. Culture refers to social capital. It means the beliefs, attitudes, habits of mind, and preferred ways of behavior of a social group. And, to repeat yet again, irregular wars are won or lost in the minds of the local people. If we do not understand those minds, what they value, and how much they value it,

success secured against terrorists and other insurgents will most likely only be temporary.

Culture is crucial, both theirs and ours. "Theirs" for the obvious reason just outlined; restated, the local people decide who wins. "Ours" because we can approach and seek to understand other cultures only through our own inevitably distorting prism. The fact is that America is a proud, ideological superpower, eager to spread and exert its "soft power" as well as prepared to apply the mailed fist of its "hard power."[51] The very strength of Americans' cultural identity is both a blessing and a hindrance. On balance, as an ingredient in the potions prepared to reduce an insurgency, American culture is a barrier to understanding effective behavior. To help offset the influence of this barrier, the armed forces have to be educated formally and by the experience gained through direct local exposure. Needless to add, if the army wages irregular warfare from a series of "Fort Apaches," isolated from the local people, it not only looks hostile, but it cannot acquire the familiarity with local opinion and mores so essential for COIN's success.

7. *No sanctuaries and no external support.* It is standard COIN doctrine to attempt to deny insurgents safe areas where they can rest, rally, regroup, recover, train, and sally forth at their discretion to wreak havoc. The sanctuaries may be protected by rugged physical terrain, complex human—which is to say urban (including refugee-camp)—terrain, or by porous international frontiers. Every military effort requires a secure base. COIN doctrine is correct to identify enemy sanctuaries as important targets. However, it must be apparent from our analysis that the key to defeating an insurgency cannot lie in the removal of sanctuaries, important though that must be. There is danger that a COIN effort could become so persuaded by the significance of sanctuary areas and assistance from abroad and of the need to interdict the latter, that the true battlespace would be downgraded. If the COIN campaign is working well, irregulars' sanctuaries and foreign support will not matter much. The struggle will be won or lost in the minds of the people that the counterinsurgency effort, civilian and military, is striving to influence

and not by harassing the irregulars' logistics. Given an American way of war that stresses aggressive offensive action against enemy forces, sanctuaries and foreign supply lines will be tempting targets for the diversion of military effort to remote areas, far away from the main centers of population.

8. *Time is a weapon.* Of all the many dimensions of strategy, time is the most intractable. Compensation for deficiencies elsewhere and corrections for errors are usually possible. But time lost is irrecoverable. The Western theory of war and strategy pays too little attention to war's temporal dimension. In particular, there is not enough recognition that time itself can be a weapon. It can be used purposefully to compensate for material or other weaknesses and to expose and intensify the vulnerability of the enemy. In irregular warfare, the materially disadvantaged combatant is obliged to try to win slowly, for no other reason than he cannot win swiftly. When Americans elect to participate in an irregular conflict, they need to know this. Also, they need to know that there may well be no practicable way in which they can hasten a decisive military outcome, a result that is certain to be unattainable. The insurgents will behave like the guerrillas poetically described by T. E. Lawrence in his classic, if rather overwritten, theorizing on "Guerrilla Warfare" and will deny the regulars worthwhile targets.[52]

A well-educated COIN force will be relatively untroubled by the elusiveness of an irregular enemy. It will understand that the battle is won with the confidence of the people the regulars protect, not by the number of dead bodies that can be strewn across distant parts of the landscape. However, COIN is slow, tedious, will face setbacks, may well be challenged by less than ideal local political partners, and will be harassed by a host of other difficulties. Most insurgents will be local, and American COIN experts will be foreign. The irregular enemy can win if it is able to outwait American patience, in the meantime create insecurity, and discourage major reforms of a kind that should alter public attitudes. The mindset needed to combat an enemy who is playing a long game is not one that comes naturally to the American soldier. To wage protracted war is not a preference in U.S. military or strategic culture. Moreover, to accept the necessity for protraction is to tolerate terms of engagement dictated by the enemy; that is not an attractive fact to recognize and explain to a doubting and increasingly impatient media and public.

9. *Undercut the irregular enemy politically.* While one is tempted to demonize an irregular enemy, label him a terrorist or worse, the local people whose allegiance is sought after will have a more nuanced view.[53] They will know some of the insurgents, and they are certain to have some sympathy with elements, at least, of their political story. Since successful COIN must speak convincingly to a public knowledgeable about local issues, including information on the character and motives of the insurgents, a COIN effort must demonstrate mastery of local conditions in terms that resonate locally.

There are many aspects to this general point about politically undercutting the irregular enemy. First, given the protracted character of an irregular conflict, there should be time, if political will is present, to address the political grievances that have fueled the insurgency. This is not to suggest abject surrender to the nominal "wish list" of the enemy. However, it is to claim that insurgents exploit genuine sources of public unrest. In its political dimension, a COIN strategy should seek to deprive the irregulars of their cause. The forces of order need to demonstrate to the public that they offer a politically superior alternative of direct local benefit.

Second, a COIN campaign and the behavior of the local government it is designed to assist must behave within the law. The irregular enemy wishes to promote chaos, uncertainty, and overreaction by the forces of order. Success in COIN is measured by the scale of the public confidence that they can live in a land of law and order, wherein they need not fear for their personal security at the hands of anyone, official or other. It follows that when the government flouts its own laws, behaves arbitrarily, abuses detainees, and generally functions according to the principle of a rough expediency, it does the insurgents' work for them. Victory or defeat in irregular warfare is about the beliefs, attitudes, and consequent behavior of the public. Everything that an American COIN effort and its local allies do to combat the irregular enemy ultimately has strategic effect, positive or negative, on the minds of that public. They are the stake and the battlespace.

The discussion in this section of irregular warfare and its implications for COIN doctrine should not be controversial. However, the ability of the U.S. military to adapt to be effective in warfare with the character described here is problematic. Self-knowledge is essential if Americans are to address the challenge of irregular warfare with good prospect of adapting successfully. The next section presents an appreciation of the traditional American way of war, a way that in many respects still permeates American behavior.

THE AMERICAN WAY OF WAR MEETS AN IRREGULAR FUTURE

The American way of war has been mentioned throughout this chapter but has remained unspecified in an orderly and detailed way. This apparent neglect is explained by the fact that my primary mission has been to consider irregular warfare in strategic perspective. Now, though, the several strands in this analysis must converge. Irregular enemies and their modes of warfare, understood strategically, are considered as a challenge to the traditional American way of war.

The "way" pertains both to war as a whole and to its military conduct in warfare. At least three of the specified features comprise a vital part of the case that holds that the United States tends to confuse principles of warfare with principles of war. If the country appreciated and generally adhered to a well-drafted and culturally embedded set of principles of war, principles that truly were Clausewitzian, its strategic and political performance in conflict after conflict should be considerably improved.[54] However, strategically, for good and ill, Americans are what they are. If they persist in failing to reap desired political rewards from their military effort, even when the effort is largely successful, there are cultural reasons for this failure. Probably Americans can only remake their strategic performance if they first remake their society, and that is a task beyond the ability of even the most optimistic agents of transformation. Moreover, one suspects that the strategic rewards would both disappoint and cost far too much in virtues sacrificed. Nonetheless, there is currently wholesale recognition in the armed forces of the seriousness and probable longevity of the menace irregular enemies pose. Deconstructing the standard American "way" and reviewing it from the perspective of countering irregulars may possibly identify pathways to improved performance. As always, though, first one must alert people to the problem.

Characteristics of the American Way of War

1. Apolitical	8. Large-scale
2. Astrategic	9. Aggressive, Offensive
3. Ahistorical	10. Profoundly Regular
4. Problem-solving, Optimistic	11. Impatient
5. Culturally Challenged	12. Logistically Excellent
6. Technology Dependent	13. Highly Sensitive to Casualties
7. Focused on Firepower	

---

1. Apolitical

Americans are wont to regard war and peace as sharply distinctive conditions. The U.S. military has a long history of waging war for the goal of victory and paying scant regard to the consequences of the course of its operations for the character of the peace that will follow. Civilian policymakers have been primarily at fault. In war after war, they have tended to neglect the Clausewitzian dictum that war is about, and only about, its political purposes. Characteristically, though certainly not invariably, U.S. military efforts have not been suitably cashed in political advantage. The traditional American separation of politics and the conduct of war is a lethal weakness when dealing with irregular enemies. Irregular conflict requires a unity of effort by all the instruments of grand strategy, and a unified high command must guide it. In that high command the political authority has to be paramount. As a general rule there can be no military solution to the challenge posed by irregulars. The principal task of the soldier is to provide the security without which decisive political progress is impossible.

2. Astrategic

Strategy is, or should be, the bridge that connects military power with policy. When Americans wage war as a largely autonomous activity and postpone worrying about peace and its politics, the strategy bridge has broken down. The conduct of war cannot be self-validating. For a leading and truly awful example of this malady, one must cite Vietnam. The United States sought to apply its newfound theory of limited war in an ill-crafted effort to employ modulated on-off-on coercion by air bombardment to influence Hanoi in favor of negotiations.[55] It is prudent to take notice of these words of wisdom from Samuel P. Huntington: "Military forces are not primarily instruments of communication to convey signals to an enemy; they are instead instruments of coercion to compel him to alter his behavior."[56]

Excellence in strategy has not been an American strength, at least not since George Washington defeated the British strategically. The major causes of the problem are twofold: first, a long-standing experience of material superiority offers few incentives for strategic calculation; and second, the "normal" theory of civil-military relations discourages tough, probing dialogue between policymaker and soldier. Unfortunately, the terrorist and the insurgent are probably functioning strategically. Indeed, they can hope to succeed in no other way. Such irregulars are playing a long game. Their tactical behavior is of little, if any, inherent significance. They do not plan and execute would-be decisive military actions. COIN is a quintessentially strategic struggle. A United States that does not really "do strategy," at least not for long, because it does not truly understand it, will be outfought and outthought by irregular enemies who must "do strategy" if they are to survive and prosper.

3. Ahistorical

As a future-oriented people whose polity has a founding ideology of faith in, hope for, and commitment to human betterment, Americans should not be expected to be respectful of what they might otherwise be inclined to allow history to teach them. A defense community led by the historically disrespectful and ill-educated is condemned to find itself surprised by events for which historical understanding could have prepared them.

The United States has a rich and extensive history of experience with irregular enemies.[57] Moreover, that experience was by no means negative in its outcomes for Americans. The trouble was, and until recently remained, that this varied experience of irregular warfare was never embraced and adopted by the army as the basis for the development of doctrine for a core competency. The army waged irregular warfare, sometimes regular war against irregulars, when it had to in an improvised manner. However, the task was always viewed officially as a regrettable diversion from preparation for "real war." Real war, of course, meant war against regular peers—the kind of war that Europeans waged against each other.

The U.S. Armed Forces have a fairly well-filled basket of experience with irregular enemies. If the military establishment is willing and able to learn and regard COIN as a necessary, enduring competency achievable through adaptable transformation, past errors demand to be recognized. COIN warfare is not a black art. Rather its principles and priorities are well known and non-controversial. All that is necessary is for the soldier to be willing and able to learn from history, recent American history at that. Unfortunately, the first and truest love of the U.S. defense community is with technology, not history. Great American strategic theorist Bernard Brodie explained for all time why history should not be neglected. He reminded that "the only empirical data we have about how people conduct war and behave under its stresses is our experience with it in the past, however much we have to make adjustments for subsequent changes in conditions."[58] An army struggling to adapt to the unfamiliar and unwelcome challenges of irregular warfare cannot afford to be ahistorical, let alone antihistorical.

4. Problem-solving, Optimistic

Holding to an optimistic public culture characterized by the belief that problems can be solved, the American way in war is not easily discouraged or deflected once it is fueled by a serious intent to succeed. That is to say not when it is made manifest in such anti-strategic sins against sound statecraft as with the "drive-by" cruise missile attacks of the late 1990s. The problem-solving faith, the penchant for the engineering fix, has the inevitable consequence of leading U.S. policy, including its use of force, to attempt the impossible.[59] After all, American history is decorated triumphantly with "impossible" achievements, typically against physical geography. Conditions are often misread as problems. Conditions have to be endured, perhaps ameliorated and tolerated, whereas by definition problems can be solved.

There are two ways in which an American way of war imbued with a problem-solving spirit is apt to stray from the path of strategic effectiveness. First, irregular enemies, terrorist-insurgents, are not usefully regarded as problems to be solved. They wage protracted war and eschew the open engagements that might produce a clear-cut military decision. Since the irregular foe cannot be brought to battle en masse, he is not a problem that the armed forces can solve tactically or operationally. Instead, following classic COIN doctrine, the problem of the insurgent is best treated as a condition that has to be addressed indirectly, as security is provided for and hopefully the trust is gained of the local people. That has to be a slow, gradual process. If one does not understand that and act accordingly, one has no future in COIN.

5. Culturally Challenged

Belatedly, it has become fashionable to berate the cultural insensitivity that has hampered American strategic performance.[60] Bear in mind American public ideology, with its emphasis on political and moral uniqueness, manifest destiny, and divine mission, is married to the multidimensional sense of national greatness. Such self-evaluation has not inclined Americans to be especially respectful of the beliefs, habits, and behavior of other cultures. This has been especially unfortunate in the inexorably competitive field of warfare. From the Indian Wars on the internal frontier to Iraq and Afghanistan in the twenty-first century, the American way of war has suffered from the self-inflicted damage caused by a failure to understand the enemy and the friends of the day. For a state that now accepts, indeed insists on, a global mandate to act as sheriff, this lack of cultural empathy, including a lack of sufficiently critical self-knowledge, is serious.

There is no mode of warfare conducted in any geographical environment wherein the enemy's strategic culture is of no importance. Even in the most extreme of warfare's technological forms, such as a large-scale "exchange" of nuclear weapons between super or great powers, the firing and targeting doctrine of the foe will not be without cultural influence. Nuclear doctrines will express calculations of military and geostrategic realities, assessments conducted by encultured strategists. Through much of the 1970s and 1980s, U.S. nuclear strategy carried promise of damage limitation for America only if Soviet nuclear strategy reciprocated in targeting restraint. Soviet attitudes toward war, including nuclear war, were of vital importance. Since culture was and indeed still is a significant dimension of warfare with nuclear weapons, how much more salient must it be in irregular conflict? Recall that the battlespace in the fight against insurgents and terrorists is in the minds of the people whose allegiance or acquiescence is the stake in the struggle. To win the trust of the people at risk requires comprehension of their beliefs, hopes, fears, and their take on their recent history, in short their culture. To acquire cultural empathy is no simple matter. It cannot be achieved inside "Fort Apache," nor can it be gained by occasional energetic and violent sweeps through "bandit country."

6. Technology Dependent

The exploitation of machinery is the American way of war. One may claim that airpower is virtually synonymous with that way of war and that its employment as the leading military instrument of choice has become routine. So at least it appeared in the 1990s, in the warm afterglow of airpower's triumph in the First Gulf War.[61] America is the land of technological marvels and extraordinary technology dependency. In the nineteenth century, a shortage of skilled craftsmen—they had tended to remain in Europe, where they prospered—obliged Americans to invent and use machines as substitutes for human skill and muscle. Necessity bred preference and then excellence, and the choice of mechanical solutions assumed a cultural significance that has endured. Unsurprisingly, the watershed was the experience of the Civil War. The way of war that succeeded in that bloody struggle was logistical and enabled by an exploitation of raw industrial power that foreign observers found awesome. Although American soldiers may profess that the human being matters most, in practice the American way of war, past, present, and prospectively future, is quintessentially and uniquely technology dependent. The army's transformation plans are awash with prudent words on the many dimensions of future conflict, but at its core lies a drive to acquire an exceedingly expensive future combat system comprising a network of enabling technologies.[62]

Given the range of potential demand that foreign policy may place on the armed forces, the only sound plan for the future has to be flexible and adaptable. The enemies of tomorrow are at least as likely to take regular, as contrasted with irregular, forms. The issue is not technology nor any particular set of weapons and support systems. Instead, the difficulty lies in the fact that the U.S. Armed Forces are culturally attuned to favoring technological solutions over other approaches, while irregular enemies pose problems of a kind where technology typically offers few advantages. Indeed, machines and dependence on them can have negative value, because although they can save American lives, they tend to isolate American soldiers from the social, and even the military, context that is the decisive battleground in irregular conflict. Whatever technology can usefully do in COIN and for counterterrorism certainly should be done. It is the misuse through overuse of technology that is at issue, not technology itself. The experience of several countries demonstrates unambiguously that there is no correlation between technical sophistication and success in the conduct of warfare against irregulars.[63] Remember the "McNamara Fence" and suchlike extravagant follies.

7. Focused on Firepower

Gen. William C. Westmoreland, the commander of the Military Advisory Command Vietnam (MACV), once famously and characteristically exclaimed at a press conference that the correct approach to counterinsurgency was "firepower."[64] It has long been the American way in warfare to send metal in harm's way in place of vulnerable flesh. This admirable expression of the country's machine-mindedness undoubtedly is the single most characteristic feature of American warmaking. Needless to say, it would seem that a devotion to firepower, while defensible, indeed necessary, encourages the armed forces to rely on it even when other modes of military behavior would be more suitable. In irregular conflicts particularly, heavy and sometimes seemingly indiscriminate, certainly disproportionate, resort to firepower solutions readily becomes self-defeating. A focus on firepower as the key to victory defined in classic military terms produces the attitude that what we do in war is service targets. Instead of being considered in his cultural context, the enemy is reduced to the dehumanized status of the object of U.S. firepower.[65] At its nadir, this characteristic was demonstrated in action in Vietnam with the prevalence of the artillery's practice of conducting unaimed harassment and interdiction fire.[66] A notable fraction of that artillery fire was expended for no better reason than that the ammunition was available in embarrassing abundance.

Regular warfare is composed of ever varying mixes of the eternal trinity of fire, movement, and shock. Irregular warfare, however, is different. There can be no decisive military engagement, because an agile, elusive, and competent irregular enemy will decline to expose himself in such a way that he can be obliterated by fire, outmaneuvered to annihilation, or destroyed physically and morally by shock effect. In COIN the rules of engagement (ROE) broadly are the reverse of those standard in regular combat. When in doubt, one should not fire. Why? Because, as a general rule, COIN must be conducted around the civilian population that comprises the conflict's center of gravity. Trigger-happiness produces undesirable collateral damage: dead and wounded civilians, damage to property, and fear of American military misbehavior. Better that an insurgent escape or an Allied soldier be killed, than a dozen or so bystanders pay the ultimate price for being in the wrong place at the wrong time. The kind of disciplined self-restraint vital to success in warfare against irregulars does not come easily or naturally to young people trained to be aggressive and kill. Nor does it come easily to officers who have well-founded anxieties about the career implications of suffering casualties. If the armed forces are serious about offering policy high competency in the conduct of war against irregulars, then they will need to curb their traditional, indeed cultural, love affair with firepower.

8. Large-scale

As a superpower, the United States tends to excel at enterprises conducted on a scale that matches its total assets. In 1985, Professor Huntington stated that "the United States is a big country, and we should fight wars in a big way."[67] More controversially, he claimed that "[b]igness not brains is our advantage, and we should exploit it."[68] No doubt these words will irritate and anger many readers. However, there is an important self-awareness in Huntington's point. As a large rich country, the United States has waged many wars, regular and irregular, domestic and foreign, as one would expect of a society amply endowed materially. Poor societies are obliged to wage war frugally. They have no choice other than to attempt to fight smarter than their rich enemies. The United States has been blessed with wealth in all its forms. Once mobilized and equipped, the U.S. Armed Forces inevitably have fought a rich person's war. From the time of the Civil War, foreign observers have been astonished by the material generosity with which American troops have been supplied and equipped. Strategic necessity is the mother of military invention, and since at least the 1860s, Americans have had little need to invent clever work-arounds for material lack. It is not self-evident that the United States is able to wage war in a materially minimalist fashion, any more than that today's volunteer soldiers and their families would tolerate campaign conditions of what would be regarded as unnecessary discomfort. The American army at war is American society at war. This is not so much a problem, rather it is a condition.

Americans have waged modern war on a shoestring, and the experience was predictably unhappy. Anyone wondering how Americans perform when the material balance is not weighted heavily in their favor will not be short of historical evidence. They could do worse than study the campaign on Guadalcanal (1942–43), or for another grim classic episode, the fate of Task Force Smith in Korea in July 1950.[69] However, these were exceptions to the rule that, because the United States was the world's greatest industrial nation, it waged its industrial age warfare on a scale that others could not hope to match. Because, though, the American way of war traditionally had to be unleashed only after a hasty surge of emergency and time-consuming mobilization, the cost was heavy for the soldiers at the sharp end. "Come as you are and with what you have got combat" is ever a bloody and extraordinarily dangerous duty. The implications of America's excellence in large-scale warfare for combatting irregular enemies are mixed but, on balance, have been negative. Warfare against a lightly armed irregular foe short of numbers is not simply a scaled down version of warfare as usual. The American strategic cultural trait of "bigness," of functioning with large footprints, is apt to be counterproductive. The more evident the American presence and influence in COIN, the less legitimate and competent the local authorities appear. The larger the American military contribution, particularly if its soldiers look hostile and behave as if they are in enemy territory, the more the U.S. presence will resemble an occupation.[70] American culture, in all senses of the term, is powerful, particularly in its hold on Americans. Large numbers of Americans, being Americans, acting like Americans, and indeed living in cultural and social little facsimiles of America, set down artificially in an alien society and comprise a challenge, even an insult, to important elements in local mores. With all the logistics deemed essential to the American way of life that the volunteer soldier expects, this is a necessary consequence of the injection of large numbers of Americans into a foreign cultural milieu. Of course, Americans can reduce their visibility by retreating into fortified bunkers or deploying away from heavily populated areas. However, to behave thus is to operate in a manner counterproductive for irregular warfare, where the battlespace, as we keep insisting, is the people.

9. Aggressive, Offensive

Geopolitics, culture, and material endowment have combined to pull the American way of war toward an aggressive, offensive style. Geopolitically viewed, the United States is effectively insular, albeit on a continental scale. The country has not faced a serious threat in North America since the War of 1812, except, of course, from its slave-holding states in 1861–65. Because of America's geopolitical isolation, in the twentieth century the country repeatedly entered wars already well underway. America had to take the initiative and move men and material across oceans. Also, it was obliged to commit to offensive operations to take back the gains made by enemies in Europe and Asia at the outset of their rampages of conquest. While U.S. political motives may have been broadly defensive, the Central and then the Axis Powers in the two world wars effectively were besieged twice by maritime coalitions. As with Iraq's seizure of Kuwait in 1990, the principal guardian of the status quo, the United States, had no military choice other than aggressive, offensive action. More often than not, an aggressor is content to take his prize and then offer an armistice and a conference to bless the crimes just committed by his offense. Prior to the creation of

NATO and the subsequent U.S. commitment to maintain a substantial garrison in Europe, the American strategic role in Eurasia was notably episodic. When an army is sent across an ocean, its society expects it to do something important, at least this is true in strategic contexts other than that of the nuclear-shadowed Cold War, which lasted roughly four decades. There are many plausible explanations for the offensive preference in the American way of war; I will cite some of the more significant among them. An aggressive, offensive style:

- is required if decisive victory is to be achieved against enemies who have to be ejected from ill-gotten gains, or otherwise taught the error of their ways.

- is mandated by a domestic political context that regards American participation in war as so extraordinary an event that it has to be completed as rapidly as possible, so that a condition of normalcy and peace can be restored.

- is fitting, because the United States only fights against evil regimes and is not minded to wage limited wars for limited political purposes, save under duress, as in Korea (1950–53). To win a war, there is no choice other than to take the offensive.

- is appropriate to America's strength and advantages. The United States is obliged to develop forces that are highly mobile. The conquest of distance has dominated America's strategic history.

- has a record of success, and it is difficult to argue with a history that appears to validate the military merits of an offensive style.

- via a succession of sometimes parallel offensive operations, was the American way, briefly in 1918, and then, of geopolitical necessity, in 1942–45.

While the American way of war can be traced back to the eighteenth century, this chapter notes that the apogée of demonstration of that "way" was, of course, 1942–45. America had, and had demonstrated on opposite sides of the world, a way of war that delivered decisive military victory. That way privileged mobility, movement at least, not necessarily skillful maneuver, command of the "commons" (the high seas and the air), and firepower. Americans sought to take war to the enemy as rapidly and destructively as the machines of industrial age warfare permitted. The problem today is that if the country's strategic future is going to be plagued more and more by challenges posed by irregular enemies, America's soldiers will lack enemy targets for their traditionally preferred style of operation. COIN warfare demotes the irregular enemy to the status of a secondary objective. Aggressive, offensive action against an enemy of uncertain location and identity is more likely to wreak political damage on the COIN endeavor, a self-inflicted wound, than on the enemy. Naturally, there is a time and place for offensive action. But, as the dominant characteristic of the official style of war, offensive action is likely to prove counterproductive against irregular enemies in many, perhaps most, circumstances. This is not to deny that irregular targets of opportunity certainly should be pursued aggressively, if the enemy is foolish enough to expose himself for discrete destruction. Also, an offensive style can be effective when it is succeeded by genuine occupation.

10. Profoundly Regular

Few, if any, armies have been equally competent in the conduct of regular and irregular warfare. The U.S. Army is no exception to this rule. Both the army and the Marine Corps have registered occasional success in irregular warfare, while individual Americans have proved themselves adept in the conduct of guerrilla warfare.[77] As institutions, however, the U.S. Armed Forces have not been friendly either to irregular warfare or to those in their ranks who were would-be practitioners and advocates of unconventional warfare or counterinsurgency.[72] American soldiers overwhelmingly have been regular in their view of, approach to, and skill in warfare. They have always prepared near exclusively for "real war," which is to say combat against an approximately symmetrical regular enemy. Irregular warfare, or low intensity conflict (LIC) as the 1960s term-of-art called it all too inclusively and therefore vaguely,[73] was regarded as a much lesser, but included, class of challenge. A good regular army has been assumed capable of turning its strengths to meet irregular enemies, whereas the reverse would not be true. Generally speaking, it has not been appreciated that LIC is not a scaled down version of "real war" but rather requires a different mindset, doctrine, and training.

The United States has a storehouse of first-hand historical experience that should educate its soldiers on the significant difference between regular and irregular warfare. While such education still has a distance to travel, it will only travel with steady endorsement from senior leadership. However, times appear to be changing for the better. Anyone in need of persuasion as to the regularity of the mindset dominant in America's military institutions need look no further than to the checkered history of the country's Special Operations Forces (SOF).

America's SOF have endured a Cinderella existence. They prospered somewhat with episodic civilian political sponsorship, but not until very recent times have they been regarded and treated as an important element in the combined arms team. For example, in the 1960s, notwithstanding the enthusiasm of "new frontiersmen" for the Green Berets in COIN, most SOF efforts were subsumed by the conventional style favored by MACV.[74] Also, in Vietnam and since, there has been tension between SOF as the expert practitioners of unconventional warfare, and SOF in the local liaison and training roles so vital for COIN. Even a regular military mind can be attracted to SOF, if their tasks comprise aggressive, offensive actions undertaken on a small scale for immediate military effect. Some special operations can simply be scaled down versions of the traditional American style in war.

The SOF are America's irregular regulars. How they are permitted to operate, and how well or poorly their duties fit into a comprehensive grand design for COIN, for example, reveals how far America's regular military establishment has moved toward incorporating an irregular dimension into its toolkit.[76] Whether or not today, for the first time, the Armed Forces will succeed in making doctrinal and operational sense of their invaluable special warriors is still in question. If they do, the strategic and political rewards should be substantial.

11. Impatient

America is an exceptionally ideological society and, to date at least, has distinguished clearly between conditions of peace and war. Americans have approached warfare as a regrettable occasional evil to be concluded as decisively and rapidly as possible. That partially moral perspective has not always sat well with the requirements of a politically effective use of force. For example, an important reason why MACV was not impressed by the promise of dedicated techniques of counterinsurgency in Vietnam was the undeniable fact that such a style of warfare was expected to take far too long to show major results. Furthermore, America's regular military minds and its domestic public have been schooled to expect military action to produce conclusive results. For example, at Khe Sahn in 1968, MACV was searching for an ever-elusive decisive victory. It was consequently outgeneraled by being lured into terrain far from the cities where the vast majority of the people had congregated. The nationwide popular rising was planned and expected by Hanoi as an urban event, with help from the Viet Cong. Following the precepts of Sun Tzu, Hanoi deceived MACV into the conviction that the war would be won or lost in rough terrain far from the cities of South Vietnam. With MACV wrong-footed into extra heavy deployments in frontier regions, the PAVN and the Viet Cong would secure urban victory leading a national popular rising. The rising did not happen, and the Viet Cong and PAVN were slaughtered in regular open warfare. Today, cultural bias toward swift action for swift victory is amplified by a mass media all too ready to report a lack of visible progress as evidence of stalemate and error.

Impatience is always a military vice, especially in the conduct of war against irregular enemies. These enemies have to use time as a weapon. We cannot claim that we have not been warned. More than seventy years ago, Mao Tse-tung described in ample detail the rationale for, character, and structure of protracted war, and with local variants it has been practiced around the world ever since by insurgents of many political persuasions.[76] It is probably no exaggeration to claim that a campaign plan fueled by impatience must prove fatal to the prospects for success in irregular warfare. An impatient combatant literally will be seeking to achieve the impossible. Unless the irregular makes a truly irreversible political error, swift and decisive success against him simply is unattainable. Terrorists and insurgents cannot be defeated rapidly. The center of gravity in irregular warfare, which is to say the local people and their allegiance, cannot be seized and held by dramatic military action. Against irregular foes, America's soldiers, and more particularly America's local allies, must be prepared to play a long game. Although the armed forces now know this, whether the American body politic shares in this enlightenment is less certain. Americans are right to be uneasy about open-ended military commitments to allies who are struggling against insurgencies. There is much to be said for U.S. forces to devote most of their distinctive strengths to keeping the ring square for local friends. This may well require the taking of suitably violent action, certainly the issuing of fearsome threats, against foreign backers of an insurgency. However, terrorists and other insurgents ultimately can only be worn down and overcome by local initiatives and steady effort, not by American COIN behavior, no matter how expertly conducted. As a general rule, there will be the odd exception: foreigners, regardless of their good intentions and the high quality of their means and methods, cannot win irregular wars.

12. Logistically Excellent

American history is a testament to the need to conquer distance. Americans at war have been exceptionally able logisticians. With a continental-size interior and an effectively insular geostrategic location, such ability has been mandatory. If war has to be waged at all, let it be waged effectively. Recalling the point that virtues also have vices, it can be argued that America frequently has waged war more logistically than strategically, which is not to deny that in practice the two nearly merge in their independence.[77] Ample support of American war-making can have the downside of encouraging a tooth-to-tail ratio almost absurdly weighted in favor of the latter. A significant reason why firepower has been the long suit in the American way of war is because repeatedly there has been an acute shortage of soldiers in the infantry. A large logistical footprint, and none come larger than the American, requires a great deal of guarding, helps isolate American troops from local people, and tends to organically grow in what has been pejoratively called the logistical snowball.[78] Of necessity America's logistical excellence has rested on mastery of the "commons." Borrowing from Alfred Thayer Mahan, who wrote of the sea as a "wide common," Barry Posen has explained how and why the United States is master not only of the high seas, but also of the new commons of the air, space, and cyberspace.[79] Should this mastery cease to be assured, the country would have difficulty waging war against anyone except Mexicans and Canadians.

Those who doubt the historical reality of a distinctive American way of war are invited to compare with other countries the quantity and quality of support deemed essential to keep American soldiers tolerably content in the field. Many critics of General Westmoreland's strategy in Vietnam failed to notice that he was always painfully short of fighting soldiers. While the U.S. military presence under his command may have totaled some 550,000, no more than 80,000 of those soldiers were "fighting men."[80] There is a crossover point where logistical sufficiency in any kind of war, regular or irregular, can slip into an excess that is a net disadvantage. In regular warfare, the traditional American way provides the infrastructure and depth of material that permits sustained combat. For example, by way of a sharp contrast, Hitler's Luftwaffe was always in desperate straits because of a lack of spare parts. In World War II, Germany and Japan fielded flashy "shop window" forces that lacked staying power. The American way is the reverse of that. However, in the conduct of irregular warfare, which almost invariably is waged on foreign soil, America's traditional way with abundant goods and services for the troops has an obvious downside. The American logistical footprint is heavy and it grows organically. The American way of war requires large bases that require protection. Those bases, dumps, and other facilities help isolate Americans from the local people and their culture, and they create a distinct economy that signals the political fact that America is on the job. Naturally, it is difficult to envisage serious measures to lighten the logistical footprint, given concerns about reenlistment, political pressures from soldiers' relatives, and soldier-citizens' notions of their rights. To succeed in COIN, the army in particular needs to adapt in the direction of lighter, more agile forces, a process already underway. In addition, it should approach the issue of its material necessities in the field from the distinctive perspective of irregular as well as regular warfare.

13. Highly Sensitive to Casualties

As with the Roman Empire, the American guardian of world order is much averse to suffering military casualties. Both super-states had and have armies that are small, too small in the opinion of many, relative to their responsibilities. Moreover, well-trained professional soldiers and volunteers are expensive to raise, train, retain, and difficult to replace. Beyond the issue of cost effectiveness, however, lies the claim that American society has become so sensitive to casualties that the domestic context for military action is no longer tolerant of potentially bloody ventures in muscular foreign governance. Careful sociological research suggests that this popular notion about the American way of war, that it must seek to avoid American casualties at almost any price, has been exaggerated.[81] Nonetheless, exaggerated or not, it is a fact that the United States has been perfecting a way in warfare that is expected, even required, to result in very few casualties. U.S. commanders certainly have operated since the Cold War under strict orders to avoid losses. The familiar emphasis on force protection as "job one," virtually regardless of the consequences for the success of the mission, is a telling expression of this cultural norm. 9/11 went toward reversing the apparent trend favoring, even demanding, friendly casualty avoidance. After all, culture does change with context. As quoted earlier, the *National Defense Strategy* document of March 2005 opens with the uncompromising declamation, "America is a nation at war." For so long as Americans believe this to be true, the social context for military behavior should be more permissive of casualties than was the case in the 1990s. Both history and common sense show that Americans will tolerate casualties, even high casualties, if they are convinced that the political stakes are vital and the government is trying hard to win. It must be noted, though, that Americans have come to expect an exceedingly low casualty rate because that has been their recent experience. This expectation has been fed by events, the evolution of a high-technology way in warfare that exposes relatively few American soldiers to mortal danger, and the low quality of recent enemies. When the context allows, it is U.S. military style to employ machines rather than people and to rely heavily on firepower to substitute for a personally more dangerous mode of combat. A network-centric army, if able to afford the equipment, carries the promise of being supported by even more real-time on-call firepower than is available today.

If the United States is serious about combating irregular enemies in a way that stands a reasonable prospect of success, it will have to continue to send its soldiers into harm's way to a degree likely to promote political discomfort. The all-service defense transformation is very much a high technology voyage into the future. The focus is on machines, the further exploitation of the computer in particular. Overall, it is not unfair to observe that this transformation, with its promise of even better performance in C^{4}ISTAR, should strengthen the American ability to wage its traditional style of war. Once detected, enemies will be tracked and then obliterated by firepower, much of it delivered from altitude. American soldiers will see little of the foe, save as a target. Civilians will be protected from suffering as victims of collateral damage, to some degree at least, by the precision with which America's forces will be able to direct their fire. A major attraction of this style of war is that few Americans will be at risk. The problem is that, except in special cases, such a high-technology dependent, stand-off style is not altogether appropriate for the conduct of war against irregulars. Certainly it is not suitable as the principal mode of operation. For American soldiers to be useful in COIN they have to be deployed "up close and personal" to the people who are the stake in the struggle. The more determinedly the army strives to avoid casualties by hiding behind fortifications and deploying with armored protection, the less likely is it to be effective in achieving the necessary relationship of trust with the people. Of course, there will be circumstances when insurgents escalate violence in urban terrain in an endeavor to tempt Americans to fight back in their preferred style with profligate resort to firepower. In stressful circumstances, it may be hard to remember that in COIN dead insurgents are not proof of success, any more than is home-side casualty avoidance by us.

CONCLUSION

Early in this study, I exposed my thinking with a three-pointed argument. By way of conclusion, I revisit those claims, with a particular view to drawing together the threads of irregular enemies and warfare, strategy, and the American way of war.

First, war and strategy have constant natures throughout history and with respect to politically motivated violence in all modes of action. It has to follow that a single general theory suffices to uncover their secrets. One can stumble on foolish references to a post-Clausewitzian era, or a pre-Clausewitzian period, but be not misled. The great Prussian, with his unfinished theory of war, is more than good enough to apply to all periods and all brands of war. However, in common with Clausewitz and, one must say, the dictates of common sense, I recognize fully that the characteristics of war evolve and different wars in the same period have distinctive features. Furthermore, the main elements that comprise the unchanging nature of war—passion, chance, reason, danger, exertion, uncertainty, and friction—though always present, must vary in their relative effect. To some degree, but only to some degree, the elements are controllable.

Strategy does have an essence. If there is a single idea that best captures that essence, it is *instrumentality*. So long as one never forgets that strategy is about the consequences of the threat and use of force and not about such use itself, one will keep to the straight and narrow. A sound grasp of strategy's essence offers no protection, at least only inadequate protection, against foolish policy or military failure. In the latter regard, it is worth quoting Col. Charles E. Callwell who wrote in his justly famous book on *Small Wars* a hundred years ago that "strategy is not, however, the final arbiter in war. The battle-field decides, and on the battle-field the advantage passes over to the regular army."[82] Callwell had been explaining how the irregular enemy in colonial warfare typically enjoyed a strategic advantage. His point was that strategic advantage is all very well, but ultimately the troops, regular or irregular, have to be able to fight well. He was not entirely correct, but we can hardly criticize him for not foreseeing the extensive politicization of irregular warfare in the twentieth century.[83] He did not anticipate a strategic context wherein the battlespace would comprise the minds of the local people.

Although irregular warfare in all its modes is different from regular combat in many respects, it is not at all distinctive from the perspective of the essence of strategy. War is war and strategy is strategy. There are no so-called new wars and old wars, nor Third Generation Wars and Fourth Generation Wars. There are only wars.[84] In its essence, strategy works identically for regular and irregular belligerents and in regular and irregular warfare. Although the characteristics of different forms of war and styles in warfare vary widely, there is a common currency in strategic effect, no matter how that effect is generated. Tactical, even operational, excellence in the waging of irregular war, or indeed any kind of war, must be at a severe discount, a waste, if it is not directed by a constant concern for its strategic effect on the course of political events. The logic of strategy is the same for wars of all kinds, even though the styles and tools of combat will differ.

The second conclusion, argument perhaps, is that the United States has a persisting strategy deficit, which reflects a political deficit in its approach to war in all its hideous forms. To put this argument in context, I argue that the United States has an enduring way of war that deserves characterization as cultural. The contemporary drive for military transformation may be hindered, even partially frustrated, by American public, strategic, and military culture. The current crop of official documents on transformation may be too optimistic in its aspirations for American military cultural, and other, change. Understandably, those documents are not eloquent on the question of the country's competence in strategy.

Of course, an American strategy deficit is a weakness that renders its armed forces victims rather than villains. However, soldiers cannot be indifferent to the fact that in conflict after conflict their effort and sacrifice do not have the strategic effect desired and expected. The armed forces need to think much harder about strategy than they have in the past. In their drive for transformation they are striving to be adaptable to a new context populated by asymmetric enemies and protracted conflicts. Once the forces grant that their tactical and operational actions have strategic meaning, which in its turn has to have political meaning, they can reconsider whether their tactical habits and preferences would benefit from further adaptation to circumstances. Soldiers have to clear their mind of the belief that they do not "do strategy." If they will read chapter 33 of T. E. Lawrence's *Seven Pillars of Wisdom*, they will discover, or be reminded of "the false antithesis between strategy . . . and tactics." Lawrence concluded that strategy and tactics "seemed only points of view from which to ponder the elements of war."[85] Armed forces' leaders, senior officials in the national security bureaucracy, and assorted experts and would-be opinion leaders perennially talk about strategy. And yet, in practice American strategic performance bears a close resemblance to the view of strategy expressed by Field Marshal Helmuth Graf von Moltke, the Prussian victor in the Wars of German Unification (1864, 1866, 1870–71). Having explained the nature of strategy in sound Clausewitzian terms, Moltke proceeded to appear to turn the master's theory on its head. He advised that "[t]he demands of strategy grow silent in the face of a tactical victory and adapt themselves to the newly created situation. *Strategy is a system of expedients* [emphasis added]."[86] To be fair to the field marshal, he was insisting only that military tactics, actually operations, be recognized as sovereign in the context of flexible pursuit of a guiding strategic idea. The events of 1914–18 and 1939–45 bear eloquent witness to the consequences of misreading Moltke's dictum. To direct attention to America's strategy deficit is not to make a fine academic point, the kind of claim to be expected of a theorist. This deficiency lies at the heart of the country's difficulties in its protracted struggles with irregular enemies.

The third conclusion is that there is a traditional American way of war that, in some respects, encourages a military style far from optimal as an approach to the challenges posed by irregular enemies. I am not quite arguing that the American way of war, a style reflecting cultural influences, will thwart the ambitions for transformation, though there are grounds for anxiety in this regard. Also, I am not claiming that a way of war is immutable. While a "way" does evolve and may adapt, it does so slowly. After all, it is deeply rooted in history, and there are good reasons why it is what it is. Also, although I am concerned to point out its weaknesses, especially its strategic deficiencies, the American way of war has major characteristic strengths. Indeed, if it did not have such strengths, then it would not have been adopted and it would not have persisted. Not everyone will agree with each characteristic that I have discerned in the American way; there is no authorized list. However, this analysis rests on the strong conviction that there has been and is such a "way," and that its strength will be a problem. The

American way of war is especially likely to be a problem, really a harassing condition, for a transformation that focuses significantly on the ability to conduct warfare against irregular enemies.

For example, the dependence on technology, the privileging of firepower, the emphasis on U.S. casualty avoidance express a mindset and doctrine that has not adapted persuasively to the distinctive conditions of irregular warfare. But, as the leading power willing and able to undertake tasks on behalf of global order and stability, the United States dare not assume that all its future foes will be of a non-state character. This means that the armed forces cannot "lighten up" comprehensively to meet the challenges posed by terrorists and insurgents. There will be regular enemies in America's strategic future, even if they are obliged by America's strengths to fight in irregular ways.

The major elements in my argument come together in this third conclusion: irregular enemies, strategy, and the traditional American way of war. Although more competent enemies will not challenge U.S. strategic effectiveness successfully, this effectiveness may fall short for reasons of America's own political, strategic, and military culture. The problems are twofold. On the one hand, Americans need to understand that irregular warfare truly is different tactically and operationally from a regular character of struggle. On the other hand, scarcely less important, Americans must never forget that strategy must rule all of warfare, regular and irregular. The traditional American way of war was designed to take down regular enemies and was not overly attentive to the strategic effect and political consequences of military action. That legacy makes the task before the agents of transformation and adaptation even greater than perhaps they have realized to date.

This chapter's subtitle poses the question: "Can the American Way of War Adapt?" My answer is "perhaps, but only with difficulty." Cultural change cannot be reliably implemented by plans, orders, and exhortation. Even negative experience is not entirely to be trusted as a certain source of sound education.

7

THE IMPLICATIONS OF PRE-EMPTIVE AND PREVENTIVE WAR DOCTRINES: A RECONSIDERATION

The United States has long maintained the option of preemptive actions to counter a sufficient threat to our national security. The greater the threat, the greater the risk of inaction—and the more compelling the case for taking anticipatory action to defend ourselves, even if uncertainty remains as to the time and place of the enemy's attack. To forestall or prevent such hostile acts by our adversaries, the United States will, if necessary, act preemptively.
—George W. Bush, 2002[1]

Preemption is the big new rule. It was created by 9/11.
—Thomas P. M. Barnett, 2004[2]

New world orders . . . need to be policed.
—Michael Howard, 2001[3]

Preemption is a leading strategic concept in this decade. However, despite its ubiquity in public discourse and its policy relevance, it is a source of great confusion. While the term is misused, in some cases deliberately one suspects, it must be admitted that strategic theorists have offered little worthwhile reading on the subject. This chapter clarifies the meaning of preemption and distinguishes it from prevention and precaution. It critically reviews the principal charges leveled against preventive warfare and uses that analysis to provide at least the bare bones of a relevant strategic theory.

Preemption is not controversial: legally, morally, or strategically. To preempt means to strike first—or attempt to do so—in the face of an attack that is either already underway or credibly imminent. The decision for war has been taken by the enemy. The victim or target state can try to disrupt the unfolding assault or may elect to receive the attack before reacting. In truth, military preemption will not always be feasible.

By way of the sharpest contrast, a preventive war is a war of discretion. It differs from preemptive war in its timing and motivation. The preemptor has no choice other than to strike rapidly; it will probably be too late even to surrender. The preventor, however, chooses to wage war, at least to launch military action, because of his fears for the future should he fail to act. In other words, the preventor strikes to prevent a predicted enemy from changing the balance of power or otherwise behaving in a manner that the preventor would judge intolerable. Naturally, the more distant the anticipated menace, the greater the degree of guesswork as to the severity and timing of the danger. A precautionary war is one waged not out of strong conviction that a dangerous threat is brewing in the target state, but rather because it is suspected that such a threat might one day emerge, and it is better to be safe than sorry. Unintentionally, of course, the decision to launch a preventive war can amount to a choice to commit suicide for fear of eventual death. A decision for war should never be regarded as a safe course of action.

The subjects of the previous chapter—strategy, irregular warfare, and the American way of war—intrude here in several important respects. Each of the large themes in chapter 6 is significant here also. Preemption and prevention are strategies subject to the general lore in the theory of strategy; they are not clever evasions of it. Although these strategies are highly relevant to conditions wherein surprise assaults are anticipated, paradoxically they are extraordinarily hard to plan and execute effectively against irregular enemies. Finally, though American culture in principle is morally and legally uncomfortable with strategies for striking first, it is happy indeed with the often advertised prospect of achieving swift and decisively successful outcomes.

INTRODUCTION: A CONFUSED DEBATE

Strategic policy issue has rarely generated so much heat, yet shed so little light, as has the twenty-first-century debate over preemption. This ancient strategic idea is not difficult to understand and explain and can be considered in the context of more than two millennia of historical experience. Nonetheless, the debate over it since September 11, 2001, would seem to have been designed to produce maximum obfuscation.

To cite a few of the willful sources of contemporary confusion: (1) the concept of preemption has been misused; (2) the vital character of the political context has not been debated realistically; (3) largely irrelevant legal and moral issues have been given their traditional outing; and (4) stunningly obvious arguments, typically critical of the ideas and practices of preemption and prevention, have been advanced as if they were pearls of eternal strategic wisdom.

We strategic theorists are guilty of failing to perform our primary professional duty. What is that duty? Carl von Clausewitz could hardly have been plainer: "The primary purpose of any theory is to clarify concepts and ideas that have become, as it were, confused and entangled."[4] Preemption is just such an idea. In order to clear the confusion, I shall attempt to rescue the concept and its much more interesting partner, prevention, from attempted intellectual control by lawyers, moralists, narrowly military defense analysts, scholastic political scientists, journalists, and politicians. The dual intention here is to place preemption and prevention where they belong in the catalog of strategic ideas, and to relate that catalog to its political context. In the latter regard, that means the role of the United States with respect to the maintenance and protection of a tolerably secure international order.

Notwithstanding its overstatement, Thomas Barnett's quotation, which heads this chapter, is accurate in one key respect: preemption as a live policy and hence strategic subject certainly owes its topicality to 9/11. It was ever thus with regard to strategic ideas. As history moves onwards, sideways, indeed frequently in a nonlinear fashion, strategic thought responds, faint but pursuing. Preemption and prevention taken together—to be defined carefully in the next section—have been contenders for "strategic concept of the decade." One cannot deny that, along with transformation, irregular warfare, asymmetrical warfare, and the return of counterinsurgency (COIN), they have secured a notable place in public discourse. However, unlike those other strategic ideas, preemption, let alone prevention, does not have definable military content. The concept is temporal and preeminently strategic, which is to say that it lurks where military behavior and policy meet.

By and large innocently, officials and commentators have spread confusion and invited needless debate. In fact, much of the public debate over preemption and prevention has been not far short of ridiculous. One can no more debate the general desirability of preemption and prevention than one can argue about the general advantages and disadvantages of war. The subject is case specific. War is always undesirable unless the alternative is anticipated to be even less desirable. What has been remarkable has been the degree to which the literature of the preemption debate has succeeded in wrenching its subject out of context. Preemption and prevention are indeed strategic ideas that can be explained and understood in the abstract. However, strategy is, above all else, a pragmatic subject and activity. Preemption has no inherent strategic merit or demerit, save in specific historical contexts. Moreover, preemption cannot sensibly be debated as if it were primarily a legal or moral issue—it is not. Preemption is a political matter utterly dependent for its feasibility on military prowess.

Recent and contemporary debate has more to do with arguments over the American role in the world than with the alleged virtues and sins of two strategic ideas. While our argument here discusses preemption as strategic theory and endeavors to locate and explain it as such, it must also strive to avoid a characteristic and long-standing weakness in American strategic studies. As befits a public and strategic culture more inclined to praise Clausewitz than to practice his wisdom, the United States continues to demonstrate an uncertain grasp of the connection between policy and military force. Bereft of political context, a debate over preemption or prevention is meaningless.

Far from providing a mere footnote to history, those who have spoken about and debated preemption and prevention have sought to address matters of the gravest significance. There is not much that can compete in importance with decisions for war or peace. Moreover, the preemption issue is not about to disappear. This chapter takes a firm stand on preemption, as it does on the all-important superior question of the U.S. role in the world, its policy and strategy. However, these pages are not a contribution to the debate over the advisability of the invasion of Iraq in 2003. Hindsight is wonderful, ever the strategist's most reliable friend. Doctrines come and go. The strategic ideas of preemption and prevention are now overdue for a well-deserved break from public overexposure, even though the political and strategic contexts that yield them their importance will remain. The policy and strategic issues of preemption and prevention are here to stay, whether Americans like it or not.

This chapter proceeds to: (1) explain and differentiate the meanings of preemption and prevention, and to place them in the recent history of strategic thought and planning; (2) consider the legal and cultural dimension of preemption and prevention; (3) provide some historical context for what otherwise could be an unduly contemporary discussion; (4) present fairly the major arguments for and against preemption and prevention, while not forgetting that as an abstract undertaking the exercise can have only limited utility; (5) develop a theory, for practice (as all strategic theory must be), of preemption and prevention for the twenty-first century; and (6) nail its colors to the mast and specify implications for policy and strategy.

DEFINITIONS

The essential first step to clarity in debate and to understanding the issues has to be the correct use of key terms. It so happens, as nearly every scholarly commentator has complained, that the so-called Bush Doctrine of 2002 either deliberately or accidentally misused the concept of preemption.

The president announced a new doctrine that had preemption in the historically organizing role once occupied by containment and deterrence.[5] What is a doctrine? Analyst M. Elaine Bunn explains, "To call preemption a doctrine implies that it is a central organizing principle for marshalling the instruments of national power in support of national objectives and that in relevant cases, action will be taken in accordance with established governing principles."[6] This is a suitably tough standard for a concept to reach before it can be the guiding light for a new doctrine. Preemption falls short of meeting that standard. More troubling, though, is the confusion created by official misuse of the concept of preemption. Even though it would be reassuring to know that the misuse has been deliberate and calculated, official language and strategic behavior have not offered such reassurance. The conceptual debate sparked by official language and behavior focused exclusively on the term preemption. This concept has been employed promiscuously to encompass any and all cases of the first use of military force intended to beat the enemy to the punch, even when that enemy is nowhere near ready to fight.

Although the official and public debate has been content to argue about the advantages and disadvantages of a multipurpose preemption, three related concepts are jostling for recognition and proper employment: preemption, prevention, and precaution. There are two underlying questions fundamental to this inquiry: (1) Under what circumstances might one strike first? (2) On what authority might one strike first?

If confident and reasonable answers can be provided to these two questions, most of the confusion in the ongoing debate should dissipate. Each of the three concepts—preemption, prevention, and precaution—has distinctive temporal meaning. In temporal distance from an imminent threat, moving from shorter to longer time available for decision, these concepts proceed in the following order: preemption, prevention, precaution. The word preemption has been employed so expansively that it has wholly overwhelmed prevention and precaution in public discourse.

Preemption

Preemption refers to the first use of military force when an enemy attack is already underway or credibly imminent. During the Cold War, these concepts were widely understood and, in the case of preemption, were adopted by both superpowers. They intended to launch their strategic nuclear forces on receipt of unambiguous warning (relying on dual phenomenology, or more) that they were under attack. Preemption would have been a desperate effort to disrupt, break up, and forestall a large-scale nuclear attack.[7] A preemptive strike would have comprised some combination of a launch on warning (LOW) and a launch under attack (LUA). The alternative would have been to launch after confirmation of attack arrival (LAA), the option otherwise known as retaliation. The verbal formula of the Cold War years held that to preempt meant "to go first in the last resort." Given the enormity of the consequences of nuclear war almost regardless of who struck first, and also given the tight timelines for launch decisions and safe escape of land-based forces, it is scarcely to be wondered that preemption was an idea, and indeed a war plan option, that was treated with great respect. Preemptive error today could have many dire consequences. But preemption in the twenty-first century against a regional menace is not going to end life on the planet. In the 1970s and 1980s, the strategic context was nowhere near so tolerant of possible error. In those decades, neither superpower could afford to be lax in its strategic conceptualization of preemption, in its contingency planning for it, or in its decision making on the preemptive option.

Strategic theory, policy, strategy, and plans for the twenty-first century need to be radically different from those suitable for the Cold War. However, the Cold War era understanding of preemption should retain its authority, even though the stakes are vastly less today. To preempt is to launch an attack against an attack that one has incontrovertible evidence either is underway or has been ordered. In such a context, the only policy and strategy question is: "Do we try to strike first to lessen the blow, or do we receive the blow and strike back?" Of course, polities' most potent military assets may be so vulnerable to attack that if they do not strike first, they would not exist to strike second. Preemption is all about self-defense. Indeed, if we define preemption properly, which is to say as the desperate last resort prior to receiving an anticipated attack, it is not really controversial. U.S. Secretary of State Daniel Webster issued the classic statement of justification for preemption in 1842. He faulted the British military initiative in attacking the steamboat *Caroline* close by Niagara Falls in 1837. The boat was conveying men and arms to fuel a rebellion in Upper Canada. In words that could hardly be bettered for their plain meaning and applicability to our missile age, Webster argued:

> Undoubtedly it is just, that, while it is admitted that exceptions growing out of the great law of self-defense do exist, those exceptions should be confined to cases in which the necessity of that self-defense is instant, overwhelming, leaving no choice of means, and no moment of deliberation.[8]

In 1914, Secretary of State Elihu Root critically modified Webster's demanding standard of imminence of threat. Root opened the gates to endless debate when he rejected the traditional American view of what would constitute an imminent threat, and instead recast policy so that it would incorporate strategic judgment. Root asserted, "the right of every sovereign state [is] to protect itself by preventing a condition of affairs in which it will be too late to protect itself."[9] Though this position is sensible, it is no longer preemption. In fact, what Root justifies is a policy of anticipatory self-defense. Exercised with self-restraint and on the basis of excellent intelligence, there is a great deal to be said in praise of the Root formula. However, it is no great stretch to interpret that formula as a legal, moral, and strategic license to wage preventive wars of discretion. Root's use of the word "preventing" is all-important.

According to Webster, preemption is not controversial. Any state finding itself under attack, or about to be so, has the right and the duty to its citizens to defend itself as effectively as it is able. In many cases, the best mode of self-defense will be a swift first strike in an attempt to limit damage. Given the assumption that an attack is underway, preemption is not really arguable—save perhaps militarily—because the aggressor has already made the decision for war.

Prevention

Prevention or preventive warfare is the subject that is most central to this chapter, just as it is what the so-called Bush Doctrine of 2002 meant when it advertised the occasional necessity for preemption. When a state preempts, it has made a choice between the option of receiving the first blow or striking first. The decision for war has been taken out of its hands. Not so with prevention. If one is uncomfortable with the tough and restrictive Webster view of justified preemption, perhaps there can be a strategically prudent alternative that falls short of waging aggressive wars of discretion. In practice, there often is a middle way, while in theory one can also identify guidance for preventive war that should restrict the discretion of fearful trigger-happy policymakers. However, once the most restrictive meaning of preemption is abandoned, the floodgates to potential policy and strategy abuse are wide open. This is a case wherein the distinction between two closely related strategic concepts is both crystal clear and vitally necessary.

Most major strategic concepts have at their core and depend on an essential insight that, if not fully appreciated, is certain to have unfortunate consequences. For example, surprisingly many people fail to understand that deterrence only works if the intended deterree chooses to be deterred. Prevention, preventive self-defense, has at its core the proposition that the preventor is able to detect and anticipate deadly menace in the future. How far in the future? Since there is no theory of preventive war, at least none known to this theorist, we must carve our own path through the jungle of conceptual confusion. Once the certainty of imminent-or-actual attack is rejected as being too passive, and therefore imprudent, in an era that is witnessing the proliferation of weapons of mass destruction (WMD), strategic theory is not able to provide much help to policy and strategy. This is not quite true, because policy and strategy are arts, not sciences. Unfortunately, futurology in its several forms—astrology, advanced methods of defense analysis, and the rest—all comes down to guesswork.[10] Of course, guesses are dressed up as calculated risks, foreseeable futures, and so forth, but former Secretary of Defense Donald H. Rumsfeld was accurate when he emphasized the significance of the unknowns and, for the truly impenetrable, the "unknown unknowns." Of recent years the DoD has privileged the deeply Clausewitzian concept of uncertainty in its view of the future. While there has been an intellectual backlash against this recent high regard for uncertainty, for the purposes of this analysis, the concept merits its official high standing.[11]

Preventive war, perhaps just a preventive strike, can be viewed as a muscular application of Root's 1914 dictum of prudence. But if a state obedient to Root's precautionary logic is determined to prevent "a condition of affairs in which it will be too late to protect itself," how much protection should it secure through the use of force? How can a doctrine of preventive war be operationalized? Is it misleading to regard preventive war as a fit subject for a doctrine? Most powerful strategic ideas are attended by potential pathologies. In the case of preventive war, a leading malady inseparable from it is a quest for absolute security.[12] A policy of preventive war amounts to an unwillingness to live with certain kinds of risk. By preventive action a state strikes to control the dangers in its external security environment—at least that is the intention. Although familiarity with history reveals that the law of unintended consequences often frustrates such attempts, when did fearful or overconfident policymakers permit themselves to be deflected from a strongly favored course by contestable caveats derived from historical experience?

The most essential distinction between preemption and prevention is that the former option is uniquely exercised in or for a war that is certain, the timing of which has not been chosen by the preemptor. In every case, by definition, the option of preventive war, or a preventive strike, must express a guess that war, or at least a major negative power shift, is probable in the future. The preventor has a choice. It can elect to tolerate the predicted adverse power shift. Alternatively, it can function grand strategically and endeavor by diplomatic, economic, subversive, and military competitive means to lessen the growing peril. Obviously, temporally the more distant the danger, the greater the uncertainty. In the early 1990s, Americans were assailed by a fashionable theory that tomorrow's great enemy would be superpower Japan. Less than a decade later, the status of the future's super threat was shared between violent Islamist fundamentalism and China.[13] While, a few years further on, Russia reemerged—erupted perhaps—as the leading menace of the day.

To consider preventive war pragmatically, one has to think in time. To preempt is to act on the basis of certain contemporary knowledge. In sharp contrast, to launch a preventive war is to act bereft of temporal certainty, or indeed of any certainty. The closer to today is the predicted maturing of danger, the less the risk of unsound prediction. However, are any temporal or other kinds of breakpoints suggested by strategic theory? Does a preventive war doctrine oblige one to consider taking forestalling military action only against states whose capabilities (and intentions?) are estimated to mature within, say, ten years, or fifteen years, or when? And just how great does an estimated threat need to be for it to warrant entry on the preventor's hit list?

If one endorses the concept of prevention, there is no evading the difficulty outlined in the preceding paragraph. All preventive war is launched because its executors believe that it is preferable to fight today rather than tomorrow. However, many predicted wars never occurred, in some cases possibly because they were predicted.[14] Also, many a state or potential coalition that could pose a deadly peril in the future failed to develop in a menacing way. Contingency, personality, surprise, and general uncertainty render strategic futurology profoundly unscientific. And the more distant the menace in time, the greater the risk of misestimation. This is not utterly to condemn preventive war as a strategic concept; that would be foolish. It is, though, to suggest in the strongest possible terms that, as an accepted policy option, it is fraught with an awesome possibility of error. Perhaps needless to say, if a state wages preventive war against a distinctly immature threat, there will be no way of ever knowing whether the war was prudent or unnecessary.

Precaution

Precautionary war, our third strategic concept, is war launched to arrest developments beyond the outer temporal or other bounds of detectable current menace. In other words, a precautionary war is a preventive war waged not on the basis of any noteworthy evidence of ill intent or dangerous capabilities, but rather because those unwelcome phenomena might appear in the future. A precautionary war is a war waged "just in case," on the basis of the principle, "better safe than sorry." It is war most usually located at the far end of the timeline from preemption through prevention in response to an ever more distantly perceived danger. Alternatively, a precautionary war can be launched strictly opportunistically, as an attempt to derive maximum benefit from a more major event. For example, had the United States proceeded from Baghdad to Damascus in 2003, the Syrian option would have been precautionary rather than preventive.

If two of the strategic concepts explained in this section, prevention and precaution, are perilously vague in real world application, at least their meaning should now be plain enough. Although it is vital to achieve strategic conceptual clarity, theoretical neatness and transparency are only two of the steps necessary toward prudent policy and strategy. The concept of preventive war has to pass the "the Brodie test." Bernard Brodie wrote:

> Strategic thinking, or "theory" if one prefers, is nothing if not pragmatic. Strategy is a "how to do it" study, a guide to accomplishing something and doing it efficiently. As in many other branches of politics, the question that matters in strategy is: Will the idea work? More important, will it be likely to work under the special circumstances under which it will next be tested? These circumstances are not likely to be known or knowable much in advance of the moment of testing, though the uncertainty is itself a factor to be reckoned with in one's strategic doctrine.[15]

The problem today is that although one can clarify the meaning of the strategic ideas, as here I hope, that essential task does not advance the building of the needful theory. There is at present no strategic theory of preventive war.

LAW AND CULTURE

Unlike the obliging certainty of the case for preemption—one is, or is soon to be, under attack—preventive action is nearly always controversial. Even if it is not controversial at the time, should it fail militarily and therefore strategically and politically, it is certain to be the subject of bitter debate. To wage preventive war is to shoot on suspicion. Should the preventive action be intended to forestall developments that require at least several years to mature, then the suspicion, though strong, could hardly offer a compelling reason for war now. If the preventive war is designed to forestall entirely a path of development that would or could be deemed threatening, then one is in the policy realm of precautionary offensive strategic behavior. The meaning of prevention is as crystal clear as its implications are inalienably uncertain. A preventive war is what a state chooses to launch in order to prevent future danger from happening. Because the future is by definition unknown and unknowable, preventive action has to entail striking on the basis of guesswork about distant threats. And threats, of course, are a matter of guesses

230 NATIONAL SECURITY DILEMMAS

about capabilities times political intentions. Though capabilities can be predicted with some confidence, political intentions can alter overnight. To wage preventive war requires a state to conduct complex cost-benefit guesswork. That exercise is expressed politely as calculation. The state comes to the conclusion that war now is preferable to war tomorrow or, at the least, to an adverse shift in the balance of power.

How, though, is the concept and policy of preventive war to be operationalized? Whereas the preemptor has only two choices, to strike first or to ride out the enemy's first strike and then strike back, the potential agent of preventive war has many choices, at least in theory. A state considering preventive war has a choice of timing: "Should we wait?" Also, if the state is functioning with a national security policy and strategy worthy of being so called, then the military option will be only one of the ways in which anticipated evils might be prevented.

Recent and indeed current history demonstrates that when there is a whiff of preventive gunpowder in the air, there will be no shortage of people and states arguing for patience and delay while diplomacy launches into action—applying economic pressures, committing bribery, and benignly effecting domestic change in the targeted preventee. Plainly, the less pressing the strategic case for prompt and hopefully decisive military behavior, the greater the nominal range of alternatives to war. Politicians eager to avoid war, up to a point an understandable and meritorious determination, will never be short of excuses to postpone hostilities. The policymaker who has read his or her Clausewitz will know that war, even preventive war, is always a gamble and that plans can be upset by the independent will and behavior of the enemy as well as by friction. Moreover, even when policymakers have excellent reason to believe the "victory is certain" briefings by advisors, they should understand that a preventive war, unlike a preventive strike or raid, may not be over when the enemy's regular forces are defeated.[16] Witness Iraq after spring 2003. A theory, let alone a policy and strategy, of preventive war has to accommodate the implications that there is more to war than warfare. A state and society militarily bested by a surprise assault cannot be assumed to be willing to cooperate with the victorious preventor.

Clausewitz's *On War*, though a timeless classic, naturally reflects the political and moral contexts of the 1820s. The principal Clausewitzian dictum, which holds that "war is merely the continuation of policy by other means," is true yet apt to mislead today.[17] War is no longer regarded as simply another tool of statecraft. Because of the twentieth century's appalling strategic history, with its two world wars and the long-standing menace of a third, peace has acquired a moral and political value it did not possess in Clausewitz's day.[18] Of course, Clausewitz's dictum retains its authority. War must be waged for political reasons and in a manner that reflects the scope of those reasons. However, war is not "merely" one option along with others such as diplomacy, economic sanctions, and political subversion. Ever since 1919 and the founding of the League of Nations in the Treaty of Versailles, war has been morally stigmatized in statecraft. Unfortunately, this rejection of politically motivated violence has taken root only unevenly around the world. It has taken command of policy almost nowhere, save possibly among the older members of the European Union (EU). Nonetheless, *On War* might misinform people who consider preventive war as a policy option.

With good reason one can claim that the Charter of the United Nations (UN) provides grounds that justify any use of force. Superficially, the Charter only licenses self-defense, which it notes is an inherent right. However, it does not restrict what a state may do in self-defense. The Charter is interpreted widely as not placing a state under the obligation to receive the first blow, or to strike first only on the basis of totally unambiguous warning that an attack is either underway or is about to be launched. In other words, the Charter's recognition of the right and duty of self-defense can be interpreted as licensing a forestalling blow on the part of the intended victim state. This is not to deny the language of Article 51, which appears to qualify the inherent right of self-defense with the conditioning phrase, "if an armed attack occurs." What, though, is an acceptable time lapse between a forestalling strike and the anticipated aggression? No legal authority provides an answer. If a state can point plausibly to a truly imminent threat, it is in the legally and morally uncontentious zone of preemption. However, the UN Charter can be interpreted as tolerating preventive war. Needless to add, such an interpretation is as legally sound and politically expedient as it is an obvious violation of the plain nominal, though not genuine political, intent of the Charter. Recall that UN members are obliged to forswear the use of force in their international relations, except, of course, in the dire circumstances of self-defense.[19]

Whether or not legal, quasi-legal, and moral issues should count for much in the U.S. debate over prevention is a matter for debate. For the moment we will withhold judgment and be satisfied with simply registering the point that war is regarded nearly universally as a qualitatively different instrument of policy from the rest of the tools in the grand strategy kit. Americans ignore or discount this fact at their political peril. The singularization of war as behavior requiring extraordinary justification is by no means strictly the product of 1914–18. The Catholic Church's just war doctrine has long sought to hold Christians to a tough standard for legitimizing the resort to war (against other Christians). Bear in mind the standard six requirements of the doctrine. Just war doctrine requires: (1) a just cause; (2) legitimate authority; (3) right intention; (4) proportionality; (5) likelihood of success; and (6) resort to war only as a last resort.[20] These potent criteria are as unambiguous in their essential meaning as they are useless as a practical guide. When is the last resort? Who has the right to decide? According to the UN Charter, every sovereign state has an inherent right of self-defense, and hence has a duty to judge on its own behalf when is its last resort.

On the resort to war, international law is highly permissive in practice. However, undoubtedly, even with its permissiveness duly granted, international law does not license powerful states to wage aggressive wars simply because they anticipate a large net benefit as a consequence. They can always find some character of preventive excuse. A preventive war can only be regarded as such if it is waged for the highly plausible and specific purpose of forestalling an extraordinary danger. If that standard is relaxed, one is back in the eighteenth- and nineteenth-century culture of statecraft. In those years, wars were waged to restore a balance of power. For example, the Crimean War (1854–56) was waged, by Britain at least, for the purpose of curbing Russia's power and influence. The France of Napoleon III, the principal instigator of the war, was motivated by a quest for glory for a fragile regime in Paris.

To repeat, there is nothing worth debating about preemption. If the attack is certain, there are only two reasons for withholding the use of force. First, it may not be feasible to preempt. If the attack is already underway, it may be highly uncertain what remains in known locations of the enemy's forces to be struck without delay. Also, it is a distinct possibility that one's military instrument is not ready to preempt. It may lack the necessary intelligence or suitable ordnance to inflict crippling damage. Second, it may be judged politically and morally important to allow the enemy to fire the first shot and thereby brand himself unquestionably as the aggressor.[21] Needless to say, the second judgment is most unlikely to be persuasive in the face of a nuclear attack. However, if the nuclear attack is very large, specifically if it is from Russia, the only state other than the United States capable of launching a nuclear attack with many hundreds or several thousands of warheads, it may be calculated that there would be no strategic advantage in preempting by way of LOW or LUA. U.S. preemption would not be able to disrupt or blunt an assault on such a scale.

Preventive war is a frightening concept with a suitably ominous ring to it. By and large, only strong states might wage it, and who or what can restrict their freedom of policy choice? Even though the difference in time between the menaces targeted by preemption and precaution may well be several years, or even longer, a highly risk averse great power might decide that prompt military prevention for assured control is better than belated efforts at forcible cure. The great or super power as good doctor of international order could persuade itself that timely force is effective preventive medicine. Recall that the default justification for the resort to war is that war has the ability to resolve dilemmas that prove resistant to all other measures. A generously calculated timely assault must preclude knowledge of whether or not any of the non-military tools of state-craft would have succeeded eventually.

STRATEGIC HISTORY

History does not provide us with a neat and convenient class of plainly preventive wars. One discovers on close examination that most wars include a preventive motive on the part of a belligerent, and sometimes on the part of both major belligerents. The presence of a preventive war motive does not warrant our classifying the subsequent hostilities as a preventive war. A preventive motive is likely to be only one urge to fight among many. With a preventive war, it is not always necessary to fire the first shot or be the first to declare war. For example, for the United States, arguably, World War II, both in Europe and in Asia-Pacific, was a preventive project. This may seem counterfactual, not to say bizarre to readers. After all, did not Japan shoot first on December 7, 1941, and did not Germany declare war on the United States quite gratuitously on December 11? In fact, the United States had been waging preventive economic warfare against Imperial Japan for at least eighteen months prior to Pearl Harbor. By a progressively tighter, eventually total blockade on finance, oil, and iron and steel, beginning selectively in July 1940, Washington hoped to coerce Japan into changing policy course in China, though the most immediate issue was the Japanese intervention in French Indochina.[22] This thoroughly futile venture required Japan to reverse its foreign policy of fifty years and abandon its dream of great power status and influence. Tokyo believed its only practical choice was to fight. The United States acted from a powerfully preventive motive, and it applied pressure with the economic and financial rather than the military instrument of grand strategy. Neither the United States nor Japan desired war in 1941, but U.S. measures of economic blockade left Japan with no alternative to war consistent with its sense of national honor. The oil embargo eventually would immobilize the Japanese Navy. Consequently, Washington confronted Tokyo with the unenviable choice between de facto complete political surrender of its ambitions in China, or war.

With respect to Germany, a subtler statesman than Adolf Hitler could have sought to remain neutral in the Asia-Pacific War. However, he elected to join his Japanese ally, notwithstanding Tokyo's fairly resolute neutrality in Germany's struggle with the USSR. Although Germany declared war on December 11, 1941, the United States had been exercising a neutrality for many months that was hugely unfriendly toward Germany. U.S. warships escorted convoys far out into the Atlantic and they had orders to sink U-boats on sight. In addition, the lend-lease transaction with Britain of bases for ships and materiel was not exactly proper behavior for a neutral state. In 1940–41, President Roosevelt did not have the domestic, hence the congressional, backing for war with Germany. However, he had a powerful preventive motive for such a commitment, if and when it became domestically feasible. The president knew that a Third Reich victorious in Europe, possibly in possession of a substantial fraction of the British Royal Navy, would pose a predictably deadly menace in the long term to the United States. He was wise to be fearful. Hitler did intend to move on from his anticipated victory in the East to the conduct of a global struggle with America. From an economically and strategically secure super-continental foundation in a conquered Eurasia, Germany would have prepared for a maritime-air conflict with the United States. Even during World War II, Germany was pouring concrete for a great new naval base at Trondheim in Norway on the Atlantic.

Pearl Harbor was a political threat to Roosevelt's policy; the American people wanted vengeance against Japan, not Germany. Fortunately, Hitler's ill-considered declaration of war solved Roosevelt's political problem for him.[23] In an obvious sense, Germany compelled the United States to wage war, though it must be

said that Hitler had shown extraordinary restraint in 1941 in tolerating unneutral U.S. activities on behalf of Britain and then Russia.
In a less obvious sense, though, the United States waged a preventive war against Germany. It entered the conflict as early as was
politically possible, with the timing dictated by Hitler and despite a
powerful domestic "pull of the Pacific."

The reasons for war are always many and mixed. This chapter
suggests that considerations of prevention typically play a role. It is
rare to find a conflict wherein there is no spore of a preventive motive
to be found. With regard to the great Cold War (1947–89), it is
standard to cite the deadly trio of geopolitics, ideology, and personality
as combining to produce the fatal brew that resulted in forty-two
years of nuclear menace.[24] However, austerely viewed, in 1946–47
both Washington and Moscow decided to wage preventive non-
military conflict. The United States was determined to prevent the
USSR from expanding its sphere of control any further, while the
USSR was determined to prevent the United States from rolling
back its hard-won gains.[25]

The so-called Bush Doctrine was historically unremarkable, notwithstanding the excitement it occasioned in 2002–3. Of course,
the historical, political, ethical, and legal contexts have changed over
a century, as they must. To launch a preventive war in the twenty-
first century requires extraordinary justification. According to one
interpretation of international law today, such a decision needs to
be justifiable with direct respect to the needs of self-defense.[26] As
noted earlier, the more distant the threat is judged to be from maturity, the more difficult it is to provide compelling arguments in
favor of forcible preventive action. One does not have to be a thoroughgoing cynic to appreciate that the emergence of a full-grown
menace most likely would be as convincing a potential justification
for preventive action as it would be too mature to be arrested definitively: It would be too late. If the menace in question includes
the threat of WMD, policymakers should be expected to consider
the precautionary principle that prevention is highly desirable, or
even essential, if there is no cure or prospect of tolerable recovery.

Prevention and preventive war suffer from a near demonic reputation that, by and large, they do not merit. Prevention is an entirely usual motive for war, albeit in company with other reasons to fight. Obviously, the concept, perhaps the principle, of preventive military action is open to abuse. An aggressive imperial or hegemonic power could wage a series of wars, all for the purpose of preventing the emergence of future challenges to its burgeoning imperium. However, that is less than a killer argument. Virtually every useful and necessary strategic concept can be abused by the unscrupulous.

DEBATING PREVENTION

Cold War historians argue that the U.S. government considered and rejected waging preventive war in the late 1940s and early 1950s in order to forestall the growth of the Soviet atomic arsenal.[27] A similar debate occurred in the early 1960s regarding the Chinese nuclear program. After the Cold War, the United States is known to have prepared seriously, in 1994 in particular, for the option of striking at North Korea's secret and illegal nuclear facilities.[28] Today, the North Korean challenge to the Non-Proliferation Treaty (NPT) regime remains, even though Pyongyang has exited, while it has been joined in the cross-hairs of would-be preventors by the Islamic Republic of Iran. The latter has become the menace of the decade and beyond and, as a result, the focus of most recent and current U.S. debate over the merit and otherwise in preventive war.[29]

Lawrence Freedman advises that "prevention can be seen as preemption in slow motion, more anticipatory or forward thinking, perhaps even looking beyond the target's current intentions to those that might be acquired along with greatly enhanced capabilities."[30] This is interesting but misleading. It blurs what should be the clear distinction between preemption and prevention.

The Bush Doctrine declared what it miscalled a preemptive intention to prevent the world's most dangerous regimes from acquiring the world's most dangerous weapons. This declaration sounded like muscular counterproliferation—a noble cause. Unfortunately, international and domestic politics, strategy, and military operations combine to provide complexities that harass and frustrate the bold counterproliferator. Even if the United States were to have a doctrine of prevention, when and where it would be applied in action would have to depend on the specific circumstances of the case at issue. President Bush and others likened the asserted doctrine of "preemption" to dominant guiding concepts from yesteryear, such as deterrence and containment. This comparison is wrong as well as dangerously misleading. Both deterrence and containment have the signal virtue that they provide a prudent, relatively low-risk default option for policy. When in doubt, deter and contain. If one elevates preemption, actually prevention, to the conceptual heights as the default option for policy, what is one saying? The answer is that when in doubt the United States will shoot on suspicion, taking preventive action on the grounds that it prefers to be safe rather than seriously regretful. To quote the ominous prose of the *National Security Strategy* document of 2002: "History will judge harshly those who saw this coming danger but failed to act."[31] To which one could reply that there will be so many dangers anticipated for the future, that the United States might well find itself engaged in more wars than it can afford or conduct effectively.

This section summarizes and presents the debate over preventive war doctrine by presenting and critiquing seven broad charges that have been leveled and repeated in recent years. These are not straw targets for easy demolition. Each has merit.

1. *Preventive war is an act of aggression.* As such, it is both illegal and immoral. Let there be no confusion over the practical meaning of a decision to wage preventive war. Such a decision translates as an unprovoked attack on another supposedly sovereign state. Of course, there is provocation, but it is not of the kind that carries weight in court. The preventive warrior is provoked by what he believes the intention of the preventee will be at some time in the future. Some commentators seek to provide justification by stretching the usual meaning of preemption. Arguably, prevention is really

preemption assessed probabilistically rather than temporally. In other words, a preventive attack is preemptive if one is sufficiently convinced that an attack will, or would, be forthcoming.[32] While I admire conceptual ingenuity, I am unconvinced by this argument. A mild version of the probabilistic judgment in lieu of temporal imminence is a conservatively prudent adherence to what has come to be known as "the precautionary principle" as an approach to risk management.[33] These concepts—precautionary principle and risk management—can serve as politically, morally, and legally more acceptable terms for preventive war.

Is preventive war illegal? Why is not such a war simply a war of aggression, since it has not been provoked by harmful behavior on the part of the target state? The answer is that no international law truly restricts the use of force. There appears to be such law, and it is located primarily in the UN Charter. However, all is not as it seems. To quote the highly relevant, if somewhat depressing, judgment of Harvard Law School's Professor David Kennedy: "Over the years, what began as an effort to monopolize force has become a constitutional regime of legitimate justifications for warfare. There is no doubt that the Charter system of principles has legitimated a great deal of warfare."[34] He proceeds to explain that

> [t]he Charter came to be read as a constitutional document articulating the legitimate justifications for warfare. Lengthy articles and books were written parsing the meaning of "aggression" and "intervention." Does economic pressure count? The conventional levers of diplomacy—the routine arrangements of commercial life—suddenly seemed arrayed on a continuum with violence. At the same time, it was hard to think of a use of force that could not be legitimated in the Charter's terms. It is a rare statesman who launches a war simply to be aggressive. There is always something to be said.[35]

We have made repeated reference to what international law, most especially in the form of the UN Charter, does and does not prohibit. It is time to be more explicit. With assistance from the distinguished legal authority, Professor Leslie C. Green, formerly of the U.S. Naval War College, let us specify the legal context for the resort to force.[36]

- The preamble to the UN Charter expresses the determination of "the peoples of the United Nations to save succeeding generations from the scourge of war."

- Article 1 of the Charter states that the first purpose of the UN is "to maintain international peace and security, and to that end: to take effective collective measures for the prevention and removal of threats to the peace, and in conformity with the principles of justice and international law, adjustment or settlement of international disputes or situations which might lead to a breach of the peace."

- Article 2 (4) of the Charter obliges members to "refrain in their international relations from the threat or use of force against the territorial integrity or political independence of any state."

- Article 51 proceeds to the heart of the matter. It affirms the

inherent right of individual or collective self-defence if an armed attack occurs against a Member of the United Nations, until the Security Council has taken the measures necessary to maintain international peace and security. Measures taken in the exercise of this right of self-defence shall be immediately reported to the Security Council and shall not in any way affect the authority and responsibility of the Security Council to take at any time such action as it deems necessary to maintain or restore international peace and security.

The contextualizing clause, "if an armed attack occurs against a Member of the United Nations," is a minor legal difficulty for the intending preventor. However, sensibly enough, it is widely held not to restrict the anticipated victim to passivity prior to the assault. That would contradict prudent exercise of the master principle of "the inherent right of individual or collective self-defence."

- Chapter VII of the Charter reserves to the Security Council authority in cases of threats to the peace or acts of aggression "to make recommendations or decide what measures shall be taken . . . to maintain or restore international peace and security." Those measures include economic as well as military action (Articles 41 and 42). Of course, Security Council behavior is always subject to potential show-stopping discipline by the exercise of its veto power by one or more of the five permanent Members.

Professor Green's excellent summary of the legal context of the subject concludes with the flat claim that "it is clear, therefore, that the Charter does not per se declare war to be illegal or merely criminal, but merely a breach of treaty subject to the sanctions embodied in that treaty."[37] Writing as a political and strategic analyst rather than a lawyer, I must add to Green's professional judgment recognition that the UN Charter is more a political than a legal document. Moreover, it is a "living" political document in legal form. Even though the more realistic among the UN's founders were not confused on this crucial point, the necessary clarity has not always been widely shared. Professional lawyers have a culture that commits them to approach world affairs legally. In addition, many people who reflexively oppose the use of force are more than happy to seize on the presumed authority of an apolitical and astrategic reading of Charter language to lend legitimacy to their moral convictions.

Some people take the view that a state can only resort to force, shoot first, if the action is strictly preemptive in self-defense, or if warfare is licensed explicitly by a resolution of the Security Council (UNSC). This interpretation of the Charter is broadly rejected for two reasons. First, it is denied in favor of the view that the inherent right of self-defense does not require a state to wait to be attacked before it can take active measures to protect itself. Second, the UNSC does not represent the moral authority of the global community, claims of convenience to the contrary notwithstanding. In practice, it is driven by the balance of influence among five highly self-regarding permanent Members whose judgments on the legality of U.S. strategic behavior, for example, will have nothing to do with considerations of law or morality.

Overall, preventive war is assuredly not prohibited by an international law that is interpreted intelligently. With respect to moral judgment, that will rest on the persuasiveness, or otherwise, of the claims advanced for anticipatory self-defense and, of course, on the interests and popular feelings at stake in a conflict. To summarize: (1) preemption is unquestionably legal; it is self-defense in the face of an unfolding and self-evidently imminent threat; (2) preventive war is legal as a forestalling move for self-defense, but as behavior, it is indistinguishable from the waging of aggressive war. As Professor Kennedy wryly suggests, aggressors always have some excuse for their misdeeds.[38]

2. *Preemption and prevention are only feasible if intelligence is immaculate.* Robert R. Tomes insists that "preemption, to be an effective component of national security strategy, requires exquisite intelligence. It requires deep insights into adversary capabilities and interests, accurate indicators and warning, prescient decision making capabilities, and superior battlefield intelligence."[39]

This statement is plausible but overstated. Although it is agreeable to have exquisite intelligence, Tomes is in danger of setting the standard so high that it cannot be met. Contra Tomes, this chapter suggests that for preemption and prevention one has to settle for intelligence that is good enough. Good enough, that is, to enable military force to do the job it is assigned. With respect to preemption, although exquisite, well-nigh perfect intelligence would be desirable, a lower quality of information will likely suffice to enable the preemptor to achieve a seriously disrupting effect. In fact, arguably, given the would-be preemptor's choices—to strike first or to be struck first—it almost does not matter how good the intelligence is. One preempts as best one can with the information available. Since it is far too late to prevent the attack, virtually any harm that can be inflicted on the enemy's confidence, plans, and forces must be welcome.

Intelligence for preventive war, or a discrete preventive strike, is a different matter. The claim that preventive military action against, for example, North Korea or Iran is not practicable because the United States and its allies lack near perfect intelligence on those countries' WMD infrastructures is as popular as it is fallacious. While there may be excellent reasons why preventive strikes against North Korea and Iran are poor ideas, the absence of truly "exquisite intelligence" is not one of them. If we believe Clausewitz rather than Sun Tzu, we know that war is a chaotic realm of uncertainty and friction and that intelligence habitually is flawed. Such is the nature of warfare. It would be absurd to claim that intelligence does not matter. Instead, the valid point is to the effect that intelligence does not need to be immaculate for it to be good enough. Certainly with regard to a nuclear program that has yet to produce operational weapons, it does not follow that because one lacks reliable information on every facility a preventive strike must fail. Fail to achieve what? A preventive strike guided by good, but assuredly not immaculate, intelligence could and should retard a nuclear program by many years. Such an enforced delay might well be judged a highly satisfactory military outcome. Of course, there is far more to the issue of prevention than strictly military considerations.

One must note in favor of this second claim critical of preventive action that less than immaculate intelligence could well prove disastrous if the target state has operational WMD, some of which escape preventive execution. The merit in active missile defense is self-evident for such a case. Recalling Imperial Germany and Grand Admiral Tirpitz's "Risk Fleet," history reveals many cases when the development of a new highly potent military capability creates a period of unusual risk, should the intended foreign target of the military program decide to prevent its completion.[40] Immediately prior to World War I, Germany's immature High Seas Fleet was not only potentially vulnerable to destruction by Britain's Royal Navy, but Russia's "Great Program" of railroad and army expansion presented Germany with the certain future that, by 1917, its enemy to the East would be more formidable.[41]

For a more complex example, as early as 1937 Hitler calculated that unless he could wage and win the wars that he needed in order to rule Europe by 1943 at the latest, Germany's enemies would have caught up in the armaments competition. What is more, the huge material resource advantages enjoyed by the British and French Empires and by the USSR—discounting the United States as a possible initial enemy—meant that Germany only had a few years wherein the balance of military assets would be to its advantage.[42] History shows that the anticipation of major shifts in the military dimension of the balance of power can be periods of acute peril. Other states may well reason "now or never."

Transnational norms about war have changed over time. In 1914, even in 1939–45, war was accepted as an inevitable, if regrettable, fact of international historical life. Today, war, and preventive war in particular, is not regarded globally as an ordinary instrument of policy. No matter how legal a preventive strike may be held to be, to launch a war, unprovoked, is to surrender the moral high ground.

In addition to the normative violation that preventive action represents today, the quality of intelligence on the target state has to be ever less reliable the further into the future one is peering. How confident can one be that intelligence on a state's political intentions is accurate even for today, let alone for a period years in the future? Also, military programs can founder for a host of reasons: change in key decision makers, lack of resources, or a shift in the state's security context, to cite only a few.

3. *Prevention is not a "silver bullet," a panacea.* Preventive war, especially a preventive strike, can be regarded by incautious commentators who do not respect Clausewitz as a definitive solution to a problem that appears resistant to all other measures. The dynamics of debate drive opposing positions further apart. From being seen as a possible answer to a pressing or even distant dilemma,

advocacy of the military option easily evolves from the status of possible answer to recommendation as the solution. For prevention even to be a live option for debate, the issue in question has to be a challenging one. Advocates of military prevention may be correct in their criticism of nonmilitary options, including long-term deterrence and containment. However, simply because deterrence is unreliable, it does not follow that a preventive strike offers the certainty of a satisfactory alternative.[43] Intelligence is bound to be imperfect. The surprise preventive attack may not achieve surprise; friction and ill luck may impede efficient execution of the assault as planned; and key elements in the target set might escape destruction or even detection. The military option cannot offer a guarantee of complete success, and incomplete success might amount to failure. Though practicable in some cases, preventive war cannot prudently be viewed as a "silver bullet," as a panacea. It is not certain to be swift, decisively victorious, and definitive in positive consequences.

4. *Preventive action, even if militarily successful, can only be assessed properly in terms of its consequences.* The familiar axiom that there is much more to war than warfare alone applies with almost spectacular accuracy to preventive action. As with all other choices in statecraft and strategy, the preventive option has to be considered in terms of expected benefits and likely costs. It is a mistake simply to compare estimates of benefits with guesses as to costs, because the two columns are dependent on each other. Should the preventive strike or war prove militarily unsatisfactory, or to have consequences that commit one to protracted warfare after the swift campaign, then the costs of the preventive option will escalate way beyond the scale of the initial calculation. There are no laws of history, but many bold decisions for action intended to resolve a current or anticipated threat have had consequences that were quite unintended and even thoroughly unanticipated.[44]

Because of the complexity of international relations, the consequences of behavior are difficult to predict. A prime attraction of the preventive option is its promise of swift and decisive action to solve a dilemma that appears likely, even certain, to be resistant to all nonforcible means. However, preventive action, even if staged only as a raid, is apt to have unanticipated costs. When debating prevention, the costs side of the ledger needs to be considered as well as the benefits. These costs can include loss of political reputation whether or not the operation is militarily successful, since preventive warfare is always a choice challengeable on political, strategic, legal, and moral grounds. Even states that share the preventor's alarmist view of a development will worry lest a decision to wage preventive warfare should become a habit. Only a faint line divides prudent prevention from an arrogant overreliance on force. How quickly does the hegemonic power draw and fire its gun? Is it disinclined to allow much time for the other tools of grand strategy to be effective or to demonstrate that they cannot work? Given the invariably controversial character of a decision to launch preventive warfare, is the preventor, no matter how powerful, prepared to withstand international condemnation of its unilateral behavior?

As a major act of statecraft, forcible preventive behavior has to be assessed beforehand on a genuinely cost-benefit basis. And the costs have to include political consequences, including first- and second-order effects. Above all else in importance, though, will be the military and other consequences of the target state's responses to the attack. It is a besetting sin of policymakers and strategists to neglect to take the independent will and capabilities of the enemy sufficiently into account. This persisting peril is never more likely to appear than in a case where a state has decided that a preventive strike, or war, is the solution to its problems. Careful consideration of enemy options, regular and irregular, military, economic, and political, should precede, not postdate, a decision to exercise the preventive option.

5. *Preventive military action prejudges the failure of other instruments of grand strategy.* Policymakers may be convinced that diplomacy, economic sanctions and bribes, and political subversion will not bring the target state to heel. However, by definition a decision for prevention action is a decision not to allow further time to pass

wherein nonmilitary tools would be used in an attempt to persuade, pressure, and coerce the adversary into mending its ways. Since there is what amounts to a global norm licensing the use of force only as the last resort, a decision for military prevention unarguably must violate that standard. Recall the rather tortured argument cited already, to the effect that a decision for prevention allegedly can rest on the substitution of believed high probability for temporal immediacy. This discussion, though not unfriendly to all cases of prevention, finds the probabilistic defense of preventive war unsatisfactory. Only a determinist uneducated in the role that contingency plays in history could believe that a relatively distant danger will mature with a probability approaching certainty. History is too rich and complex, as well as liable to deliver one or two of Rumsfeld's unknowns and "unknown unknowns," for one to be sure that only military action now can prevent intolerable danger much later.

6. *To wage preventive war, even to endorse it as policy, sets a highly undesirable precedent that encourages the resort to force in international relations.* This claim is true, up to a point at least. Furthermore, to proclaim the necessity for preemption, as the United States has of recent years, is to imply that war is not only an acceptable instrument of policy, but that it is a fairly ordinary one. In other words, to endorse a doctrine of preemption-meaning-prevention is to challenge the slow and erratic, but nevertheless genuine, growth of a global norm that regards the resort to war as an extraordinary and even desperate measure. A policy that favors military prevention proclaims that it is acceptable to decide coolly and in good time that war is preferable to the conditions predicted for "peace." One can argue that a decision to prevent reflects necessity, but that is not convincing. Preventive war is a war of discretion. And the world is full of people, including many among Western publics, who would never choose to go to war so long as there was an alternative, virtually no matter how humiliating that alternative might be.

Does a policy of prevention, let alone actual preventive behavior, set a dangerous precedent? In principle, the answer has to be "yes." In practice, some assert there is and needs to be a double standard.[45] It is claimed, not unreasonably in the view of this chapter, that because the United States has an extraordinary responsibility for maintaining world order, it is permitted to act, indeed sometimes it has to act, in ways that would not be acceptable if practiced by others. The justification is international security. As the principal guardian or sheriff of world order, albeit admittedly self-appointed, the United States must allow itself the policy and strategy to fulfill its unique responsibilities.[46] The taking of occasional preventive action can be necessary if regional order and peace with security are to be protected. Washington should not be impressed by criticism of its preventive war policy by those states that seek to exercise political power without responsibility in the UN.

No matter what international law affirms to the contrary, all states are not sovereign equals. The UNSC is a great power club, as was the Council of the League of Nations before it and as, explicitly, was the "Concert System" that functioned usefully from time to time between 1814 and the dismissal of German Chancellor Otto von Bismarck in 1890. The purpose, character, and restricted permanent membership of the UNSC underlines the point that the maintenance of world order can only rest on recognition of the realities of power relations and the contemporary norms that generally govern those relations. Given what world order requires of the United States, or indeed of any guardian state or institution, the claim for a special license to use force is not only reasonable, it is essential. If U.S. behavior should set a precedent, that would be unfortunate. However, it would be a price worth paying if the alternative had to be a world sheriff armed only with blanks.

7. *A policy that favors preventive warfare expresses a futile quest for absolute security.* It could do so. Most controversial policies contain within them the possibility of misuse. In the hands of a paranoid or boundlessly ambitious political leader, prevention could be a policy for endless warfare. However, the American political system, with its checks and balances, was designed explicitly for the

purpose of constraining the executive from excessive folly. Both the Vietnam and the contemporary Iraqi experiences reveal clearly that although the conduct of war is an executive prerogative, in practice that authority is disciplined by public attitudes. Clausewitz made this point superbly with his designation of the passion, the sentiments, of the people as a vital component of his trinitarian theory of war.[47] Power can be, and indeed is often, abused, both personally and nationally. A state could possibly acquire a taste for the apparent swift decisiveness of preventive warfare and overuse the option. The easy success achieved against Taliban Afghanistan in 2001 provided fuel for the urge to seek a similarly rapid success against Saddam Hussein's Iraq. In other words, the delights of military success can be habit forming.

On balance, claim seven is not persuasive, though it certainly contains a germ of truth. A country with unmatched wealth and power, used to physical security at home—notwithstanding half a century of nuclear danger and a high level of gun crime—is vulnerable to demands for policies that supposedly can restore security. However, we ought not to endorse the argument that the United States should eschew the preventive war option, because it could lead to a futile, endless search for absolute security. One might as well argue that the United States should adopt a defense policy and develop capabilities shaped strictly for homeland security approached in a narrowly geographical sense. Since a president might misuse a military instrument that had a global reach, why not deny the White House even the possibility of such misuse? In other words, constrain policy ends by limiting policy's military means.

This argument has circulated for many decades and, it must be admitted, it does have a certain elementary logic. However, the claim that a policy that includes the preventive option might lead to a search for total security is unconvincing. Of course, folly in high places is always possible, which is one of the many reasons why popular democracy is the superior form of government. It would be absurd to permit the fear of a futile and dangerous quest for absolute security to preclude prevention as a policy option.

STRATEGIC THEORY AND PREVENTIVE WAR

I have taught strategic theory and worked as a strategic theorist for more than forty years. Up to this time and including the present, I have never come across a strategic theory of preventive war worthy of the ascription. The political and technical feasibility of preemption was studied endlessly during the Cold War, with both superpowers electing to attempt it on the basis of unambiguous warning of attack. Preventive war was debated within government from time to time, but on the evidence publicly accessible today, it never came close to acceptance as policy. As for the strategic studies literature, the cupboard is virtually bare. There is no strategic theory of prevention. If prevention were regarded as a powerful strategic concept similar in function, domain, and possibly even authority to deterrence and containment, then the absence of theory would be hard to explain. The reality is that prevention is not a strategic concept akin to deterrence and containment, or to limited war or arms control. This study asserts that there is both a lesser and a dominant compelling reason why strategic theorists appear to have neglected prevention as a strategic idea.

The lesser reason why the library of working strategic concepts is bereft of notable treatments of preventive war is because theorists dismissed it as being a political, not a strategic, subject.[48] Prevention does not lend itself to the kind of rational choice analysis that has been responsible for much of modern strategic theory; it lacks a distinctive logical structure. It is not a strategic idea at all, rather it is political. The dominant reason for theorists' apparent neglect of preventive war is that such war lacks a distinguishable character. It is war that policymakers decide to wage by way of anticipatory self-defense. When strategic theorists come to intellectual grip with the concept of preventive war, they discover that the adjective refers to matters that defy their expertise, while the noun, war, is already treated competently in the theories provided by Clausewitz, Sun Tzu, and Thucydides. The subject is war. When or if policymakers bank on the potency of the adjective, preventive, they neglect at their peril the eternal nature of war and warfare.

Given the negative judgments now delivered, what can be argued by way of an alternative to theory for preventive war? Whether or not a theory is possible, and I believe it is not, what do we most need to understand about this controversial idea? The following offers the bare bones of the functional equivalent of a theory of preventive war.

1. *Preventive war is war, and preventive warfare is warfare.* It is not a distinctive genus of war and warfare. The distinguishing characteristics of preventive action are motive and timing, though the former is so well represented historically that it is not especially useful as a discriminator. Timing is by far the superior marker.

2. *If preventive war is simply war, it has to follow that it cannot require a unique strategic theory for its understanding and guidance.* It must be governed by the same features that characterize all wars and warfare. To understand preventive war, read and reread Clausewitz's general theory carefully.

3. *Preventive war is a gamble because war is always such.* Preventive timing and leading motive do not negate the authority of the Clausewitzian judgment that "no other [than war] human activity is so continuously or universally bound up with chance. And through the element of chance, guesswork and luck come to play a great part in war."[49]

4. *The state or other security entity that launches a preventive war starts with an advantage.* It has selected the timing for combat and it has the initiative. However, these advantages diminish should the war be other than a single campaign. All attacks lose momentum over time; many adversaries are able to rally, regroup, and counterattack. It is not safe to assume that the victim-preventee will be a helpless target set. Even if a preventive regular character of war achieves rapid victory, it has been fairly common in history for that victory to be marred by "the war after the war." At the core of Clausewitz's trinitarian theory of war was his insistence on the universal salience of the complex and highly variable relations among

passion or hatred, chance, and reason. While a state's army may be beaten, its public might not accept that verdict.

5. *When considering preventive military action, the assessment must include anticipated and possible costs, as well as expected benefits.* Policymakers, in common with the rest of us, are vulnerable to the censoring effect of their desires and convictions.

6. *A prudent anticipation of high costs should not necessarily be a showstopper for proposals for preventive war.* Cost-free, casualty-free warfare is a fantasy. This is not to deny that Kosovo in 1999 was a casualty-free enterprise for NATO. However, this remarkable historical episode was the exception that proves the rule. If the case for prevention is believed to be compelling, then even the certainty of daunting costs of many kinds cannot be permitted to close down the option from live consideration. Each historical case has to be examined on its own terms at the time. There are no metrics, there is no methodology, to which one can delegate the decision to act or not to act.

These six points, and the body of inquiry behind them, enables this chapter to specify key implications for U.S. policy and strategy. It may be necessary to emphasize that these implications express the personal beliefs of the author. Although the claims and recommendations are historically and analytically grounded, they are undeniably controversial in a few cases.

CONCLUSION

1. *Preemption is not controversial.* It is not always feasible or effective, but its inherent desirability cannot be challenged.

2. *To be willing to act preventively requires a determination to proceed in the teeth of much, even great, political opposition.* The United States has to be willing to strike preventively, only occasionally.

3. *The United States should not have, indeed does not need, an explicit doctrine, so miscalled, of prevention (or preemption, meaning prevention).* Its global role as principal guardian of world order

requires it to maintain the capability to behave preventively— and to be willing to use it.

4. *In order to approach the preventive war option prudently, the United States has to accept the necessity for using military force for political ends.*

5. *To wage preventive warfare successfully requires very good intelligence, as does warfare of any character.* It does not require immaculate intelligence. A requirement for the best is the enemy of the good enough.

6. *Military prevention is not, and cannot be, a doctrine, let alone the dominant national security doctrine.* It should be regarded as "an occasional stratagem," certainly not "as the operational concept of choice."[50] To go to war, even just to stage a limited campaign, is to enter the highest realm of chance, risk, uncertainty, friction, and potentially exorbitant costs. Deterrence is infinitely preferable, if and when it can work.

7. *To endorse the prevention option is to be willing to gamble on military success.* In some cases, the damage required to be inflicted must be close to 100 percent (e.g., if nuclear-armed missiles are the prime targets).[51] However, in other instances, military perfection would not be necessary in order for the strike or campaign to achieve worthwhile strategic and political goals.

8. *In most cases, preventive military action should have the character of a raid, not an invasion.* The United States is not capable of remaking culturally alien societies so that they become shining examples of successful American-style globalization. If the job is impracticable, as I claim, it cannot be sound policy and strategy to make the attempt.

9. *Since this chapter endorses prevention as a rare, but still vitally necessary, option, it judges these to be the most essential criteria for a decision to act*:

- Force must be the last resort, not temporally, but with respect to the evidence-based conviction that the non-military instruments of policy cannot succeed.

- There must be persuasive arguments to the effect that the conditions to be forcibly prevented would be too dangerous to tolerate.

- The benefits of preventive military action must be expected to be far greater than the costs.

- There must be a high probability of military success.

- There should be some multinational support for the preventive action; indeed the more, the better. However, the absence of blessing by the world community cannot be permitted to function politically as a veto.

Because of my strong agreement with the relevant judgment expressed, these words of John Lewis Gaddis close this chapter:

Like most other nations, we got to where we are by means that we cannot today, in their entirety, comfortably endorse. Comfort alone, however, cannot be the criterion by which a nation shapes its strategy and secures its safety. The means of confronting danger do not disqualify themselves from consideration solely on the basis of the uneasiness they produce.[52]

8

THE MERIT IN
ETHICAL REALISM

The deepest fear of my war years, one still with me, is that these happenings had no real purpose. Just as chance often appeared to rule my course then, so the more ordered paths of peace might well signify nothing or nothing much.
—J. Glenn Gray, 1967[1]

As typically is the case with national security books, ethical discussion has intruded here only rarely. Because most strategists like to think of themselves professionally as hard-nosed realists, they are inclined to view questions about values as being only of minor practical significance. Of course, while they acknowledge in principle the legitimacy and even the authority of ethical rules, they find little if any space for the moral dimension in what they must regard as a pragmatic profession. Good strategy is workable strategy. In the memorable words of a great German field marshal, it is a "system of expedients."[2] In this closing chapter I argue that it is nearly always inexpedient to ignore or affront the ethical sensibilities of stakeholder communities, including one's own. In a statement of exemplary clarity, David J. Lonsdale preaches from the heartland of the transnational strategic studies profession:

> Strategic studies seeks to present an amoral analysis of military affairs. By doing so, we can objectively assess actions and/or individuals that as moral beings may cause us concern. In the search for best practice in strategic affairs we can, and should, be able to disentangle moral judgments from strategic ones.[3]

On first reading, Lonsdale seems simply to be explaining a basic distinction between objective strategic judgment and subjective moral judgment. On second reading, however, one begins to wonder whether the idea of "amoral analysis" can be pragmatically sound. After all, war, its preparation and actual conduct, is a profoundly human activity, and Lonsdale grants rightly that people are "moral beings." Can we distinguish our strategic selves, including our behavior as strategic players, from our moral selves? Should we try to do so? More to the point, is it strategically sound to try to distinguish supposedly objective strategic judgment from subjective moral judgment?

As a practicing strategist, I am convinced that strategy's ethical dimension is not subjectively irrelevant; rather it is integral to supposedly objective analysis, calculation, decision, and behavior. Martin van Creveld approaches the target when he persuasively claims that "compared with the willingness or lack of it, in men (and women) to die for their cause, virtually all questions of policy, organization, doctrine, training, and equipment pale into insignificance."[4] Motives for the willingness to risk death vary widely, but usually it seems that they include what can only be termed a moral element.[5] Soldiers need to regard their behavior, as well as their mission, as "right conduct" in a critical measure. In other words, the moral is strategic and the strategic is moral. The specific content of an individual's "moral" sanction may vary from that of other individuals, though generally not dramatically. The strategist who discounts or ignores the ethical dimension weakens his ability to grasp the nature of the human function that we call "strategic."

What is the relevance of this ethical dimension to the preceding chapters wherein the issue of values was rarely prominent? The answer is that the analysis of every subject has had some ethical content, though admittedly its presence generally has not been made explicit. Chapter 1 recognized the potency for statecraft and war, indeed for politics generally, of Thucydides' immortal triad: "Fear, honor, and interest."[6] On examination, the second of these broad categories of motives reveals itself as the repository of what we understand by ethics. It is sensible to approach the Greek historian's insight inclusively. By "honor" we should understand not only a concern for reputation as well as self-regard for dignity, but also a determination to behave honorably. Of course, the precise content of what is deemed honorable is fairly specific to culture, but this does not invalidate the point made here. Norms, values, morals, and ethics do not rule the world, but save for the sad cases of truly deviant or sick personalities, they are always powerful shapers, even drivers, of thought and behavior. For good or ill in Lonsdale's sense of objectively strategic terms, we are "moral beings." The potential sources of moral authority are several, but that does not matter. What matters is that each of America's national security "dilemmas" has an ethical dimension that contributes net positively or negatively to the strategic effectiveness of Americans.

✦ ✦ ✦

Security, personal or national, is a subjective quality. It cannot be measured or purchased directly. Chapter 1 paints a fairly grim portrait of contemporary U.S. national security. It suggests evidence in support of the thesis that this is proving to be yet another "snafu'ed" era. But, is this entirely fair? The chapter argues also, somewhat in mitigation of undeniable American failures, that to err is only human. Furthermore, it explains that policy and strategic performance are subject to the phenomenon common to all complex enterprises known as the "normal accident."[7]

One might argue that the first decade of the twenty-first century, despite the troubles, challenges, and dilemmas addressed in these chapters, constitutes a golden age for American security. How can this possibly be true, given the anxieties represented by the existence of a newly minted Department of Homeland Security and the unending American commitments to the conflicts in Iraq and Afghanistan? Although this decade is blighted for America in comparison with the 1990s, still the concept of a "happy time" has limited merit, for North America at least. If one contrasts the current state of U.S. national security with its possible, even probable, future condition, one discovers that the situation could be a great deal worse.[8]

To be specific: (1) though sometimes difficult, U.S. relations with the other members of the "greater economic powers" club known as the G8, at worst are only troubled, they are not confrontational, let alone militarily confrontational; (2) what used to be known officially as the Global War on Terror (GWOT) has not been won on any assessment, but neither has it been lost in an obvious sense; (3) although the current U.S. positions in Iraq and Afghanistan are far from ideal, or from those anticipated back in the heady optimism from late 2001 until summer 2003, many Americans understand that "failure is not an option"[9]; (4) the principal institutions for multinational cooperation, in some cases governance, in which the United States has a major stake are still open for business (e.g., the United Nations, the World Bank, and NATO); (5) most predicted global non-military threats to international security have yet to appear in catastrophic forms—for examples, severely adverse climate change, disease pandemics, and organized crime—though a financial crash has occurred; and (6) the United States remains "number one" in sufficient respects to warrant unique categorization as the global hegemonic power.

By hegemonic we mean, restrictively, only that the country is the global leader to the degree to which other polities agree to be led. The United States is the sole country able to take the lead when military intervention is necessary, even if arguably, to restore or maintain regional order. Resentful and disadvantaged would-be rivals will always harass U.S. hegemonic leadership in action. Nonetheless, Washington effectively is alone as the world's sheriff.[10] Others, for their own reasons, may choose to join the posse, and the authority of U.S. policing behavior will vary with the apparent quantity and quality of political legitimacy conferred on it by that vaporous notional entity, the international community. The community does not move in mysterious ways, but rather in predictably self-interested ways through the political, not moral, machinations of the UN Security Council. This is not to deny relevance to the ethical dimension cited earlier. However, it is to claim that "honor" and honorable behavior are judged relatively, according to the norms of local culture. The self-interested policies and actions of states typically lend themselves without undue difficulty to persuasive local ethical justification. When there is a clash, one can count on local consequentialist reasoning triumphing over absolute standards.

Some readers may have noticed that the "golden age" argument, such as it is, has been advanced only in distinctly modest voice and strictly in comparison with how much worse the future may be. Since the future lies before us entirely unsullied by the unsavory deeds that frequently are triggered by "fear, honor, and interest," it is tempting to view the twenty-first century as an open-ended opportunity for the human race to mend its security ways. Unfortunately, if history is any guide, and recall that it is the only one available, the future is no more likely to yield to the logic of a single grand narrative than did the past. If U.S. national security comprises not one master challenge, but rather a range of challenges, greater and smaller, how much more fragmented is the challenge posed by global security?

When we list the contemporary and anticipated major challenges to U.S. national security, there is everything to be said in favor of interrogating them to see if they could be exploited as opportunities. We have to recognize that not all challenges are practicable opportunities. One could argue that the U.S. decision to oust the Ba'athist tyranny in Baghdad was motivated as much by the desire to create a unique opportunity to fire up a democratic revolution in the Arab world, as it was to destroy the regime in power. In other words, Saddam Hussein's Iraq was defined as a challenge substantially for the purpose of generating a great opportunity for (U.S. defined) change. Alas, the vision of an opportunity proved to be a chimera. As much to the point, even if there was an opportunity to kick-start an Arab renaissance via a democratic revolution, Americans lacked the knowledge and the skills necessary to enable Arabs to carry through such an epoch-reshaping process. It is not sufficient just to wish to improve the world; in addition, one needs to know how to do it.[11] The United States does not do colonial governance well. Were a General Douglas MacArthur available to play viceroy, as did the original in Japan in 1945 and long after, it might be a different matter. However, it is not helpful to compare the U.S. record in remaking post-war Japan with its like mission in post-Saddam Iraq. The contexts are too different. Among other contrasts, MacArthur inherited a Japan with a fully functioning government, whereas in 2003 nothing much was functioning in Iraq. Also, notwithstanding the prescient quip from then Secretary of State Colin Powell to the effect that a successful invader "owns" what he conquers, Americans came to liberate, not to possess. As this text has argued, we are largely prisoners of our culture and of the political context for our behavior.

Americans are prone to define challenges as opportunities, because they tend to be future-oriented and optimistic, and to believe in progress. Societies that have known a great deal more tragedy than has the American—always excepting the Civil War and its aftermath, particularly in the South, of course—are far less inclined to believe that their best years are yet to come. An important reason why it is beneficial for global security that the United States is the contemporary hegemonic power is that Americans typically are convinced that problems of all sizes can be solved. Most especially, they believe that humans can advance in their well being and inter-communal civility because of the agencies of technology and the right ideas. A freedom-loving, commercially fairly free-trading, democratic America acknowledges no limits to what it might accomplish. As a very American saying has it, "the impossible is only a problem for which a solution has yet to be found." This is an attractive assumption and attitude, even though it can be a recipe for disaster. It stands in stark contrast to the culturally pervasive pessimism that rules in many societies.

Unfortunately, perhaps, U.S. national security does not face a single Great Dilemma in the twenty-first century. While Islamist violence is the most pressing concern of the 2000s, one cannot be sure that this will remain the case in the 2010s, 2020s, and beyond. Moreover, even if the current jihad were the entirety of the U.S. national security problem, present and future, if this truly were the "long war" that Washington has identified, how could the challenge be addressed? Since the Roman answer of utmost violence is not available for us, culturally or practically, the most we can do is provide assistance to the Islamic world as it endeavors to reform itself. To shift focus, adverse and especially abrupt climate change constitutes a severe threat to national and global security. However, will this threat of uncertain exact character and timing be abrupt? Although climate change eventually may have implications for national military security, the quest for alleviation of the emerging crisis is currently not in need of a military effort.

The sources of insecurity consist of a disaggregated array of troubles and dilemmas. Moreover, as this book has striven to explain, many challenges are more akin to conditions than to problems. Chapter after chapter addressed either persisting or recurring dilemmas (e.g., How to define victory? How to deter? How to cope with the prospect of surprise?). The American engineering spirit promotes a cultural privileging of structural solutions on a large scale. Let us build multinational institutions. Let us devise ever more rigorous rules of right behavior. Let us expand the realm of political, economic, and social freedom. Occasionally, let us do by force what only we Americans are able to do by force as the sheriff of world order, so as to punish the rogues and remind what should be a global community about the need for good manners.

◆ ◆ ◆

The dominant reason why this concluding chapter emphasizes the diversity of U.S. national security dilemmas, rather than votes for one Master Menace, is because history has a way of mocking futurists' predictions. The official and societal demand for insight into the future is understandably insatiable. On many occasions, I have been embarrassed by being introduced to an audience as an expert on the future. No one is, or can be, such an expert. We can, however, achieve a highly variable knowledge and understanding, albeit always with some contestable content, of the human historical experience with security challenges, opportunities, and of course, dilemmas. The liberal historian Arthur M. Schlesinger Jr. offered and endorsed sound advice on the value of history for the present:

> It is useful to remember that history is to the nation as memory is to the individual. As persons deprived of memory become disoriented and lost, not knowing where they have been and where they are going, so a nation denied a conception of the past will be disabled in dealing with its present and its future. "The longer you look back," said Winston Churchill, "the further you can look forward." America needs history as never before.[12]

Virtue does not reliably bring its own reward on this earth. But, although good intentions in statecraft frequently lead to unfortunate unintended consequences, a narrow and brutal pursuit of national self-interest is apt to prove self-defeating. Statesmen often flout domestic norms of decent behavior when they act for their country. Governments commit acts for which individuals would, at least should, be executed. Because of the integral and irremovable human dimension to national and international security, however, notably unprincipled statecraft can have lethal consequences for its authors.

We are moral beings. It is true that we differ from society to society, certainly from civilization to civilization, in the details of our ethics as well as in the weighting we assign to particular founts of ethical authority. It is true, also, that our ethics, which are part of our culture, are not unrelated to our interests as we perceive them. Unethical behavior is wont to be action taken that harms the interests of others. Naturally enough, those others will be motivated to resist. A favorable balance of power most likely will deteriorate if it is sustained by methods judged unacceptable abroad and even at home. And, if the purpose behind the accumulation of national power is revealed to be the ruthless pursuit of yet more national power, it is a certainty that the hegemon of today will face an exciting future comprising "interesting times" in the familiar words of the Chinese proverb. A Golden Rule of sustainable hegemony holds that the hegemon must serve others if it is to serve itself well enough.

I close this chapter by returning to where it began, with the dilemma posed by moral philosopher and U.S. Army combat veteran, J. Glenn Gray. What is it all about? Does the grand narrative of U.S. national security policy signify nothing much? Perhaps there is no grand narrative, no binding thread that joins the past to the present and the future. I do not believe this. Rather I contend that the continuities in historical experience with security challenges and opportunities are vastly more impressive than the discontinuities. The contemporary dilemmas probed in detail in these chapters, whether regarded as challenges or opportunities, or both, are generically identifiable throughout the past 2,500 years. They are evident in all of recorded history, which is to say they can be traced from the time of Herodotus and his younger contemporary, Thucydides, to the present. This thought is comforting as well as depressing. Whether or not the course of strategic history is finite, statesmen and strategists are responsible for coping adequately with the dilemmas both extant and anticipated. History, which is to say the competing views of historians, suggests that the future will reveal ever familiar, though seemingly novel, national security dilemmas.

NOTES

Foreword

1. Walter Millis, *Military History* (Washington, DC: Service Center for Teachers of History, 1961), 16–18.

2. Goldwater-Nichols Department of Defense Reorganization Act of 1986, Section 104 (a) (1) of Section 603, title 10, United States Code.

3. U.S. Defense Department, *Conduct of the Persian Gulf War: Final Report to Congress* (Washington, DC: U.S. Government Printing Office, April 1992), 31.

4. Though often translated from German to English as ". . . *by* other means" the preposition *with* more accurately reflects that war does not supplant the "other means," which in the United States are usually categorized as diplomacy, economics, and information.

5. Arnold Beichman, "Revolution in the Warfare Trenches," *Washington Times*, January 31, 1996, 17.

6. Ibid.

7. Carl von Clausewitz, *On War*, trans. Michael Howard and Peter Paret (Princeton NJ: Princeton University Press, 1976), 75, hereafter cited as Clausewitz.

8. Ibid., 89.

9. Ibid., 594.

Chapter 1: Portrait of an Era

1.   General Sir Nevil Macready, Commander-in-Chief Ireland, quoted in Charles Townshend, *The British Campaign in Ireland, 1919–1921: The Development of Political and Military Policies* (Oxford: Oxford University Press, 1975), 85.

2.   Barry Turner, quoted in Isabel V. Hull, *Absolute Destruction: Military Culture and the Practices of War in Imperial Germany* (Ithaca, NY: Cornell University Press, 2005), 3.

3.   Clausewitz.

4.   J. C. Wylie, *Military Strategy: A General Theory of Power Control* (Annapolis, MD: Naval Institute Press, 1989), 66.

5.   See Colin S. Gray, *After Iraq: The Search for a Sustainable National Security Strategy* (Carlisle, PA: Strategic Studies Institute, U.S. Army War College, forthcoming).

6.   On "normal accidents" and related matters, see Scott D. Sagan, *The Limits of Safety: Organizations, Accidents, and Nuclear Weapons* (Princeton, NJ: Princeton University Press, 1993). I have extended the domain of the "normal accident" concept from its home in engineering to international politics.

7.   Bruce Fleming, "Can Reading Clausewitz Save Us from Future Mistakes?" *Parameters* XXXIV (Spring 2004), 62–76.

8.   See Colin S. Gray, *Fighting Talk: Forty Maxims on War, Peace, and Strategy* (Westport, CT: Praeger Security International, 2007), 134–137.

9.   Admiral Ellis, quoted in R. A. Renner, "America's Asymmetric Advantage: The Utility of Airpower in the New Strategic Environment," *Defence Studies* 4 (Spring 2004), 103.

10.   Much of the detail of "the American way" in action on the ground in Iraq was extraordinarily inappropriate to local conditions. See Thomas G. Ricks, *Fiasco: The American Military Adventure in Iraq* (New York: The Penguin Press, 2006); and the utterly amazing book by Rajiv Chandrasekaran, *Imperial Life in the Emerald City: Inside Baghdad's Green Zone* (London: Bloomsbury, 2008). The latter work would strain the suspension of disbelief were it presented as fiction.

11.   Robert B. Strassler, ed., *The Landmark Thucydides: A Comprehensive Guide to the Peloponnesian War*, rev. ed., trans. Richard Crawley (New York: Free Press, 1996), 43.

12.   Richard K. Betts, "A Disciplined Defense: How to Regain Strategic Solvency," *Foreign Affairs* 86 (November/December 2007), 67–80. Even if Americans can afford to be profligate in paying for national security, they should demand better value for money than has been secured of recent years.

13.   Wylie, *Military Strategy* 14.

14. See Michael I. Handel, *Masters of War: Classical Strategic Thought*, 3rd ed. (London: Frank Cass, 2001), 345–351.

15. Clausewitz, 119–121.

16. For the theory of strategy see my forthcoming book, *The Strategy Bridge*.

17. Donald H. Rumsfeld, "America Is a Nation at War," *The National Defense Strategy of the United States of America* (Washington, DC: U.S. Department of Defense, March 2005), 1.

Chapter 2: Defining and Achieving Decisive Victory

1. Clausewitz.

2. Peter G. Tsouras, ed., *The Daily Telegraph Dictionary of Quotations* (London: Greenhill Books, 2005), 466.

3. Raymond Aron, "The Evolution of Modern Strategic Thought," in *Problems of Modern Strategy*, ed. Alastair Buchan (London: Institute for Strategic Studies, 1970), 25.

4. "The Elusive Character of Victory," *The Economist* (November 24, 2001), 11–12; Conrad Black, "What Victory Means," *The National Interest* 66 (Winter 2001/02), 155–164. Recent scholarship includes Robert Martel, *The Meaning of Victory* (Boulder, CO: Lynne Rienner Publishers, 2006); and William C. Martel, *Victory in War: Foundation of Modern Military Policy* (Cambridge: Cambridge University Press, 2007).

5. Thomas C. Schelling, *Arms and Influence* (New Haven, CT: Yale University Press, 1966), 31.

6. See Azar Gat, *The Origins of Military Thought: From the Enlightenment to Clausewitz* (Oxford: Clarendon Press, 1989), ch. 7, esp. 199.

7. Clausewitz, 75.

8. Michael Quinlan, *Thinking about Nuclear Weapons* (London: Royal United Services Institute for Defence Studies, 1997), 19.

9. Colin S. Gray and Keith B. Payne, "Victory Is Possible," *Foreign Policy* 39 (Summer 1980), 14–27. The title, picked by the editor of the journal, would have been improved had the words "but improbable," been added.

10. Colin S. Gray, "Nuclear Strategy: The Case for a Theory of Victory," *International Security* 4 (Summer 1979), 54–87.

11. Edward N. Luttwak, *On the Meaning of Victory: Essays on Strategy* (New York: Simon and Schuster, 1986), 289.

12. The commitment to "prevail" in a nuclear war was written in the new *Defense Guidance, 1984–1988,* document which was inevitably leaked to the *Washington Post*. For a relevant quotation, see Lawrence Freedman,

The Evolution of Nuclear Strategy, 3rd ed. (Basingstoke UK: Palgrave Macmillan, 2003), 388.

13. Casper W. Weinberger, *Annual Report to the Congress, Fiscal Year 1986* (Washington, DC: U.S. Government Printing Office, February 4, 1985), 45.

14. Casper W. Weinberger in the *New York Times*, August 9, 1982.

15. For example, Stephen Kotkin, *Armageddon Averted: The Soviet Collapse, 1970–2000* (Oxford: Oxford University Press, 2001). A different opinion animates Peter Schweizer, *Victory: The Reagan Administration's Secret Strategy That Hastened the Collapse of the Soviet Union* (New York: Atlantic Monthly Press, 1994); and William E. Odom, *The Collapse of the Soviet Military* (New Haven, CT: Yale University Press, 1998). Odom notes that "a program of U.S. military modernization based on new technologies confronted the Soviet military with another challenge it could not hope to meet." 876.

16. See Mark Bowden, *Black Hawk Down* (London: Bantam Press, 1999), on Somalia; Robert C. Owen, ed., *Deliberate Force: A Case Study in Effective Air Campaigning* (Maxwell AFB, AL: Air University Press, January 2000), on Bosnia 1995; Benjamin S. Lambeth, *NATO's Air War for Kosovo: A Strategic and Operational Assessment* (Santa Monica, CA: RAND, 2001); and idem, *Air Power Against Terror: America's Conduct of Operation Enduring Freedom* (Santa Monica, CA: RAND, 2005).

17. Robert H. Scales, Jr., *Certain Victory: The U.S. Army in the Gulf War* (Washington, DC: Office of the Chief of Staff, 1993); Norman Friedman, *Desert Victory: The War for Kuwait* (Annapolis, MD: Naval Institute Press, 1991). The Air Force story was told in Richard P. Hallion, *Storm over Iraq: Air Power and the Gulf War* (Washington, DC: Smithsonian Institution Press, 1992); and, in ways not wholly beloved by the USAF hierarchy, in its commissioned *Gulf War Air Power Survey* (GWAPS) (5 vols.) See Thomas A. Keaney and Eliot A. Cohen, *Gulf War Air Power Survey, Summary Report* (Washington DC: U.S. Government Printing Office, 1993). The official Air Force reaction to the GWAPS volumes was not notably dissimilar from the Royal Navy's distancing response to the volumes of the official history of Naval Operations in the Great War written by Julian S. Corbett.

18. For an influential British dissenting voice, and his second thoughts, see Michael Howard, "Mistake to Declare this is a War," *RUSI Journal* 146 (December 2001), 1–4, reprinted in Michael Howard, *Liberation or Catastrophe? Reflections on the History of the Twentieth Century* (London: Hambledon Continuum, 2007), 175–180, 181–190.

19. Writing about 1940, Williamson Murray and Allan R. Millett have commented that "for the Germans, the victory over France suggested that everything was possible for the Third Reich." *A War to be Won: Fighting the Second World War* (Cambridge, MA: Harvard University Press, 2000), 89.

20. Save with reference to politically meaningless and morally abominable

destructive potential, nuclear armaments almost certainly rendered the two superpowers less powerful than they would have been without the nuclear discovery. Today, nuclear arms are the weapons of the weak, not the strong. The U.S. Government is thoroughly disinterested in its nuclear arsenal, save only for its uncertain residual value to help deter the threat or use of weapons of mass destruction against U.S. interests. Clark A. Murdock makes the interesting, if ultimately unconvincing, argument that the 2001–02 Nuclear Posture Review of the George W. Bush administration has so "mainstreamed" nuclear weapons that their value for deterrence has been needlessly impaired. *The Department of Defense and the Nuclear Mission in the 21st Century*, A Beyond Goldwater-Nichols Phase 4 Report (Washington, DC: Center for Strategic and International Studies, March 2008). Usable American military power is thoroughly conventional. The nuclear emphasis in contemporary Russian military doctrine attests to Moscow's appreciation of the weakness of its conventional forces. Victory over Georgia in 2008 was not proof of Russian military excellence.

21. Russell F. Weigley, *The Age of Battles: The Quest for Decisive Warfare from Breitenfeld to Waterloo* (Bloomington: Indiana University Press 1991), xiii.

22. Ibid.

23. For presentations of the realist paradigm, see Colin S. Gray, "Clausewitz Rules, OK? The Future is the Past—with GPS," in *The Interregnum: Controversies in World Politics, 1989–1999,* ed. Michael Cox, Ken Booth, and Tim Dunne (Cambridge: Cambridge University Press, 1999), 161–182; John J. Measheimer, *The Tragedy of Great Power Politics* (New York: W.W. Norton, 2001); and Jonathon Haslam, *No Virtue Like Necessity: Realist Thought in International Relations since Machiavelli* (New Haven, CT: Yale University Press, 2002).

24. The most intelligent discussion of "the origins of great wars" is T.C.W. Blanning, *The Origins of the French Revolutionary Wars* (London: Longman, 1986), ch. 1. Also see Stephen van Evera, *Causes of War: Power and the Roots of Conflict* (Ithaca, NY: Cornell University Press, 1999); and Dale C. Copeland, *The Origins of Major War* (Ithaca, NY: Cornell University Press, 2000). It is surprising how many scholars fail to grasp both the vital distinction between the causes of war and the causes of peace, and the need for theory to explain periods of peace as well as outbreaks of war.

25. Weigley, *Age of Battles,* 543.

26. See Michael Howard, "When are Wars Decisive?" *Survival* 41 (Spring 1999), 129.

27. For an insightful discussion of the relationship between the conduct of war and the securing of a tolerable peace, see Brian Bond, *The Pursuit of Victory: From Napoleon to Saddam Hussein* (Oxford: Oxford University Press, 1996).

28. Howard, "When are Wars Decisive?" 135.

29. Clausewitz, 75.

30. "Few wars, in fact, are any longer decided on the battlefield, if indeed they ever were. They are decided at the peace table. Military victories do not themselves determine the outcome of wars; they only provide political opportunities for the victors—and even those opportunities are likely to be limited by circumstances beyond their control." Howard, "When are Wars Decisive? 130. Howard comes close to overstating a persuasive point.

31. Readers tired of the literature that is largely dismissive of U.S. and ARVN (Army of the Republic of Vietnam) military efforts, could do worse than examine the evidence and arguments in Mark W. Woodruff, *Unheralded Victory: Who Won the Vietnam War?* (New York: Harper Collins, 1999); C. Dale Walton, *The Myth of Inevitable U.S. Defeat in Vietnam* (London: Frank Cass, 2002); and Mark Moyar, *Triumph Forsaken: The Vietnam War, 1954–1965* (Cambridge: Cambridge University Press, 2006). On the events of 1972, see Dale Andrade, *Trial by Fire: The 1972 Easter Offensive, America's Last Vietnam Battle* (New York: Hippocrene Books, 1995).

32. See Colin S. Gray, *Modern Strategy* (Oxford: Oxford University Press, 1999), ch. 1; and Richard K. Betts, "Is Strategy an Illusion?" *International Security* 25 (Fall 2000), 5–50.

33. Colin S. Gray, "Why Strategy is Difficult," *Joint Force Quarterly* 22 (Summer 1999), 6–12.

34. On the McNamara years, see Alain Enthoven and K. Wayne Smith, *How Much Is Enough? Shaping the Defense Program, 1961–1969* (New York: Harper and Row, 1971).

35. See Terence Zuber, "The Schlieffen Plan Reconsidered," *War in History* 6 (July 1999), 262–305; Annika Mombauer, "Of War Plans and War Guilt: The Debate Surrounding The Schlieffen Plan," *Journal of Strategic Studies* 28 (October 2005), 857–885; and Antulio J. Echevarria II, *After Clausewitz: German Military Thinkers Before the Great War* (Lawrence: University Press of Kansas, 2000), 193–194.

36. Clausewitz, 75, 77.

37. Richard P. Henrick, *Crimson Tide* (New York: Avon Books, 1995), 75. I am grateful to Richard Betts for bringing this brilliant interpretation of Clausewitz to my notice.

38. For the best of modern scholarship, see the different views in Martin van Creveld, *Supplying War: Logistics from Wallenstein to Patton* (Cambridge: Cambridge University Press 1977); John A. Lynn, ed., *Feeding Mars: Logistics in Western Warfare from the Middle Ages to the Present* (Boulder, CO: Westview Press, 1993); and especially Thomas M. Kane, *Military Logistics and Strategic Performance* (London: Frank Cass, 2001).

39. Hew Strachan observes of the war in German East Africa that "both the climate . . . and the insect life . . . were strategically decisive." *The First World War*, vol. 1: *To Arms* (Oxford: Oxford University Press, 2001), 504.

Also see the monumental scholarly study by Edward Paice, *Tip and Run: The Untold Tragedy of the Great War in Africa* (London: Phoenix, 2008), for the full horror of conducting warfare in one of the unhealthiest places on earth.

40. See Lawrence Freedman, ed., *Strategic Coercion: Concepts and Cases* (Oxford: Oxford University Press, 1998); and Stephen J. Cimbala, *Coercive Military Strategy* (College Station: Texas A&M University Press, 1998).

41. Clausewitz, 607.

42. See Gray: *Modern Strategy*, 19–23; and *Weapons for Strategic Effect: How Important is Technology?* Occasional Paper 21 (Maxwell AFB, AL: Center for Strategy and Technology, Air War College, January 2001).

43. Victor Davis Hanson, *Why the West Has Won: Carnage and Culture from Salamis to Vietnam* (London: Faber and Faber, 2001), risks taking a powerful culturalist thesis a step too far.

44. Jeremy Black, *War in the New Century* (London: Continuum, 2001), vii.

45. Hanson, *Why the West Has Won*, ch. 4.

46. The most comprehensive treatment is Horst Boog and others, *Germany and the Second World War*, vol. 4: *The Attack on the Soviet Union* (Oxford: Clarendon Press, 1998).

47. Black, *War in the New Century*, viii. He argues that war's multiple contexts are fatal for RMA theory.

48. Quoted ibid., 2.

49. For reasons none too hard to glean from Michael Burleigh, *The Third Reich: A New History* (London: Macmillan, 2000).

50. Clausewitz, 85.

51. Ibid., 86.

52. See J. P. Harris, *Amiens to the Armistice: The BEF in the Hundred Days' Campaign, 8 August–11 November 1918* (London: Brassey's, 1998).

53. A proposition argued persuasively in Murray and Millett, *War to Be Won*, 483.

54. Antoine Henri de Jomini, *The Art of War* (1838; Novato, CA: Presidio Press, 1992), 325.

55. Ibid., 70.

56. See Strachan, *The First World War*, 1: 724.

57. John Shy, "Jomini," in *Makers of Modern Strategy: from Machiavelli to the Nuclear Age*, ed. Peter Paret (Princeton, NJ: Princeton University Press, 1986), 183–184.

58. Edward N. Luttwak, *Strategy: The Logic of War and Peace*, 2nd ed. (Cambridge, MA: Harvard University Press, 2001).

59. Daniel Gouré gushed as follows: "RMA advocates need fear no longer [that others might exploit the RMA first]. The RMA they predicted is here and the USA holds an unquestionable, perhaps even unchallengeable lead. The war in Afghanistan demonstrates the reality of the RMA and shows just how far the USA has come in owning and exploiting it." "Location, Location, Location," *Jane's Defence Weekly*, February 27, 2002.

60. J. F. C. Fuller, *Armament and History* (London: Eyre and Spottiswoode, 1946). For an outstanding discussion, see Eliot Cohen, "Technology and Warfare," in, *Strategy in the Contemporary World: An Introduction to Strategic Studies*, 2nd ed., ed. John Baylis and others (Oxford: Oxford University Press, 2007), 141–159.

61. See Andrew F. Krepinevich Jr., *The Army and Vietnam* (Baltimore: Johns Hopkins University Press, 1986), esp. 112–127, 168–172; and Shelby Stanton, *The 1st Cav in Vietnam: Anatomy of a Division* (Novato, CA: Presidio Press, 1999).

62. For Russian perspectives on their Afghan experience, see Lester W. Grau, ed., *The Bear Went over the Mountain: Soviet Combat Tactics in Afghanistan* (London: Frank Cass, 1998). For Afghan perspectives it would be difficult to better Mohammad Yousaf and Mark Adkin, *Afghanistan—The Bear Trap: The Defeat of a Superpower* (Barnsley, UK: Leo Cooper, 2001), esp. ch. 11, "Wonder Weapons—Gunships versus Stingers."

63. Alfred Thayer Mahan, *The Influence of Sea Power upon the French Revolution and Empire, 1793–1812* (Boston: Little Brown, 1898), 1: 102. I thank Jon Sumida for bringing this Mahanian dictum to my attention.

64. Hanson, *Why the West Has Won*, 360.

65. Cohen, "Technology and Warfare," 152–153.

66. The question of substitution of strength for weakness among strategy's dimensions is central to the argument in Colin S. Gray, *Strategy for Chaos: RMA Theory and the Evidence of History* (London: Frank Cass, 2002).

67. John Ferling, *Almost a Miracle: The American Victory in the War of Independence* (New York: Oxford University Press, 2007), is outstanding, though readers need to be alert to the modicum of patriotic history in the story as told.

68. Colin S. Gray, "Thinking Asymmetrically in Times of Terror," *Parameters* 32 (Spring 2002), 5–14.

69. As Eliot Cohen has noted, the military and strategic effectiveness of America's information-led RMA cannot be assessed properly until it is tested in combat against more worthy foes than have been trounced thus far. "Technology and Warfare," 149.

70. Robert M. Utley, *Cavalier in Buckskin: George Armstrong Custer and the Western Military Frontier* (Norman, OK: University of Oklahoma Press, 1988), 206.

Custer never thought like an Indian. With most of his peers, therefore, he was doomed to fight Indians with the techniques of conventional warfare.

For a century the army fought Indians as if they were British or Mexicans or Confederates. Each Indian war was expected to be the last, and so the generals never developed a doctrine or organization adapted to the special problems posed by the Indian style of fighting.

Also see Sam C. Sarkesian, *America's Forgotten Wars: The Counterrevolutionary Past and Lessons for the Future* (Westport, CT: Greenwood Press, 1984), which is a neglected minor classic

71. Charles E. Heller and William A. Stofft, eds., *America's First Battles, 1776–1965* (Lawrence: University Press of Kansas, 1986), is valuable.

72. See Michael C. C. Adams, *Our Masters the Rebels: A Speculation on Union Military Failure in the East, 1861–1865* (Cambridge, MA: Harvard University Press, 1978). The title tells nearly all.

73. The classic text is Charles A. Callwell, *Small Wars: A Tactical Textbook for Imperial Soldiers* (1906 ed.; Novato, CA: Presidio Press, 1990).

74. See John Haldon, *Warfare, State and Society in the Byzantine World, 565–1204* (London: UCL Press, 1999), ch. 2.

75. See Edward Spiers, "The Late Victorian Army, 1868–1914," in *The Oxford Illustrated History of the British Army*, ed. David Chandler and Ian Beckett (Oxford: Oxford University Press, 1994), 189–214; T.R. Moreman, *The Army in India and the Development of Frontier Warfare, 1889–1947* (London: Macmillan, 1998); and John Gooch, ed., *The Boer War: Direction, Experience and Image* (London: Frank Cass, 2000).

76. At least if modern scholars are to be believed. See Adrian Keith Goldsworthy, *The Roman Army at War, 100 BC–AD 200* (Oxford: Oxford University Press, 1996), ch. 3.

77. Sun Tzu, *The Art of War*, Ralph D. Sawyer, trans. (Boulder, CO: Westview Press, 1994), 179.

78. There is much to recommend this thought of Ralph Peters: "In this age of technological miracles, our military needs to study mankind." *Fighting for the Future: Will America Triumph?* (Mechanicsburg, PA: Stackpole Books, 1999), 172.

79. See Keith B. Payne, *The Fallacies of Cold War Deterrence and a New Direction* (Lexington: University Press of Kentucky, 2001).

80. See, for example, Philip Smucker, "Blunders that let bin Laden slip away," the *Daily Telegraph*, London, February 23, 2002.

81. On the logic of international competition, see Mearsheimer, *The Tragedy of Great Power Politics*.

82. Robert Allan Doughty, *The Breaking Point: Sedan and the Fall of France, 1940* (Hamden, CT: Archon Books, 1990), tells the story of tactical and operational disaster.

83. See David M. Glantz and Jonathan House, *When Titans Clashed:*

How the Red Army Stopped Hitler (Lawrence: University Press of Kansas, 1995); and Robert M. Citino, *Blitzkrieg to Desert Storm: The Evolution of Operational Warfare* (Lawrence: University Press of Kansas, 2004), chs. 2–3.

84. See Victor Davis Hanson, *The Western Way of War: Infantry Battle in Classical Greece* (London: Hodder and Stoughton, 1989); Stephen Mitchell, "Hoplite Warfare in Ancient Greece," in *Battle in Antiquity*, ed. Alan B. Lloyd (London: Gerald Duckworth, 1996), 87–105; and J. E. Lendon, *Soldiers and Ghosts: A History of Battle in Classical Antiquity* (New Haven, CT: Yale University Press, 2005).

85. Mao Tse-tung, attrib., *On Guerrilla Warfare*, Samuel B. Griffith, trans. (New York: Frederick A. Praeger, 1961), 52.

86. See Michael I. Handel, *Masters of War: Classical Strategic Thought*, 3rd ed. (London: Frank Cass, 2001), Appendix B: "The Weinberger Doctrine."

Chapter 3: Maintaining Effective Deterrence

1. Although this monograph is wholly original, I wish to acknowledge the strong, pervasive influence of two works: Keith B. Payne, *Fallacies of Cold War Deterrence and a New Direction* (Lexington: University Press of Kentucky, 2001); and Lawrence Freedman, *Deterrence* (Cambridge: Polity Press, 2004).

2. Payne, *Fallacies of Cold War Deterrence*, 36–37.

3. A fine analytical review of the scholarly literature on deterrence is provided in Freedman, *Deterrence*. Those who would like to sample this literature might try Robert Jervis, "Deterrence Theory Revisited," *World Politics* 31 (January 1979), 289–324; Robert Jervis, Richard Ned Lebow, and Janice Gross Stein, *Psychology and Deterrence* (Baltimore: Johns Hopkins University Press, 1985); Paul K. Huth, *Extended Deterrence and the Prevention of War* (New Haven, CT: Yale University Press, 1988); Paul C. Stern and others, eds., *Perspectives on Deterrence* (New York: Oxford University Press, 1989); Richard Ned Lebow and Janice Gross Stein, *We All Lost the Cold War* (Princeton, NJ: Princeton University Press, 1994); Frank C. Zagare and D. Marc Kilgour, *Perfect Deterrence* (Cambridge: Cambridge University Press, 2000); and Patrick Morgan, *Deterrence Now* (Cambridge: Cambridge University Press, 2003).

4. This notion is well developed in Freedman, *Deterrence*.

5. In modern times, Glenn Snyder rigorously laid out the conceptual distinction between deterrence by denial or by punishment. See his *Deterrence and Defense* (Princeton, NJ: Princeton University Press, 1961).

6. "'Strategic thinking,' or 'theory' if one prefers, is nothing if not pragmatic. Strategy is a 'how to do it' study, a guide to accomplishing something and doing it efficiently." Bernard Brodie, *War and Politics* (New York: Macmillan, 1973), 452.

7. For some relevant history, see Lawrence Freedman, *The Evolution of Nuclear Strategy*, 3rd ed. (London: Palgrave Macmillan, 2003); and Colin S. Gray, *Strategic Studies and Public Policy: The American Experience* (Lexington: University Press of Kentucky, 1982).

8. Michael Howard, "Lessons of the Cold War," *Survival* 36 (Winter 1994–95), 161, 164.

9. Henry Kissinger, *Diplomacy* (New York: Simon and Schuster, 1994), 608.

10. George Friedman and Meredith Lebard, *The Coming War with Japan* (New York: St. Martin's Press, 1991); Richard Bernstein and Ross H. Munro, *The Coming Conflict with China* (New York: Alfred A. Knopf, 1997). Books whose titles begin with the formula, "the coming war with . . . ," seem to have market appeal.

11. The historian was Dennis Showalter. He is quoted in Williamson Murray, "Thinking about Revolutions in Military Affairs," *Joint Force Quarterly* 16 (Summer 1997), 69.

12. The two-MTW paradigm was given a rough time in Steven Metz, ed., *Revising the Two MTW Force Shaping Paradigm* (Carlisle, PA: Strategic Studies Institute, U.S. Army War College, April 2001).

13. Robert C. Owen, ed., *Deliberate Force: A Case Study in Effective Air Campaigning* (Maxwell AFB, AL: Air University Press, January 2000); Benjamin S. Lambeth, *NATO's Air War for Kosovo: A Strategic and Operational Assessment* (Santa Monica, CA: RAND, 2001). Also see the persuasive indictment in Frederick W. Kagan, *Finding the Target: The Transformation of American Military Policy* (New York: Encounter Books, 2006).

14. See Daniel Gouré and Jeffrey M. Ranney, *Averting the Defense Train Wreck in the New Millennium* (Washington, DC: Center for Strategic and International Studies, 1999).

15. Aron, "The Evolution of Modern Strategic Thought," 25.

16. See John Mueller, "Harbinger or Aberration? A September 11 Provocation," *The National Interest* 69 (Fall 2002), 45–50; and Walter Laqueur, "Left, Right, and Beyond: the Changing Face of Terror," in *How Did This Happen? Terrorism and the New War*, eds. James F. Hoge, Jr., and Gideon Rose (Oxford: Public Affairs, 2001), 71–83.

17. Lawrence Freedman, "The Third World War?" *Survival* 43 (Winter 2001), 61–87.

18. Michael Howard was adamantly of the opinion that it was a "Mistake to Declare this a War," *RUSI Journal* 146 (December 2001), 1–4.

19. Clausewitz, 88–89.

20. For somewhat alternative views of the American role, see: Andrew J.

Bacevich, *American Empire: The Realities and Consequences of U.S. Diplomacy* (Cambridge, MA: Harvard University Press, 2002); Colin S. Gray, *The Sheriff: America's Defense of the New World Order* (Lexington: University Press of Kentucky, 2004); idem., *After Iraq: The Search for a Sustainable National Security Strategy* (Carlisle, PA: Strategic Studies Institute, U.S. Army War College, forthcoming).

21. Colin S. Gray, *Strategy for Chaos: Revolutions in Military Affairs and the Evidence of History* (London: Frank Cass, 2002), argues for the conduct of RMAs as strategic behavior.

22. Eliot A. Cohen, "The Mystique of U.S. Air Power," *Foreign Affairs* 73 (January/February 1994), 109–24, is very much to the point. Also see Benjamin S. Lambeth, *The Transformation of American Air Power* (Ithaca, NY: Cornell University Press, 2000).

23. William J. Clinton, *A National Security Strategy of Engagement and Enlargement* (Washington, DC: The White House, July 1994). Perhaps one might be permitted the comment that some strategies are more strategic than others.

24. Henry Kissinger, *Does America Need a Foreign Policy? Toward a Diplomacy for the 21st Century* (New York: Simon and Schuster, 2001), 19.

25. For some endeavors to understand the changed roles and significance of nuclear weapons after the Cold War, see Keith B. Payne, *Deterrence in the Second Nuclear Age* (Lexington: University Press of Kentucky, 1997); T.V. Paul, Richard J. Harknett, and James J. Wirtz, eds., *The Absolute Weapon Revisited: Nuclear Arms and the Emerging International Order* (Ann Arbor, MI: University of Michigan Press, 1998); Colin S. Gray, *The Second Nuclear Age* (Boulder CO: Lynne Rienner Publishers, 1999); and John Baylis and Robert O'Neill, eds., *Alternative Nuclear Futures: The Role of Nuclear Weapons in the Post-Cold War World* (Oxford: Oxford University Press, 2000).

26. See Bruce Hoffman, *Inside Terrorism*, rev. ed. (London: Victor Gollancz, 2006); and Walter Laqueur, *The New Terrorism: Fanaticism and the Arms of Mass Destruction* (New York: Oxford University Press, 1999).

27. George W. Bush, *The National Security Strategy of the United States of America* (Washington, DC: The White House, September 2002), 15.

28. Ibid.

29. "Rumsfeld Interview," the *Times* (London), February 10, 2003.

30. Steven Metz and Douglas V. Johnson II, *Asymmetry and U.S. Military Strategy: Definition, Background, and Strategic Concepts* (Carlisle, PA: Strategic Studies Institute, U.S. Army War College, January 2001); and Roger W. Barnett, *Asymmetrical Warfare: Today's Challenge to U.S. Military Power* (Washington, DC: Brassey's, 2003), are particularly thoughtful and rewarding treatments of this slippery concept.

31. Clausewitz, 75.

32. See Ken Booth, *Strategy and Ethnocentrism* (London: Croom Helm, 1979); and Peter J. Katzenstein, ed., *The Culture of National Security: Norms and Identity in World Politics* (New York: Columbia University Press, 1996).

33. John Lewis Gaddis, *The Long Peace: Inquiries into the History of The Cold War* (New York: Oxford University Press, 1987). Also see Norman Friedman, *The Fifty-Year War: Conflict and Strategy in the Cold War* (Annapolis, MD: Naval Institute Press, 2000); and Odd Arne Westad, ed., *Reviewing the Cold War: Approaches, Interpretations, Theory* (London: Frank Cass, 2000).

34. John Shy has noticed that some of the criticism of modern American strategic thought is "very like the standard critique of Jomini. The criticism is that strategists in the nuclear age employ abstract methods like model building and systems analysis that reduce war to an operational exercise, transforming it thereby into an unrealistic but extremely dangerous game." Critics argue that the Jominian approach followed, albeit largely unknowingly, by American theorists, "lifts 'strategy' out of its real-world context, demonstrably increasing the risk of major miscalculations." "Jomini" in *Makers of Modern Strategy: from Machiavelli to the Nuclear Age*, ed. Peter Paret (Princeton, NJ: Princeton University Press, 1986), 183. John Weltman expressed a similar thought elegantly when he wrote that "[t]he development of nuclear strategy represented an attempt at a Jominian solution to a problem that was essentially Clausewitzian in nature. Rules were propounded and calculations elaborated, designed to ensure with certainty the successful accomplishment of a wide range of national goals through the deployment, threat, or even use of nuclear weapons." Weltman described convincingly the invention and development of "rules and calculations for nuclear weapons 'intended' to ensure the deterrence of undesired actions." He contrasted the cutting edge of American strategic analysis with the apparent fact that the outcome of conflicts and crises "turned far more on the attitudes, expectations, perceptions and behavior of the antagonists, than they did on sophisticated calculations about the results of hypothetical clashes of armed forces in battle." *World Politics and the Evolution of War* (Baltimore: Johns Hopkins University Press, 1995), 152. This outstanding book deserves to be better known.

35. Those in need of a rapid education in what might be deficient in the deterrence theory that we have inherited from past decades, could do worse than consult Payne, *Deterrence in the Second Nuclear Age; Fallacies of Cold War Deterrence*; and his major work, *The Great American Gamble: Deterrence Theory and Practice From the Cold War to the 21st Century* (Fairfax, VA: National Institute Press, 2008).

36. This significant distinction is usually credited to Patrick M. Morgan, *Deterrence: A Conceptual Analysis* (Beverly Hills, CA: Sage Publications, 1977), ch. 2.

37. Different kinds of deterrence are well-explained in Freedman, *Deterrence*.

38. See Thomas C. Schelling, *Arms and Influence* (New Haven, CT: Yale University Press, 1966); Alexander L. George, David K. Hall, and William E. Simons, *The Limits of Coercive Diplomacy: Laos, Cuba, Vietnam* (Boston: Little, Brown, 1971); Lawrence Freedman, ed., *Strategic Coercion: Concepts and Cases* (Oxford: Oxford University Press, 1998); Stephen J. Cimbala, *Coercive Military Strategy* (College Station: Texas A&M University Press, 1998); and Daniel Byman and Matthew Waxman, *The Dynamics of Coercion: American Foreign Policy and the Limits of Military Might* (Cambridge: Cambridge University Press, 2002).

39. Bush, *National Security Strategy*, 2002, 29. Richard L. Kugler, "Dissuasion as a Strategic Concept," *Strategic Forum* (INSSS/NDU) 196 (December 2002), provides a first-rate discussion.

40. Donald H. Rumsfeld, *Annual Report to the President and the Congress* (Washington, DC: Department of Defense, 2002), 18.

41. Stephen Metz and Raymond Millen, *Future War/Future Battlespace: The Strategic Role of American Landpower* (Carlisle, PA: Strategic Studies Institute, U.S. Army War College, March 2003), 7. The same thought animates Michael Mandelbaum, "Is Major War Obsolete?" *Survival* 40 (Winter 1998–99), 20–38; and Mary Kaldor, *New and Old Wars: Organized Violence in a Global Era* (Cambridge: Polity Press, 1999).

42. Alexander L. George is probably the most consistent and rigorous advocate of inducement as an integral part of a broad strategy of influence, including deterrence and coercion. See George and Richard Smoke, *Deterrence in American Foreign Policy: Theory and Practice* (New York: Columbia University Press, 1974); and George, "The Role of Force in Diplomacy: A Continuing Dilemma for U.S. Foreign Policy," in *The Use of Force after the Cold War*, ed. H. W. Brands (College Station: Texas A&M University Press, 2000), 59–92.

43. By strategy I mean the use made of force and the threat of force for the ends of policy. This is a light update of Clausewitz's definition: "Strategy [is] the use of engagements for the object of the war." Clausewitz, 128; Colin S. Gray, *Modern Strategy* (Oxford: Oxford University Press, 1999), 17.

44. Rumsfeld, *Annual Report*, 2002, 85.

45. Clausewitz, Bk. VIII is often cited, but is it read and understood? Sometimes one has the impression that many defense analysts are more comfortable with the pre-1827 Clausewitz who did not complicate his theory of war with political considerations.

46. I advance and defend the golden age thesis in my *Strategic Studies and Public Policy*, ch. 4. The major innovative works that framed this period

were William W. Kaufmann, ed., *Military Policy and National Security* (Princeton, NJ: Princeton University Press, 1956); Herman Kahn, *On Escalation: Metaphors and Scenarios* (New York: Frederick A. Praeger, 1965); and Schelling, *Arms and Influence.*

47. Writing to introduce a genuinely stellar collection of essays prepared for a conference in 1968, the first Director of the Institute for Strategic Studies, Alastair Buchan, gave a strong impression that modern strategic thought was a job well done.

> The collection of essays, prepared as papers for this conference . . . is therefore, largely concerned with a retrospective analysis of how strategic ideas, doctrines and policies have developed over the last fifteen or twenty years. Though they attack the subject from many different angles and national viewpoints, the reader may find a common thread in the views of many writers that the greater conceptual battles about the nature and limitations of modern strategy, the breaking of the mould of traditional thought on the subject, are now largely over and that the problems of the future are not so much philosophical or conceptual as political, that is the alignment or realignment of our notions as to what constitutes "security" or "stability" or "influence" with the pressures of international politics and the rapid form of technological change.

Buchan, *Problems of Modern Strategy*, Foreword.

48. Antoine Henri de Jomini, *The Art of War* (1838, Novato, CA: Presidio Press, 1992), 323

49. Ibid., 325.

50. Michael C. Desch, "Culture Clash: Assessing the Importance of Ideas in Security Studies," *International Security* 23 (Summer 1998), 145.

51. I appreciate that the structure of international security politics in the Cold War was never quite this simple. Both superpowers were troubled by a small "awkward squad" of allies, friends, and dependents of convenience, who were never under completely reliable control. This is emphasized in John Lewis Gaddis, *The Cold War* (London: Allen Lane, 2006).

52. This subject is treated persuasively in Payne, *Fallacies of Cold War Deterrence*, 7–15.

53. Ibid., 10.

54. Ibid., 12.

55. For a potent contemporary assessment, see Hedley Bull, "Strategic Studies and Its Critics," *World Politics* 20 (July 1968), 269–283.

56. Clausewitz, 75.

57. But, preventive war did have its day as an option of strategic interest. See Marc Trachtenberg, *History and Strategy* (Princeton, NJ: Princeton University Press, 1991), ch. 3.

58. Some blows for common sense are well struck in Stephen M. Walt, "Rigor or Rigor Mortis? Rational Choice and Security Studies," *International Security* 23 (Spring 1999), 5–48.

59. Clausewitz, 119.

60. Ibid.

61. Ibid., 121.

62. Ibid., 120.

63. Daniel J. Hughes, ed., *Moltke on the Art of War: Selected Writings*, trans. Hughes and Harry Bell (Novato, CA: Presidio Press, 1993), 45.

64. Barry Watts has done his best, though it may have been mission impossible. See his challenging monograph, *Clausewitzian Friction and Future War*, McNair Paper 68 rev. ed. (Washington, DC: Institute for National Strategic Studies, National Defense University, August 2004). Stephen J. Cimbala, *Clausewitz and Chaos: Friction in War and Military Policy* (Westport, CT: Praeger Publishers, 2001), ventures boldly where many fear to tread.

65. Clausewitz, 101.

66. Metz and Millen, *Future War/Future Battlespace*, viii, 12.

67. Ralph Peters, *Beyond Terror: Strategy in a Changing World* (Mechanicsburg, PA: Stackpole Books, 2002), 22–65.

68. Ibid., 22–23.

69. I am pleased to borrow the metaphor from Peters. Ibid., 22.

70. This argument is especially well developed in Freedman, *Deterrence*.

71. This is the fundamental message of Payne, *Fallacies of Cold War Deterrence*.

72. I analyze the value of the general theory of strategy in my forthcoming book, *The Strategy Bridge: Theory for Practice*.

73. This advice has been pressed with great consistency for several decades by Alexander George. See George and Smoke, *Deterrence in American Foreign Policy*; and George, "The Role of Force in Diplomacy."

74. The importance of local, including individual leaders', beliefs is a theme in Payne, *Fallacies of Cold War Deterrence*. Also see John Mueller, "The Impact of Ideas on Grand Strategy," in *The Domestic Bases of Grand Strategy*, ed. Richard Rosecrance and Arthur A. Stein (Ithaca, NY: Cornell University Press, 1993), 48–62.

75. The most sacred book expressing the neorealist persuasion is Kenneth N. Waltz, *Theory of International Politics* (Reading, MA: Addison-Wesley

Publishing Company, 1979). John J. Mearsheimer, *The Tragedy of Great Power Politics* (New York: W.W. Norton, 2001), is a major example of the genre. For useful background, see Jonathan Haslam, *No Virtue Like Necessity: Realist Thought in International Relations since Machiavelli* (New Haven, CT: Yale University Press, 2002).

76. Antulio J. Echevarria II, *Clausewitz's Center of Gravity: Changing Our Warfighting Doctrine—Again!* (Carlisle, PA: Strategic Studies Institute, U.S. Army War College, September 2002), 19.

77. Mao Tse-tung, attrib., *On Guerrilla Warfare*, trans. Samuel B. Griffith (New York: Frederick A. Praeger, 1961), 52.

78. See Clark A. Murdock, *The Department of Defense and the Nuclear Mission in the 21st Century*, A Beyond Goldwater-Nichols Phase 4 Report (Washington, DC: Center for Strategic and International Studies, March 2008).

79. See the excellent case studies in Talbot C. Imlay and Monica Duffy Toft, eds., *The Fog of Peace and War Planning: Military and Strategic Planning under Uncertainty* (Abingdon, UK: Routledge, 2006).

80. Metz and Millen, *Future War/Future Battlespace*, 24.

81. From a large literature, see Robert A. Pape, *Bombing to Win: Air Power and Coercion in War* (Ithaca, NY: Cornell University Press, 1996); and Gian P. Gentile, *How Effective is Strategic Bombing? Lessons Learned from World War II to Kosovo* (New York: New York University Press, 2001).

82. Julian S. Corbett, *Some Principles of Maritime Strategy* (1911; Annapolis, MD: Naval Institute Press, 1988), 16.

83. J. C. Wylie, *Military Strategy: A General Theory of Power Control* (Annapolis, MD: Naval Institute Press, 1989), 72.

84. Clausewitz, 607. Again this is an argument handled exceptionally well in Freedman, *Deterrence*.

85. Clausewitz, 585.

86. Ibid., 605.

87. Keith Payne points out that it is something of a heroic task to expect to be able to deter nuclear use by a regional power facing conventional defeat at American hands. In his words: "In the future, Washington will want results from its deterrence policy that it said were not possible for the Soviet Union vis-à-vis NATO during the Cold War: confidence that it can deter an opponent's threat of WMD escalation even while projecting power and defeating that opponent on or near its own soil." *Fallacies of Cold War Deterrence*, 185.

88. Metz and Millen, *Future War/Future Battlespace*, 23.

89. Ibid.

90. See Stephen Biddle, *Afghanistan and the Future of Warfare: Implications for Army and Defense* (Carlisle, PA: Strategic Studies Institute, U.S. Army War College, November 2002); and Jonathan House, *Combined Arms Warfare in the Twentieth Century* (Lawrence: University Press of Kansas, 2001).

91. The high priest of "dominant weapon" theory was the British theorist, J. F. C. Fuller. See his remarkable little book, *Armament and History* (London: Eyre and Spottiswoode, 1946).

92. See Susan L. Marquis, *Unconventional Warfare: Rebuilding U.S. Special Operations Forces* (Washington, DC: Brookings Institution Press, 1997). I have offered some strategic analysis of the value of SOF in my *Explorations in Strategy* (Westport, CT: Praeger Publishers, 1998), chs. 7–9; and "Handfuls of Heroes on Desperate Ventures: When do Special Operations Succeed?" *Parameters* 29 (Spring 1999), 2–24.

93. See the comment in Eliot A. Cohen, "Kosovo and the New American Way of War," in *War Over Kosovo: Politics and Strategy in a Global Age*, ed. Andrew J. Bacevich and Cohen (New York: Columbia University Press, 2001), 55–56.

94. Max Boot, *The Savage Wars of Peace: Small Wars and the Rise of American Power* (New York: Basic Books, 2002), offers a timely reminder of the historically rich variety of the American military landpower experience, and it does not even deal with the Army's major role on the country's internal frontier.

Chapter 4: Transformation and Strategic Surprise

1. S. Douglas Smith, book review, *Naval War College Review* 57 (Winter 2004), 147.

2. Arthur C. Clarke, quoted in Primo Levi, *The Search for Roots—A Personal Anthology* (London: Allen Lane, 2001), 188. I am grateful to John B. Sheldon for bringing this wise judgment by Clarke to my notice.

3. Colin S. Gray, *Strategic Studies and Public Policy: The American Experience* (Lexington: University Press of Kentucky, 1982), chs. 3–4; Saki Dockrill, *Eisenhower's New-Look National Security Policy, 1953–61* (New York: St. Martin's Press, 1996); and Lawrence Freedman, *The Evolution of Nuclear Strategy*, 3rd ed. (Basingstoke, UK: Palgrave Macmillan), 2003, ch. 6.

4. U.S. strategic offensive force loadings increased from 330 warheads in 1950 to 1,418 by 1954. Natural Resources Defense Council, "Table of US Strategic Offensive Force Loadings, 1945–75, 1976–2012," August 21, 2004. http://nrdc.org/nuclear/nudb/datab1.asp Estimates for the Soviet Union remain uncertain. See Thomas B. Cochran and others, *Nuclear Weapons Databook*, vol. 4: *Soviet Nuclear Weapons* (New York: Harper and Row, 1989), 25; Steven J. Zaloga, *Target America: The Soviet Union and the Strategic Arms Race, 1945–1964* (Novato, CA: Presidio Press, 1993); and Pavel Podvig, ed.,

Russian Strategic Nuclear Forces (Cambridge, MA: MIT Press, 2004).

5. See Richard K. Betts, *Surprise Attack: Lessons for Defense Planning* (Washington, DC: Brookings Institution, 1982), chs. 6–9; and John J. Mearsheimer, *Conventional Deterrence* (Ithaca, NY: Cornell University Press, 1983), ch. 6.

6. Barnett, *Asymmetrical Warfare*, is particularly useful.

7. Donald H. Rumsfeld, *Annual Report to the President and the Congress* (Washington DC: Department of Defense, 2002), 10–11. http:// www.defenselink.mil/execsec/adr2002/index.htm

8. For example, in his path-breaking study of friction, Barry D. Watts concedes as follows: "The objection, which has been consciously ignored to this point, is that the unified concept of a general friction *(Gesamtbegriff einer allgemeinen Friktion)* embraces so much of war that it does not provide a very precise instrument for analyzing the phenomena at issue." *Clausewitzian Friction and Future War,* McNair Paper 68, rev. ed. (Washington, DC: National Defense University, August 2004), 77.

9. An outstanding analysis is Michael I. Handel, "Intelligence and the Problem of Strategic Surprise," in *Paradoxes of Intelligence: Essays in Honor of Michael I. Handel,* ed. Richard K. Betts and Thomas G. Mahnken (London: Frank Cass, 2003), 1–58.

10. See Keith B. Payne, *The Fallacies of Cold War Deterrence and a New Direction* (Lexington: University Press of Kentucky, 2001).

11. Roberta Wohlstetter introduced the vital distinction between "noise" and "signals" in her book, *Pearl Harbor: Warning and Decision* (Stanford, CA: Stanford University Press, 1967).

12. John Gray, *Al Qaeda and What It Means to Be Modern* (London: Faber and Faber, 2003), 27.

13. Clausewitz, 75; and J. C. Wylie, *Military Strategy: A General Theory of Power Control* (Annapolis, MD: Naval Institute Press, 1989), 77–78. "So it is proposed here that a general theory of strategy should be some development of the following fundamental theme: The primary aim of the strategist in the conduct of war is some selected degree of control of the enemy for the strategist's own purpose; this is achieved by control of the pattern of war; and this control of the pattern of war is had by manipulation of the center of gravity of war to the advantage of the strategist and the disadvantage of the opponent."

14. Richard K. Betts, *Enemies of Intelligence: Knowledge and Power in American National Security* (New York: Columbia University Press, 2007), is first rate.

15. See Scott D. Sagan, *The Limits of Safety: Organizations, Accidents, and Nuclear Weapons* (Princeton, NJ: Princeton University Press), 1993.

16. James Wirtz, "Theory of Surprise," in *Paradoxes of Strategic Intelligence*, 103.

17. Edward N. Luttwak, "Strategy," in *The Oxford Companion to American Military History*, ed. John Whiteclay Chambers (Oxford: Oxford University Press, 1999), 684.

18. John R. Boyd, "A Discourse on Winning and Losing," briefing, August 1987; David S. Fadok, "John Boyd and John Warden: Air Power's Quest for Strategic Paralysis," in *The Paths of Heaven: Airpower Theory*, ed. Phillip S. Meilinger (Maxwell Air Force Base, AL: Air University Press, 1997), 357–398; Grant T. Hammond, *The Mind of War: John Boyd and American Security* (Washington, DC: Smithsonian Institution Press, 2001); Robert Coram, *Boyd: The Fighter Pilot Who Changed the Art of War* (Boston: Little, Brown, 2002); and Frans P. B. Osinga, *Science, Strategy and War: The Strategic Theory of John Boyd* (Abingdon, UK: Routledge, 2007).

19. Clausewitz, 75.

20. Wirtz, "Theory of Surprise," 103.

21. B. H. Liddell Hart, *History of the First World War* (London: Pan Books, 1972), 325.

22. Ibid.

23. See Williamson Murray and Allan R. Millet, *A War to be Won: Fighting the Second World War* (Cambridge, MA: Harvard University Press, 2000), chs. 2–4.

24. See Colin S. Gray, *The Sheriff: America's Defense of the New World Order* (Lexington: University Press of Kentucky, 2004).

25. Clausewitz, 85.

26. Ibid., 101.

27. Antulio J. Echevarria II, *Toward an American Way of War* (Carlisle, PA: Strategic Studies Institute, U.S. Army War College, March 2004), v. Also see Russell F. Weigley, *The American Way of War: A History of U.S. Military Strategy and Policy* (Bloomington, IN: Indiana University Press, 1973); and Benjamin Buley, *The New American Way of War: Military Culture and the Political Utility of Force* (Abingdon, UK: Routledge, 2008).

28. See Sam C. Sarkesian, *America's Forgotten Wars: The Counterrevolutionary Past and Lessons for the Future* (Westport, CT: Greenwood Press, 1984); and Max Boot, *The Savage Wars of Peace: Small Wars and the Rise of American Power* (New York: Basic Books, 2002). American experience in waging war against irregulars was distilled in the U.S. Marine Corps, *Small Wars Manual, 1940* (Washington, DC: U.S. Government Printing Office, 1940).

29. Robert M. Citino, *The German Way of War: From the Thirty Years' War to the Third Reich* (Lawrence: University Press of Kansas, 2005), is essential.

30. B. H. Liddell Hart, *Strategy: The Indirect Approach*, rev. ed. (London: Faber and Faber, 1967), 366.

31. A. K. Cebrowski, *Military Transformation: A Strategic Approach* (Washington, DC: Department of Defense, Fall 2003).

32. Peter Browning, *The Changing Nature of Warfare: The Development of Land Warfare from 1792 to 1945* (Cambridge: Cambridge University Press, 2002), 7.

33. See Stuart E. Johnson and Martin C. Libicki, eds., *Dominant Battlespace Knowledge*, rev. ed. (Washington, DC: National Defense University Press, April 1996).

34. U.S. Army, *The Way Ahead* (Washington, DC: U.S. Army, Spring 2004), 1.

35. See *Military Review*, Special Edition, "Counterinsurgency Reader" (October 2006); and, above all else, U.S. Army and Marine Corps, *Counterinsurgency Field Manual* (Chicago: University of Chicago Press, 2007). Also useful is Joseph R. Cerami and Jay W. Boggs, eds., *The Interagency and Counterinsurgency Warfare: Stability, Security, Transition, and Reconstruction Roles* (Carlisle, PA: Strategic Studies Institute, U.S. Army War College, December 2007).

36. See Colin S. Gray, *Modern Strategy* (Oxford: Oxford University Press, 1999), ch. 5, "Strategic Culture as Context."

37. Norman Friedman, *The Fifty-Year War: Conflict and Strategy in the Cold War* (Annapolis, MD: Naval Institute Press, 2000), is persuasive on the U.S. contribution to the fall of the USSR.

38. U.S. Army, *Army Campaign Plan* (Washington, DC: Office of the Deputy Chief of Staff, U.S. Army, April 12, 2004), 3.

39. The literature on strategic culture has expanded of recent years. See Ken Booth, *Strategy and Ethnocentrism* (London: Croom Helm, 1979); Alastair Iain Johnston, *Cultural Realism: Strategic Culture and Grand Strategy in Chinese History* (Princeton, NJ: Princeton University Press, 1995); Michael C. Desch, "Culture Clash: Assessing the Importance of Ideas in Security Studies," *International Security* 23 (Summer 1998), 141–170; Victor Davis Hanson, *Why the West Has Won: Carnage and Culture from Salamis to Vietnam* (London: Faber and Faber, 2001); John A. Lynn, *Battle: A History of Combat and Culture* (Boulder, CO: Westview Press, 2003); Jeremy Black, *Rethinking Military History* (London: Routledge, 2004), esp. ch. 9; Lawrence Sondhaus, *Strategic Culture and Ways of War* (London: Routledge, 2006); and Buley, *New American Way of War*.

40. The issue of culture versus material circumstances is well handled in Colin Dueck, *Reluctant Crusaders: Power, Culture, and Change in American Grand Strategy* (Princeton, NJ: Princeton University Press, 2006).

41. Colin S. Gray: *Nuclear Strategy and National Style* (Lanham, MD:

University Press of America, 1986); and *Modern Strategy*, ch. 5.

42. Robert Kagan, *Paradise and Power: America and Europe in the New World Order* (London: Atlantic Books, 2003), overstates a fundamentally sound argument.

43. See Bacevich, *American Empire*; Gray, *The Sheriff*; and Niall Ferguson, *Colossus: The Rise and Fall of the American Empire* (London: Allen Lane, 2004).

44. Edward N. Luttwak, "Toward Post-Heroic Warfare," *Foreign Affairs* 75 (May/June 1995), 109–122. Luttwak showed the way, but Christopher Coker has provided the heavy guns in a quartet of outstanding works: *Humane Warfare* (London: Routledge, 2001); *Waging War Without Warriors? The Changing Culture of Military Conflict* (Boulder, CO: Lynne Rienner Publishers, 2002); *The Future of War: The Re-Enchantment of War in the Twenty-First Century* (Oxford: Blackwell Publishing, 2004); and *The Warrior Ethos: Military Culture and the War on Terror* (Abingdon, UK: Routledge, 2007). There is a sense in which Coker has written the same book four times, but still they are necessary reading. Even when one disagrees with him, as I do frequently, one is obliged to recognize the superior quality of Coker's argument and writing.

45. See Peter D. Feaver and Richard H. Kohn, eds., *Soldiers and Civilians: The Civil-Military Gap and American National Security* (Cambridge, MA: MIT Press, 2001), 467.

46. "Technology is driving everyone, terrorist and armies alike, to the same tactics. What is more, most of the technology is commercially available. . . . As we have seen, the United States and Al Qaeda took the same approach to war. That is because many groups can now compete at the same level as many nation-states, and everyone is adopting similar methods, because that is what works." Bruce Berkowitz, *The New Face of War: How War Will Be Fought in the 21st Century* (New York: Free Press, 2003), 16, 18. While there is some merit in Berkowitz's claims, his general assertion of tactical commonality is a misleading fallacy.

47. Clausewitz, 605.

48. Emily Goldman and Andrew L. Ross, "Conclusions: The Diffusion of Military Technology and Ideas—Theory and Practice," in *The Diffusion of Military Technology and Ideas*, ed. Goldman and Leslie C. Eliason (Stanford, CA: Stanford University Press, 2003), 390.

49. Paul Hirst, *War and Power in the 21st Century: The State, Military Conflict and the International System* (Cambridge: Polity Press, 2001), 9.

50. In the early 1980s, the creaking leaders of the USSR persuaded themselves that the tough talk of the Reagan administration signaled more than mere rhetoric, it reflected an intention to act, even at the highest level of violence. See Ben B. Fischer, *A Cold War Conundrum: The 1983 War Scare*, CSI 97-10002 (Washington, DC: Center for the Study of Intelligence, Central Intelligence Agency, September 1997); Peter Vincent Pry, *War Scare: Russia*

and America on the Nuclear Brink (Westport, CT, Praeger Publishers, 1999), Part 1; and Richard Rhodes, *Arsenals of Folly: The Making of the Nuclear Arms Race* (New York: Simon and Schuster, 2008), ch. 9.

51. In decades to come, Russia might decide that China is its principal foe and that the United States would be an ideal ally.

52. This claim is explained and defended at length in my book, *Another Bloody Century: Future Warfare* (London: Weidenfeld and Nicolson, 2005).

53. Wirtz is convincing when he argues that "relying on the element of surprise, however, is extraordinarily risky." "Theory of Surprise," 105. Surprise may not be achieved. Even if the enemy is caught unawares, the anticipated effects of the surprise might well prove disappointing. If the attacker was driven to resort to surprise by awareness of his inferiority in a war of attrition, any measure of surprise effect short of decisive victory should mean a war that could not be won. Had the attacker not succumbed to the temptation to gamble on surprise, he would not have dared to take the initiative. Such, of course, should be true for a rational and reasonable leadership. It so happens that risk assessment and risk tolerance vary dramatically from person to person and regime to regime.

54. See my book-in-progress, *The Strategy Bridge: Theory for Practice*.

55. Clausewitz, 606.

56. Ibid., 85. Clausewitz's distinction between war's "objective" nature, which is unchanging, and its "subjective" nature, which is ever on the move, is well deployed and explained in Antulio J. Echevarria II, *Globalization and the Nature of War* (Carlisle, PA: Strategic Studies Institute, U.S. Army War College, March 2003). Clausewitz's concept of the subjective nature of war is identical in meaning to our contemporary reference to the character of war.

57. U.S. Army, *Army Campaign Plan*, 2

58. The classic explanation is Samuel P. Huntington, *The Soldier and the State: The Theory and Politics of Civil-Military Relations* (New York: Vintage Books, 1964), ch. 1. For a bold challenge to the classic view, see Eliot A. Cohen, *Supreme Command: Soldiers, Statesmen, and Leadership in War* (New York: Free Press, 2002).

59. Historians disagree, as is their wont, on whether or not the manner of war termination in 1918 and the character of the Versailles settlement rendered a "second round" inevitable. Nothing is strictly inevitable, but the facts that German society did not feel defeated, the homeland did not suffer damage, the army returned generally in good order and bearing its arms, and the terms imposed at Versailles were deemed universally to be outrageously unjust, manifestly comprised potent fuel for possible exploitation by the unscrupulous in the future. On top of the failings of the unloved Weimar Republic and the desire for revenge over 1918–19, the Great Depression provided the additional push needed for Germans to gamble on the Nazi solution to their troubles.

60. Beatrice Heuser, *Reading Clausewitz* (London: Pimlico, 2002), 19, 138–42, is especially helpful.

61. Clausewitz, 610.

62. From the still burgeoning, forbiddingly large literature on Vietnam, see particularly Andrew F. Krepinevich, *The Army and Vietnam* (Baltimore: Johns Hopkins University Press, 1986); and C. Dale Walton, *The Myth of Inevitable U.S. Defeat in Vietnam* (London: Frank Cass, 2002). The latter demonstrates how well the United States performed in Vietnam, at least as measured by anxieties in Hanoi, despite its commission of gross political, strategic, and military errors. Mark Moyar, *Triumph Forsaken: The Vietnam War, 1954–1965* (Cambridge: Cambridge University Press, 2006), is so uncompromisingly revisionist and bold in its arguments and assertions that it is probably responsible for many cases of cardiac arrest.

63. On the important issue of whether war is too serious a business to be left to the generals, or, alternatively, too serious to be left to the politicians, see Cohen, *Supreme Command*.

64. For a notable scholarly work on the sources of high military performance, see Stephen Biddle, *Military Power: Explaining Victory and Defeat in Modern Battle* (Princeton, NJ: Princeton University Press, 2004). Unfortunately, Biddle does not attempt to address the problem that dominates my text. Modern battle is not the American challenge. Rather does the difficulty lie in waging war effectively for desirable political ends.

65. See Colin S. Gray, *Explorations in Strategy* (Westport, CT: Praeger Publishers, 1998), ch. 7, "The Nature of Special Operations."

66. *The Economist*, April 3, 2004, 94.

Chapter 5: Recognizing and Understanding Revolutionary Change in Warfare: The Sovereignty of Context

1. Clausewitz, 89.

2. Ibid., 606.

3. Ibid., 54.

4. Andrew W. Marshall, *Statement on "Revolutions in 'Military Affairs,'"* before the Senate Armed Services Committee, Subcommittee on Acquisition and Technology, May 5, 1995. In a letter to the author dated August 24, 1995, Dr. Marshall wrote to say that "I think the period we are in has a lot of similarities to the 20s and 30s and that we are in the early 20s. We have only the beginnings of the ideas about the appropriate concepts of operations and organizations. The innovations will be harder this time because there appear to be few new distinctive platforms." A key early document was Andrew W. Marshall, *Some Thoughts on Military Revolutions*, Memorandum for the Record,

OSD Office of Net Assessment, July 27, 1993. Marshall sponsored the research which led to an outstanding collection of case studies on the 1920s and 1930s. See Williamson Murray and Allan R. Millett, eds., *Military Innovation in the Interwar Period* (Cambridge: Cambridge University Press, 1996).

5. For example, as in Frederick W. Kagan, *Finding the Target: The Transformation of American Military Policy* (New York: Encounter Books, 2006). Also see the valuable study, Robert R. Tomes, *US Defense Strategy from Vietnam to Operation Iraqi Freedom: Military Innovation and the new American Way of War, 1973–2003* (Abingdon, UK: Routledge, 2007).

6. Suitable skepticism suffuses Milan Vego, "Effects-Based Operations: A Critique," *Joint Force Quarterly* 41 (2nd qtr.), 51–57; and Antulio J. Echevarria II, *Challenging Transformation's Cliches* (Carlisle, PA: Strategic Studies Institute, U.S. Army War College, December 2006).

7. As a concept history is ambiguous. It can refer to what happened, whether or not we are well informed about it. But also it can refer to what historians have written. Modern intellectual fashion has tended to be dismissive of history as an accessible past. Instead, we are invited to have only low expectations of the veracity in historical writing. In a recent essay Antulio J. Echevarria corners the "the trouble with history." He tells us that "the problem is not so much that history is a 'fable agreed upon,' as Napoleon reportedly said, but that except for those accounts that blatantly contradict or disregard the available facts, the reader cannot determine *objectively* which history is more accurate than another. Ultimately, historical truth, like beauty, remains in the eye of the beholder [emphasis in the original]." "The Trouble with History," *Parameters* XXXV (Summer 2005), 81. Echevarria is right with his post-modern view. Nonetheless, I decline to be intimidated by his formidable logic. I persist in regarding historical study as a practicable search for truth. Perhaps I should say for a plausible approach to truth. The trouble with "The Trouble with History," is that it will be read and cited to confirm anti-historical bias in a U.S. defense community not overly inclined to respect the past.

8. Williamson Murray and MacGregor Knox, "Thinking About Revolutions in Warfare," in *The Dynamics of Military Revolution, 1300–2050*, ed. Knox and Murray (Cambridge: Cambridge University Press, 2001), 7, 12.

9. Andrew F. Krepinevich, "Cavalry to Computer: the Pattern of Military Revolutions," *The National Interest* 37 (Fall 1994), 30.

10. Richard O. Hundley, *Past Revolutions, Future Transformation: What Can the History of Revolutions in Military Affairs Tell Us about Transforming the U.S. Military?* MR-1029-DARPA (Santa Monica, CA: RAND, 1999), 9. Mercifully, this study is untroubled by postmodern qualifications of judgment.

11. Ibid.

12. Ibid

13. Jeremy Black, "A Military Revolution? A 1660–1792 Perspective," in *The Military Revolution Debate: Readings on the Military Transformation of Early Modern Europe*, ed. Clifford J. Rogers (Boulder, CO: Westview Press, 1995), 98.

14. It is worth noting that Black's objection to the RMA concept is not of the post-modernist kind. He writes with confidence in the belief that the past is accessible to understanding. Moreover, in common with this theorist, Black does not subscribe to the view that "history" is a beauty contest between competing fables.

15. Jeremy Black, *Rethinking Military History* (London: Routledge, 2004), 225.

16. The title tells all in the notable, perhaps notorious, revolutionary tract and period piece, Bill Owens, *Lifting the Fog of War* (New York: Farrow, Straus, Giroux, 2000).

17. The best discussion is provided by the studies in Knox and Murray, eds., *The Dynamics of Military Revolution, 1300–2050*.

18. Hundley, *Past Revolutions, Future Transformations*, 27.

19. Colin S. Gray: *Weapons for Strategic Effect: How Important is Technology?* Occasional Paper 22 (Maxwell AFB, AL: Center for Strategy and Technology, Air War College, January 2001); *Strategy for Chaos: Revolution in Military Affairs and the Evidence of History* (London: Frank Cass, 2002).

20. Clausewitz, 566.

21. Not infrequently, a technological shortfall creates a demand for a supply of heroes. Such supply soon can be exhausted.

22. See Bruce I. Gudmundsson, *Stormtroop Tactics: Innovation in the German Army, 1914–1818* (New York: Praeger, 1989). This excellent book suffers a little from teutophilia. The author is slightly baffled by the indisputable fact that the German Army lost the war. American admirers of German military prowess often can seem almost embarrassed to have to concede that, by the way, the superior military team lost!

23. The story is well told in Williamson Murray, "May 1940: Contingency and Fragility of the German RMA," *Dynamics of Military Revolution, 1300–2050*, in Knox and Murray, eds., 154–74. Robert Allan Doughty, *The Breaking Point: Sedan and the Fall of France, 1940* (Hamden, CT: Archon Books, 1990), is classic.

24. There can be no doubting the sincerity of the U.S. Army's current interest in counterinsurgency. See the new manual, The U.S. Army and Marine Corps, *Counterinsurgency Field Manual* (Chicago: The University of Chicago Press, 2007). Also see *Military Review*, Special Edition, "Counterinsurgency Reader" (October 2006). Robert R. Jones, "Relearning Counterinsurgency Warfare," *Parameters* XXXIV (Spring 2004), 16–28, offers

a plausible message for today. Relevant background is to be found in Andrew F. Krepinevich, *The Army and Vietnam* (Baltimore: Johns Hopkins University Press, 1986); and Stuart Kinross, *Clausewitz and America: Strategic thought and practice from Vietnam to Iraq* (Abingdon, UK: Routledge, 2008).

25. I developed this point in my article, "RMAs and the Dimensions of Strategy," *Joint Force Quarterly* 17 (Autumn/Winter 1997–98), 50–54.

26. Clausewitz, 605.

27. Ibid., 89.

28. Near perfect examples were the Anglo-French wars of the very late seventeenth, the eighteenth, and the early nineteenth centuries. The political, and hence strategic, contexts did vary significantly from war to war. Nonetheless, the geopolitical-geostrategic challenge to English, then British, security posed by France essentially was stable for more than a century.

29. George W. Bush, *The National Security Strategy of the United States of America* (Washington, DC: White House, September 2002), is amazingly forthright in its declaration of a U.S. intention to remain strategically preeminent.

30. Colin S. Gray, *The Sheriff: America's Defense of the New World Order* (Lexington: University Press of Kentucky, 2004).

31. In a famous purple passage in his book, *Paradise and Power: America and Europe in the New World Order* (London: Atlantic Books, 2003), Robert Kagan explained the strategic context for the global sheriff. "Americans are 'cowboys,' Europeans love to say. And there is truth in this. The United States does act as an international sheriff, self-appointed perhaps but widely welcomed nonetheless, trying to enforce some peace and justice in what Americans see as a lawless world where outlaws need to be deterred or destroyed, often through the muzzle of a gun. Europe, by this Wild West analogy, is more like the saloonkeeper. Outlaws shoot sheriffs, not saloonkeepers. In fact, from the saloonkeeper's point of view, the sheriff trying to impose order by force can sometimes be more threatening than the outlaws, who may just want a drink." 36–37.

32. See Qiao Liang and Wang Xiangsui, *Unrestricted Warfare: Assumptions on War and Tactics in the Age of Globalization*, FBIS trans. (Beijing: PLA Literature Arts Publishing House, February 1999).

33. A well regarded short paper on "The Current Revolution in the Nature of Conflict" (July 2005), prepared by Chris Donnelly at Britain's Defence Academy for the attention of the secretary of defense, had this to say: "We think of them [revolutions in the nature of conflict] as 'military events.' But in fact the principal drivers tend to be economic, social or political rather than military-technical. They are not just revolutions in the nature of battle." 1.

34. First-rate studies of military innovation in the interwar years, its execution and its detection, monitoring, and comprehension, include: Ernest

May, ed., *Knowing One's Enemies: Intelligence Assessment before the Two World Wars* (Princeton, NJ: Princeton University Press, 1984); Wesley K. Wark, *The Ultimate Enemy: British Intelligence and Nazi Germany, 1933–1939* (Ithaca, NY: Cornell University Press, 1985); Murray and Millett, *Military Innovation in the Interwar Period*; Harold R. Winton and David R. Mets, eds., *The Challenge of Change: Military Institutions and New Realities, 1918–1941* (Lincoln: University of Nebraska Press, 2000); Thomas G. Mahnken, *Uncovering Ways of War: US Intelligence and Foreign Military Innovation, 1918–1941* (Ithaca, NY: Cornell University Press, 2002); and John Ferris, *Intelligence and Strategy: Selected Essays* (London: Routledge, 2005), ch. 3, "Image and Accident: Intelligence and the Origins of the Second World War."

35. The authoritative, quasi-official, German history of World War II, is unambiguous in its judgment on the implications of Hitler's frank outlining of his plans for expansion to the country's military and diplomatic leaders on November 5, 1937. "From this point onwards Hitler was not pursuing a policy at the risk of war, but a war policy, which he had thought out in advance and had been preparing since 1933." Wilhelm Deist et al., *Germany and the Second World War*, vol. 1: *The Build-up of German Aggression* (Oxford: Clarendon Press, 2000), 638.

36. The Rimland concept was developed in the early 1940s by the Yale-based Dutch-American political scientist, Nicholas J. Spykman. See his books: *America's Strategy in World Politics: The United States and the Balance of Power* (New York: Harcourt, Brace, 1942); and *The Geography of the Peace* (1944; Hamden, CT: Archon Books, 1969).

37. Clausewitz, 610.

38. Hew Strachan shares this concern of mine in his important article, "The Lost Meaning of Strategy," *Survival* 47 (Autumn 2005), 33–54.

39. Clausewitz, 183.

40. Ibid.

41. See Peter J. Schoomaker, *2004 Army Transformation Roadmap* (Washington, DC: Department of the Army, July 2004).

42. See Donald H. Rumsfeld, *Transformation Planning Guidance* (Washington, DC: Department of Defense, April 2003).

43. "The thesis of this book is clear—but as yet little understood: the way we make war reflects the way we make wealth . . ." Alvin and Heidi Toffler, *War and Anti-War: Survival at the Dawn of the 21st Century* (Boston: Little, Brown, 1993), 3.

44. See Rohan Gunaratna, *Inside Al Qaeda: Global Network of Terror* (New York: Columbia University Press, 2002); and Steve Coll, *Ghost Wars: The Secret History of the CIA, Afghanistan, and bin Laden, from the Soviet Invasion to September 10, 2001* (London: Penguin Books, 2004). The historical context is brilliantly explained from a viewpoint rarely considered

seriously by Westerners, in M. J. Akbar, *The Shade of Swords: Jihad and the Conflict between Islam and Christianity* (London: Routledge, 2002).

45. There has been a revival of interest in the power of ideas to shape minds, societies, policy, and the course of history. An exemplar of this trend is Michael Burleigh, *The Third Reich: A New History* (London: Macmillan, 2000), which presents Nazism as a political religion.

46. Edward N. Luttwak, "Toward Post-Heroic Warfare," *Foreign Affairs* 74 (May/June 1995), 109–122.

47. Although I recommend careful study of warfare's social-cultural context, I must admit to a certain unease. It is some small comfort to note that other scholars, Richard K. Betts and Hew Strachan, have flagged the same disquiet. Specifically, it is possible to become so enamored of the possible significance of social and cultural factors, among many others, that one's strategic analysis ceases to be very strategic. In short, one may drown in context. A good idea, for example that context is vitally significant, becomes a bad idea if it promotes so much extra-strategic study that strategic analysis all but disappears. Given the long-standing strategy deficit that has plagued American performance in war, the last thing one wishes to encourage is any further dilution of this essential focus. Strategic studies become security studies, and security studies potentially include just about everything, a condition that Strachan rightly condemns thus: "By being inclusive they [security studies] end up by being nothing." "Lost Meaning of Strategy," 47. Also, see Betts, "Should Strategic Studies Survive?" *World Politics* 50 (October 1997), 27.

48. Paul Kennedy, *The Rise and Fall of the Great Powers: Economic Change and Military Conflict from 1500 to 2000* (New York: Random House, 1987). Kennedy's main argument is to the effect that military greatness imposes such an enervating economic burden that it proves unsustainable. It carries the economic seeds of its own future destruction, always provided rival states do not write finis to the imperial story in the nearer term. A more recent analysis with the same historical sweep that also is highly regarded by scholars, is John Darwin, *After Tamerlane: The Rise and Fall of Global Empires, 1400–2000* (London: Penguin Books, 2008).

49. The clearest and most persuasive analysis is Murray and Knox, "Thinking About Revolutions in Military Affairs."

50. Stephen Biddle, *Afghanistan and the Future of Warfare: Implications for Army and Defense Policy* (Carlisle, PA: Strategic Studies Institute, U.S. Army War College, November 2002). Also see Biddle, *Military Power: Explaining Victory and Defeat in Modern Battle* (Princeton, NJ: Princeton University Press, 2004), 37–38.

51. The distinguished British scientist, Martin Rees, advises that although "there are physical limits to how finely silicon microchips can be etched by present techniques . . . new methods are already being developed that can

print circuits on a much finer scale, so 'Moore's Law' need not level off." Rees proceeds to speculate that "quite different techniques—tiny crisscrossing optical beams, not involving chip circuits at all—may increase computing power still further." *Our Final Century: Will Civilization Survive the Twenty-First Century?* (London: Arrow Books, 2003), 16.

52. Mahnken, *Uncovering Ways of War.*

53. See Murray and Millett, *Military Innovation in the Interwar Period*; and Thomas G. Mahnken, "Beyond Blitzkrieg: Allied Responses to Combined Arms Armored Warfare during World War II," in *The Diffusion of Military Technology and Ideas,* ed. Emily O. Goldman and Leslie C. Eliason (Stanford, CA: Stanford University Press), 243–266.

54. In support of this claim I cite the now well-known fact that for forty years there were major difference between U.S. and Soviet approaches to nuclear strategy. Those differences were not, as many Americans believed in the 1960s and 1970s, the result of Soviet strategic intellectual backwardness, neither did they simply reflect distinctive paths in weapons choices driven by respective technological prowess. Instead, U.S. and Soviet strategies for nuclear weapons, and their motives and proposals for strategic arms limitation, were the product mainly of distinguishably different strategic and military cultures. This author was a participant-observer of this long running controversy. See Colin S. Gray, *Nuclear Strategy and National Style* (Lanham, MD: Hamilton Press, 1986).

55. A fine set of studies on the diffusion of technology and ideas concludes with the important judgment that "an innovation developed and honed in one setting is rarely transplanted wholly to another without modification. Historically, states have either adapted innovations to make them functionally effective in their new setting, or selected certain aspects of the model to adopt. Few chapters identify instances of faithful emulation. Departure from original patterns occurs because the environment and values in the importing society usually diverge from those of the source." Emily O. Goldman and Andrew L. Ross, "Conclusion: the Diffusion of Military Technology and Ideas—Theory and Practice," in *The Diffusion of Military Technology and Ideas*, ed. Goldman and Eliason, 386.

56. David J. Lonsdale, *Alexander: Killer of Men. Alexander the Great and the Macedonian Art of War* (London: Constable, 2005), 198. For the full story, see the same author's excellent book, *Alexander the Great: Lessons in Strategy* (Abingdon, UK: Routledge, 2007).

57. Lonsdale, *Alexander: Killer of Men,* 198.

58. Martin C. Libicki, "The Emerging Primacy of Information," *Orbis* 40 (Spring 1996), 261–274.

59. Bruce Berkowitz, *The New Face of War: How War Will Be Fought in the 21st Century* (New York: Free Press, 2003), 179.

60. J. C. Wylie, *Military Strategy: A General Theory of Power Control* (Annapolis, MD: Naval Institute Press, 1989), 72.

61. Brian W. Blouet, ed., *Global Geostrategy: Mackinder and the Defence of the West* (London: Frank Cass, 2005), is a helpful collection of essays that treats many of the key themes in geopolitics.

62. See Thomas A. Keaney and Eliot A. Cohen, *Revolution in Warfare? Air Power in the Persian Gulf* (Annapolis, MD: Naval Institute Press, 1995). This book is a revised version of the Summary volume of the Gulf War Air Power Survey, published in 1993.

63. This maxim of eternal worth is well presented in Williamson Murray and Mark Grimsley, "Introduction: On Strategy," in *The Making of Strategy: Rulers, States and War*, ed. Murray, MacGregor Knox, and Alvin Bernstein (Cambridge: Cambridge University Press, 1994), 22. The authors qualify the maxim astutely with an all too pertinent observation, "but few can discern what is possible."

64. The scholarly literature on this subject is of high quality and has much merit, even though, paradoxically, it tends to come to unsound conclusions and offers unreliable advice for policy and strategy. See Martin van Creveld, *The Transformation of War* (New York: Free Press, 1991); John Keegan, *A History of Warfare* (London: Hutchinson, 1993); Mary Kaldor, *New and Old Wars: Organized Violence in a Global Era* (Cambridge: Polity Press, 1999); Colin McInnes, *Spectator-Sport War: The West and Contemporary Conflict* (Boulder, CO: Lynne Rienner Publishers, 2002); James C. Kurth, "Clausewitz and the Two Contemporary Military Revolutions: RMA and RAM," in *Strategic Logic and Political Rationality: Essays in Honor of Michael I. Handel*, ed. Bradford A. Lee and Karl F. Walling (London: Frank Cass, 2003), 274–297; Christopher Coker, *Waging War Without Warriors? The Changing Culture of Military Conflict* (Boulder, CO: Lynne Rienner Publishers, 2002); Christopher Coker, *The Future of War: The Re-Enchantment of War in the Twenty-First Century* (Oxford: Blackwell Publishing, 2004); Herfried Münkler, *The New Wars* (Cambridge: Polity Press, 2005); and Isabelle Duyvesteyn and Jan Angstrom, eds., *Rethinking the Nature of War* (London: Frank Cass, 2005).

65. Chris Donnelly observes that "there is today an almost total lack of media correspondents and editors who really understand defence and security issues." "The Current Revolution in the Nature of Conflict," 4.

66. "But in terms of the history of warfare, the most significant point about the war with Iraq is perhaps the fact that soldiers are accountable as in no other age for the war that they fight. Not just for winning the war, which is all that mattered in centuries past, but for every action that takes place on the battlefield." Eleanor Goldsworthy, "Warfare in Context," *RUSI Journal* 148 (June 2003), 19.

67. See the timely, well argued, but dangerously enticing article, Robert

H. Scales, Jr., "Culture-Centric Warfare," U.S. Naval Institute *Proceedings* 130 (October 2004), 32–36.

68. Especially Murray and Millett, *Military Innovation in the Interwar Period*. And one should not forget the monumental three-volume study of comparative military effectiveness led by these authors in the mid to late 1980s, also with the sponsorship of Marshall's Office of Net Assessment. See Allan R. Millett and Williamson Murray, eds., *Military Effectiveness*, 3 vols. (Boston: Allen and Unwin, 1988). These outstanding books have much to say that is relevant to the understanding of revolutionary change in warfare. There is no denying, though, that they do suffer noticeably from some important conceptual shortfalls. There is a pervasive theory deficiency which most plausibly is attributable to the fact that the project was conducted almost entirely by professional historians, without the conceptual discipline from social science that it needed. This judgment may well result in my being removed from a few Christmas card lists.

69. Murray and Knox, "Conclusion: The Future Behind Us," 192–193.

70. Unfortunately for the theorist who relies heavily on the "evidence" of the past, history is almost maliciously well endowed with inconvenient exceptions to favored postulates, theories, and meta-narratives. As Napoleon said, "there is no authority without exception . . ." Napoleon, *The Military Maxims of Napoleon*, David G. Chandler trans. (New York: Macmillan, 1988), 70, "Maxim XLII."

71. For the industrial points see Guido Knapp's study of Admiral Wilhelm Canaris, Head of the *Abwehr*, in his book, *Hitler's Warriors* (Stroud, UK: Sutton Publishing, 2005), 324. General Leutnant Friedrich von Paulus, the chief planner for Barbarossa with his appointment to be senior Quartermaster on the Army General Staff, was not seriously troubled by doubts about the quality of the intelligence on which he based his planning, any more than he was by doubts about the logistical feasibility of the campaign. Ibid., 200–202. Political and strategic assumptions dominated the analysis. Since the campaign, which is to say the war, was confidently expected to destroy the fielded Red Army close to the recently advanced frontiers of the Soviet Union, and because the entire venture was calculated to last little more than six weeks, perhaps two to three months, what did it matter how many additional divisions the enemy might raise, or how many tanks his factories could produce? For the statistics cited in the text on the Soviet and NKVD order of battle, for the Red Army see Horst Boog et al., *Germany and the Second World War*, vol. 4: *The Attack on the Soviet Union* (Oxford: Clarendon Press, 1998), 320–325; while for the NKVD see David Glantz, *Colossus Reborn: The Red Army at War, 1941–1943* (Lawrence: University Press of Kansas, 2005), ch. 5.

72. Antulio J. Echevarria II, *After Clausewitz: German Military Thinkers Before the Great War* (Lawrence: University Press of Kansas, 2000). Also see Niall Ferguson, *The Pity of War* (London: Allen Lane, 1998), 101; and especially

Hew Strachan, *The First World War*, vol. 1: *To Arms* (Oxford: Oxford University Press, 2001), 98–99. Although military leaders almost everywhere expected a lengthy military conflict, they were assured by civilian economic experts that this could not happen because a general war must precipitate a no less general financial collapse which would render further hostilities impossible. This was a significant illusion prior to 1914.

73. These are not uncontested judgments. See Stephen Peter Rosen, "Military Effectiveness: Why Society Matters," *International Security* 19 (Spring 1995), 5–31; and for a more skeptical view, Michael C. Desch, "Culture Clash: Assessing the Importance of Ideas in Security Studies," *International Security* 23 (Summer 1998), 141–170. For a scholarly work which offers case studies of six countries, India, Nigeria, Japan, Australia, Russia, and Germany, see John Glenn, Darryl Howlett, and Stuart Poore, eds., *Neorealism Versus Strategic Culture* (Burlington, VT: Ashgate Publishing, 2004).

74. Mahnken, *Uncovering Ways of War*.

75. Ibid., 179–180.

76. Black, *Rethinking Military History*, 13–22.

77. Clausewitz, 89.

78. I am grateful to Antulio Echevarria of the Army War College, Strategic Studies Institute, for assisting my Clausewitzian education by emphasizing to me the extent of the potential differences of relative influence among the trinitarian elements. He is right, but his valid point does not dissuade me from insisting upon the overall authority of Clausewitz's absolute claim that "all wars are things of the *same* nature [emphasis in the original]." Clausewitz, 606.

79. With reference to airpower, examples of the potential for the strategically confusing influence of a radical change in warfare include the German development of an unduly short-range air force, one much hampered additionally by many unsound operational and technical choices. The defects of the *Luftwaffe* may well have cost Germany the war. Also, the United States pursued its all-geographies nuclear revolution in the 1950s and 1960s with such dedication that the armed forces were desperately short of effective close ground support aircraft in Vietnam, a role partially filled by the helicopter gunship. Furthermore, in the 1960s the U.S. military discovered that its prospective excellence in the delivery of nuclear ordnance in Europe had not equipped it well to conduct old-fashioned aerial dogfights. There was a need for fighters to have guns as well as bomb racks and rockets. The subsequent development of the loved and hated A-10 *Warthog*, was a reluctant recognition by the Air Force that in some wars it had no choice but to share the glory with the Army.

80. Gray, *Strategy for Chaos*, esp. 274–275.

81. Lonsdale, *Alexander: Killer of Men*, 230. My argument is heavily

indebted to this first rate work and its successor, *Alexander the Great: Lessons in Strategy*. I am grateful to Dr. Lonsdale for his patient and enthusiastic efforts to explain why Alexander merits billing as the finest strategist in history. I am largely convinced; a judgment I have not sought to conceal in the text. Not even awful movies can seriously dent Alexander's popular reputation, though they can certainly threaten to do so. It does need to be noted, however, that Alexander did manage to lose the confidence of his army, though not his charisma as leader and commander.

82. See Michael C. C. Adams, *Our Masters the Rebels: A Speculation on Union Military Failure in the East, 1861–1865* (Cambridge, MA: Harvard University Press, 1978).

83. A diagram in my *Strategy for Chaos*, 126, Fig. 5.2, illustrates this incontrovertible claim forbiddingly: "The 17 Dimensions of Strategy." Deservedly, this diagram may have lost me some of my less tolerant readers.

84. See my chapter, "The American Way of War: Critique and Implications" in *Rethinking the Principles of War: The Future of Warfare*, Anthony McIvor, ed. (Annapolis, MD: Naval Institute Press, 2005), 13–40.

85. Clausewitz, 75.

86. Gray, *Strategy for Chaos*, ch. 3, "RMA Dynamics."

87. See Keith B. Payne, *The Fallacies of Cold War Deterrence and a New Direction* (Lexington: University Press of Kentucky, 2001); while Colin S. Gray, *The Second Nuclear Age* (Boulder, CO: Lynne Rienner Publishers, 1999), explains the proposition of two nuclear ages.

88. This is the convincing overall conclusion to the studies collected in Goldman and Eliason, *The Diffusion of Military Technology and Ideas.*

89. Murray and Knox, "Conclusion: The Future Before Us," 193.

90. Ibid., 185.

Chapter 6:   Irregular Enemies and the Essence of Strategy: Can the American Way of War Adapt?

1.   Stuart Kinross, "Clausewitz and Low-Intensity Conflict," *The Journal of Strategic Studies* 27 (March 2004), 54.

2.   Sam C. Sarkesian, *America's Forgotten Wars: The Counterrevolutionary Past and Lessons for the Future* (Westport, CT: Greenwood Press, 1984), 245.

3.   Charles E. Callwell, *Small Wars: A Tactical Textbook for Imperial Soldiers* (1906; Novato, CA: Presidio Press, 1990), 23.

4.   Clausewitz, 89.

5. The cyclical view of strategic history is presented and defended in Colin S. Gray, *Another Bloody Century: Future Warfare* (London: Weidenfeld and Nicolson, 2005).

6. Clausewitz, 141, 578.

7. Colin S. Gray, *Villains, Victims and Sheriffs: Strategic Studies for an Inter-War Period,* an inaugural lecture at the University of Hull, January 12, 1994 (Hull, UK: University of Hull Press, 1994), reprinted in *Comparative Strategy* 13 (October–December 1994), 353–369.

8. Donald H. Rumsfeld, *The National Defense Strategy of the United States of America* (Washington, DC: U.S. Department of Defense, March 2005), 1.

9. See Colin S. Gray, *The Sheriff: America's Defense of the New World Order* (Lexington: University Press of Kentucky, 2004). I seem to specialize in controversial concepts and metaphors. My characterization of the United States as the contemporary global sheriff is about as popular as was my description of the 1990s as an inter-war period.

10. Callwell, *Small Wars,* 21.

11. Thomas X. Hammes, *The Sling and the Stone: On War in the 21st Century* (St. Paul, MN: Zenith Press, 2004).

12. For a basic education see Clausewitz, esp. Book 3, ch. 1. Also try: Colin S. Gray, *Modern Strategy* (Oxford: Oxford University Press, 1999), ch. 1; Richard K. Betts, "Is Strategy an Illusion?" *International Security* 25 (Fall 2000), 5–50; and Hew Strachan, "The Lost Meaning of Strategy," *Survival* 47 (Autumn 2005), 33–54.

13. Sun Tzu, *The Art of War,* Ralph D. Sawyer, trans. (Boulder, CO: Westview Press, 1994); Robert B. Strassler, ed., *The Landmark Thucydides: A Comprehensive Guide to "The Peloponnesian War,"* Richard Crawley, trans., rev. ed. (New York: Free Press, 1996).

14. I was tempted to claim that intellectual mastery of the strategic mode of reasoning equips one to succeed in war, regular or irregular. On further reflection, however, it rapidly became clear that although skill as a strategist is always desirable, it cannot guarantee decisive victory. The enemy may be led by strategists who are yet more skilled, or, more likely, the balance of advantage and disadvantage may be so heavily weighted to one's disadvantage that no measure of strategic excellence is able to provide sufficient compensation. In the text I warn against treating COIN theory and the discovery of culture as panaceas. I could just as well warn against the elevation of strategy to panacea status. The American defense community periodically, albeit briefly, succumbs to what can fairly be termed "strategism," meaning an infatuation with strategy.

15. Andrew F. Krepinevich, Jr., *The Army and Vietnam* (Baltimore:

Johns Hopkins University Press, 1986), ch. 6.

16. Clausewitz, 177.

17. Russell F. Weigley, *The American Way of War: A History of United States Strategy and Policy* (New York: Macmillan, 1973), is now the classic treatment of this contestable concept.

18. Sun Tzu, *Art of War*, 179.

19. In the 1970s, a few American defense analysts and regional experts made the startling suggestion that the Soviet Union might not have signed on for a common theoretical, hence policy, enlightenment. Significant period pieces included: Richard Pipes, "Why the Soviet Union Thinks It could Fight and Win a Nuclear War," *Commentary* 64 (July 1977), 21–34; Jack L. Snyder, *The Soviet Strategic Culture: Implications for Limited Nuclear Operations,* R-2154-AF (Santa Monica, CA: RAND, September 1977); and Fritz Ermath, "Contrasts in American and Soviet Strategic Thought," *International Security* 3 (Fall 1978), 138–155.

20. Robert H. Scales, Jr., "Culture-Centric Warfare," U.S. Naval Institute *Proceedings* 130 (October 2004), 32–36.

21. The clearest statement of this fact is in Samuel P. Huntington, *American Military Strategy*, Policy Paper 28 (Berkeley, CA: Institute of International Studies, University of California, Berkeley, 1986).

22. Mao Tse-tung, *Selected Military Writings* (Beijing: Foreign Languages Press, 1963).

23. Robert R. Tomes, "Relearning Counterinsurgency Warfare," *Parameters* XXXIV (Spring 2004), 16–28, is very much to the point. From a very large literature, Ian F. W. Beckett, *Modern Insurgencies and Counter-Insurgencies: Guerrillas and Their Opponents since 1750* (London: Routledge, 2001), provides invaluable historical perspective, while Donald W. Hamilton, *The Art of Insurgency: American Military Policy and the Failure of Strategy in Southeast Asia* (Westport, CT: Praeger Publishers, 1998), provides some focus.

24. Steven Metz and Raymond Millen, *Insurgency and Counterinsurgency in the 21st Century: Reconceptualizing Threat and Response* (Carlisle, PA: U.S. Army War College, Strategic Studies Institute, November 2004); Michael F. Morris, "Al Qaeda as Insurgency," *Joint Force Quarterly* 39 (4th qtr. 2005), 41–50.

25. Ralph Peters, "In Praise of Attrition," *Parameters* XXXIV (Summer 2004), 24–32.

26. All will be revealed in my forthcoming book, *The Strategy Bridge*.

27. The use of time as a weapon to outlast the regular foreign enemy of an insurgency is a significant theme in Jeffrey Record, *The Wrong War: Why We Lost in Vietnam* (Annapolis, MD: Naval Institute Press, 1998), 67, 178–179.

28. See Susan L. Marquis, *Unconventional Warfare: Rebuilding U.S. Special Operations Forces* (Washington, DC: Brookings Institution Press, 1997).

29. Clausewitz, 178.

30. My early efforts to apply cultural analysis to contemporary strategy were focused on superpower nuclear issues. These efforts eventually were collected in *Nuclear Strategy and National Style* (Lanham, MD: Hamilton Press, 1986). For a vigorous methodological assault on my endeavors, see Alastair Iain Johnston, *Cultural Realism: Strategic Culture and Grand Strategy in Chinese History* (Princeton, NJ: Princeton University Press, 1995), esp. ch. 1. I replied to his critique in my *Modern Strategy*, ch. 5. The primary issue between us was, and remains, whether culture merely influenced behavior or was evidenced in behavior. Johnston was seeking a methodology for the study of culture, whereas I was proceeding empirically without overmuch concern for the feasibility of theory building. I have always been attracted to Callwell's advice that "theory cannot be accepted as conclusive when practice points the other way." *Small Wars,* 270. For those who wish to explore the highways and byways of strategic culture, they could do worse than sample the following: Ken Booth, *Strategy and Ethnocentrism* (London: Croom Helm, 1979); Carl G. Jacobsen, ed., *Strategic Power: USA/USSR* (New York: St. Martin's Press, 1990); Peter J. Katzenstein, ed., *The Culture of National Security: Norms and Identity in World Politics* (New York: Columbia University Press, 1996); Michael C. Desch, "Culture Clash: Assessing the Importance of Ideas in Security Studies," *International Security* 23 (Summer 1998), 141–170; Victor Davis Hanson, *Why the West Has Won: Carnage and Culture from Salamis to Vietnam* (London: Faber and Faber, 2001); John A. Lynn, *Battle: A History of Combat and Culture: From Ancient Greece to Modern America* (Boulder, CO: Westview Press, 2003), for a more critical view of culture's strategic responsibility; and John Glenn, Darryl Howlett and Stuart Poore, eds., *Neorealism Versus Strategic Culture* (Aldershot, UK: Ashgate, 2004).

31. Eliot A. Cohen, *Supreme Command: Soldiers, Statesmen, and Leadership in Wartime* (New York: Free Press, 2002), is essential contemporary reading on American civil-military relations. The "normal" American theory of those relations, which describes and praises the separation of soldiers from politics, was presented in the study by Samuel P. Huntington, *The Soldier and the State: The Theory and Politics of Civil-Military Relations* (New York: Vintage Books, 1964).

32. Clausewitz, 177 ff.

33. Cohen, *Supreme Command.*

34. Clausewitz, 610, 607.

35. Ibid., 605.

36. The contemporary literature that directly addresses the difficulties

of strategic performance is not extensive, but most people should find it useful. For some examples, see David Jablonsky, "Why Is Strategy Difficult?" in *The Search for Strategy: Politics and Strategic Vision*, ed. Gary L. Guertner (Westport, CT: Greenwood Press, 1993), 3–45; Colin S. Gray, "Why Strategy Is Difficult," *Joint Force Quarterly* 22 (Summer 1999), 6–12; and Richard K. Betts, "The Trouble with Strategy: Bridging Policy and Operations," *Joint Force Quarterly* 29 (Autumn/Winter 2001–2002), 23–30.

37. Clausewitz, 608.

38. Cohen's *Supreme Command* is essential, but by no means is it the last word on the subject.

39. I feel a little uncomfortable quoting this ironic cliché. At a conference, I was told by the former soldier who was the source of the deadly admission, that he had misspoken in stressful circumstances and could not clarify his meaning or retract the phrase before the damage was done. Friction happens! I hope that the person in question can find it in his generous heart to forgive me.

40. Clausewitz, 104.

41. Especially useful studies include: J. Paul de B. Taillon, *The Evolution of Special Forces in Counter-Terrorism: The British and American Experience* (Westport, CT: Praeger Publishers, 2001); Alastair Finlan, "Warfare by Other Means: Special Forces, Terrorism and Grand Strategy," in *Grand Strategy in the War Against Terrorism*, ed. Thomas R. Mockaitis and Paul B. Rich (London: Frank Cass, 2003), 92–108; preeminently, James D. Kiras, *Rendering the Mortal Blow Easier: Special Operations and the Nature of Strategy* (London: Routledge, 2006); Derek Leebaert, *To Dare and to Conquer: Special Operations and the Destiny of Nations from Achilles to Al Qaeda* (Boston: Little, Brown, 2006); and Christopher K. Ives, *US Special Forces and Counterinsurgency in Vietnam: Military Innovation and Institutional Failure, 1961–1963* (Abingdon, UK: Routledge, 2007).

42. Three first-rate books by Lewis Sorley are essential reading: *Thunderbolt: From the Battle of the Bulge to Vietnam and Beyond: General Creighton Abrams and the Army of His Times* (New York: Simon & Schuster, 1997); particularly his *A Better War: The Unexamined Victories and Final Tragedy of America's Last Years in Vietnam* (New York: Harcourt Brace, 1999); and *Honorable Warrior: General Harold K. Johnson and the Ethics of Command* (Lawrence: University Press of Kansas, 1998). Although this chapter is not specifically about Vietnam, it keeps intruding into the narrative and analysis despite my best efforts. Most of the literature, certainly the overwhelming bulk of expert opinion on America's performance—political, strategic, and military—is strongly negative. Therefore, for some balance, it is suitable to recommend three thoughtful books, one based on firsthand (Australian) experience, which tell a rather more up-beat story of the American effort. Mark W. Woodruff, *Unheralded Victory: Who Won the Vietnam War?* (New York:

Harper Collins, 1999). Also see C. Dale Walton, *The Myth of Inevitable U.S. Defeat in Vietnam* (London: Frank Cass, 2002); and Mark Moyar, *Triumph Forsaken: The Vietnam War, 1954–1965* (Cambridge: Cambridge University Press, 2006), the first volume in a two-book, "in your face," rewriting of the history of the war. There is no question that Americans can be effective in the conduct of irregular warfare against revolutionary enemies. For example, see Michael A. Hennessy, *Strategy in Vietnam: The Marines and Revolutionary Warfare in I Corps, 1965–1972* (Westport, CT: Praeger Publishers, 1997). The trouble was that the Army was not committed to an effective strategy. For a longer historical perspective, see Max Boot, *The Savage Wars of Peace: Small Wars and the Rise of American Power* (New York: Basic Books, 2002.

43. Some worrying possibilities were discussed in the influential article by Barry R. Posen, "Command of the Commons: The Military Foundation of U.S. Hegemony," *International Security* 28 (Summer 2003), 5-46. Posen was not enthusiastic about American commitments to continental warfare.

44. Krepinevich, *The Army and Vietnam*, 7.

45. See Gray, *Another Bloody Century,* ch. 6, "Irregular Warfare and Terrorism."

46. Clausewitz's chapter on "The People in Arms" recognized the occasional potency of guerrilla action viewed as a military tactic by an outraged people against an invader. Such warfare was extensive in his years as a serving soldier (1792–1831). But, sensibly enough, he recognized that irregulars could succeed only in highly permissive circumstances. Clausewitz, Book 6, ch. 26. Certainly it is true to claim that he devoted very little explicit attention to people's war in its several styles. Nonetheless, I believe that Ian Beckett's unappreciative comments on Clausewitz's treatment of guerrilla warfare are too negative. *Modern Insurgencies and Counter-Insurgencies,* 14. Clausewitz theorized better than he may have known for irregular warfare, as I argue in this chapter. Also see Kinross, "Clausewitz and Low-Intensity Conflict."

47. See Roger Trinquier, *Modern Warfare: A French View of Counterinsurgency* (New York: Praeger, 1964); and for a judicious explanation, Peter Paret, *French Revolutionary Warfare from Indo-China to Algeria: The Analysis of a Political and Military Doctrine* (New York: Frederick A. Praeger, 1964).

48. Callwell, *Small Wars*, 38.

49. Clausewitz, 605.

50. For a persuasive set of scholarly studies of the phenomenon of cultural adaptation, see Emily O. Goldman and Leslie C. Eliason, eds., *The Diffusion of Military Technology and Ideas* (Stanford, CA: Stanford University Press, 2003). Williamson Murray and Allan R. Millett, eds., *Military Innovation in the Interwar Period* (Cambridge: Cambridge University Press, 1996), also has much to say of value on the subject of distinctive national responses to common technological opportunities.

51. "Soft power" is shorthand for the many means of gaining influence that fall short of threatening or taking action that must kill people and break things. The founding modern text is Joseph S. Nye, Jr., *Bound to Lead: The Changing Nature of American Power* (New York: Basic Books, 1990). It is an attractive concept. It is a little less attractive in conflicts with rogues and irregulars because they tend to be less easily seduced by some aspect of American culture and ideology than are more normal aspirants for the better, which is to say American, way of life. Also, the appealing belief that the slow but cumulatively engaging potency of soft power should preclude the necessity for having to resort to brutal hard power, may be wrong. When soft power fails over a lengthy period, time, the most unforgiving dimension of strategy, will have been lost for effective action. The case of Iran today promises to be a classic case in illustration of this point.

52. T. E. Lawrence, "Guerrilla Warfare," entry in *Encyclopedia Britannica: A New Survey of Universal Knowledge*, 14th ed., vol. 10 (1929; London: Encyclopedia Britannica, 1959 revision), esp. 950B. In his *Seven Pillars of Wisdom: A Triumph* (New York: Doubleday, 1991), Lawrence drew upon the insight that "it seemed a regular soldier might be helpless without a target, owning only what he sat on, and subjugating only what, by order, he could poke his rifle at." 192. His undoubted brilliance as a practitioner and theorist of guerrilla warfare is not well communicated, even to this admirer, by his purple prose, overstatements, underappreciation of the salience of context, and vanity. Still, the high quality of his thought and his record of success do survive the literary pretensions.

53. This important but frequently overlooked point is made usefully in Adam Roberts, "The 'War on Terror' in Historical Perspective," *Survival* 47 (Summer 2005), 112.

54. An essay in my *Strategy and History: Essays on Theory and Practice* (Abingdon, UK: Routledge, 2006), 81–87, compares and contrasts the two concepts, "From Principles of Warfare to Principles of War: A Clausewitzian Solution," and provides a suggested list of entries for the latter, ones worthy of such prestigious selection.

55. See Stephen Peter Rosen, "Vietnam and the American Theory of Limited War," *International Security* 7 (Fall 1982), 83–113; Mark Clodfelter, *The Limits of Air Power: the American Bombing of North Vietnam* (New York: Free Press, 1989); and Robert A. Pape, *Bombing to Win: Air Power and Coercion in War* (Ithaca, NY: Cornell University Press, 1996), ch. 6.

56. Huntington, *American Military Strategy*, 16. The intellectual godfather of coercive diplomacy, American-style, was Thomas C. Schelling. See his timely, influential tour de force, *Arms and Influence* (New Haven, CT: Yale University Press, 1966). Another American period piece that had traceable real-world consequences was Herman Kahn, *On Escalation: Metaphors and Scenarios* (New York: Praeger, 1965). Coercion is analyzed in a scholarly way

in Stephen J. Cimbala, *Coercive Military Strategy* (College Station: Texas A&M University Press, 1998); Lawrence Freedman, ed., *Strategic Coercion: Concepts and Cases* (Oxford: Oxford University Press, 1998); and Daniel Byman and Mathew Waxman, *The Dynamics of Coercion: American Foreign Policy and the Limits of Military Might* (Cambridge: Cambridge University Press, 2002).

57. Sarkesian, *America's Forgotten Wars*; John M. Collins, *America's Small Wars: Lessons for the Future* (Washington, DC: Brassey's (U.S.), 1991); and Boot, *The Savage Wars of Peace*.

58. Bernard Brodie, "The Continuing Relevance of *On War*," in Clausewitz, 54.

59. See Stanley Hoffman, *Gulliver's Troubles: On the Setting of American Foreign Policy* (New York: McGraw-Hill, 1968).

60. Scales, "Culture-Centric Warfare."

61. Eliot A. Cohen: "The Mystique of U.S. Air Power," *Foreign Affairs* 73 (January/February 1994), 109–124; "The Meaning and Future of Air Power," *Orbis* 39 (Spring 1995), 189–200. In addition, for careful historical perspective, Benjamin S. Lambeth, *The Transformation of American Air Power* (Ithaca, NY: Cornell University Press, 2000), is essential.

62. For example, U.S. Army, *2004 Army Transformation Roadmap* (Washington, DC: Office of the Deputy Chief of Staff, U.S. Army Operations, Army Transformation Office, July 2004).

63. Two British COIN experts judge that "generally speaking the less sophisticated the army, the better able it has been to defeat insurgency." I. W. Beckett and John Pimlott, "Introduction," to *Armed Forces and Modern Counter-Insurgency*, ed. Beckett and Pimlott (New York: St. Martin's Press, 1985), 10. A similarly reserved attitude towards technology has been expressed by the outstanding British soldier of his generation, a man with an abundance of relevant personal experience, General Sir Rupert Smith, in his book *The Utility of Force: The Art of War in the Modern World* (London: Allen Lane, 2005), esp. 400–401. Many of his comments echo the standard empirically based lore on how to wage COIN intelligently. The dominant concept in Smith's book is his belief that the chief challenge facing Western armies is the necessity to function effectively "amongst the people."

64. Quoted in Boot, *The Savage Wars of Peace*, 294.

65. The bluntest competent assault to date on this military cultural preference is to be found in Frederick W. Kagan, "War and Aftermath," *Policy Review* 120 (August and September 2003), 27. "It is a fundamental mistake to see the enemy as a set of targets. The enemy in war is a group of people."

66. Boot, *The Savage Wars of Peace*, 301. In 1966, for example, two-

thirds of the American shells expended were fired at no known targets. Also see Record, *The Wrong War*, ch. 3.

67. Huntington, *American Military Strategy*, 15.

68. Ibid., 16.

69. The pattern of military sacrifice mandated by a public culture of unpreparedness is well told in Charles E. Heller and William A. Stofft, eds., *America's First Battles, 1776–1965* (Lawrence: University Press of Kansas, 1986), esp. ch. 9 on Korea.

70. This is not to deny that small SOF training teams can make, indeed have and should be allowed to make, a crucial difference in the ability of local clients to combat insurgents and terrorists. However, there are no free gifts in warfare. Even a well-conducted advisory enterprise carries the risk of donating the irregular enemy visible, hopefully barely visible in this case, apparent evidence of American imperialism and of official failure when unaided.

71. See Sarkesian, *America's Forgotten Wars*; Collins, *America's Small Wars*; Anthony James Joes, *America and Guerrilla Warfare* (Lexington: University Press of Kentucky, 2000); and Boot, *The Savage Wars of Peace*.

72. See Krepinevich, *The Army and Vietnam*.

73. For an important study from the period, written by a gifted and highly experienced British serving soldier, a true period piece, see Frank Kitson, *Low Intensity Operations* (London: Faber and Faber, 1971).

74. Krepinevich, *The Army and Vietnam*, 230–232.

75. I explored the conditions permissive for the success of SO in my, "Handfuls of Heroes on Desperate Ventures: When do Special Operations Succeed?" *Parameters* XXIX (Spring 1999), 2–24. I suspect strongly that by emphasizing SO as unconventional warfare I may have appeared to undervalue SOF in their several COIN roles.

76. Mao Tse-tung, "On Protracted War (May 1938)," in his *Selected Military Writings*, 187–266.

77. See Herman Hattaway and Archer Jones, *How the North Won: A Military History of the Civil War* (Urbana: University of Illinois Press, 1983), 720, for the primacy of logistics; and Thomas M. Kane, *Military Logistics and Strategic Performance* (London: Frank Cass, 2001), for a superior explanation of logistics as an essential enabler of strategy.

78. Henry E. Eccles, *Military Concepts and Philosophy* (New Brunswick, NJ: Rutgers University Press, 1965), 83. "All logistic activities naturally tend to grow to inordinate size, and unless positive control is maintained this growth continues until, like a ball of wet snow, a huge accumulation of slush obscures the hard core of essential combat support and the mass becomes unmanageable. This snowball effect permeates the entire structure of military organization and effort."

79. Alfred Thayer Mahan, *The Influence of Sea Power upon History, 1660–1783* (London: Methuen, 1965), 25; Posen, "Command of the Commons."

80. Peter M. Dunn, "The American Army: The Vietnam War, 1965–1973," in *Armed Forces and Modern Counter-Insurgency*, ed. Beckett and Pimlott, 103.

81. Peter D. Feaver and Richard H. Kohn, eds., *Soldiers and Civilians: the Civil-Military Gap and American National Security* (Cambridge, MA: MIT Press, 2001). Also see Paul Cornish, "Myth and Reality: U.S. and U.K. Approaches to Casualty Aversion and Force Protection," *Defense Studies* 3 (Summer 2003), 121–128.

82. Callwell, *Small Wars*, 90.

83. This development is well handled in Beckett, *Modern Insurgencies and Counter-Insurgencies*.

84. Mary Kaldor, "Elaborating the 'New War' Thesis," in *Rethinking the Nature of War*, ed. Isabelle Duyvesteyn and Jan Angstrom (London: Frank Cass, 2005), 210–224; Hammes, *Sling and the Stone*.

85. Lawrence, *Seven Pillars of Wisdom*, 192.

86. Daniel J. Hughes, ed., *Moltke On the Art of War: Selected Writings* (Novato, CA: Presidio Press, 1993), 47.

Chapter 7: The Implications of Preemptive and Preventive War Doctrines: A Reconsideration

1. George W. Bush, *The National Security Strategy of the United States of America* (hereafter cited as *NSS*) (Washington, DC: White House, September 2002), 15.

2. Thomas P. M. Barnett, *The Pentagon's New Map: War and Peace in the 21st Century* (New York: Berkeley Books, 2004), 261.

3. Michael Howard, *The Invention of Peace and the Reinvention of War* (London: Profile Books, 2002), 124.

4. Clausewitz, 132.

5. In his speech at West Point on June 1, 2002, President Bush notably demoted deterrence and containment. He said,

> for much of the last century, America's defense relied on the Cold War doctrines of deterrence and containment. In some cases, those strategies still apply. But new threats also require new thinking. Deterrence—the promise of massive retaliation against nations—means nothing against shadowy terrorist networks with no nations or citizens to defend. Containment is not possible when unbalanced dictators with weapons of mass destruction can deliver those weapons as missiles or secretly provide them to terrorist allies.

The president insisted, "We must take the battle to the enemy." And he announced, "Our security will require transforming the military you will lead—a military that must be ready to strike at a moment's notice in any dark corner of the world. And our security will require all Americans to be forward-looking and resolute, to be ready for preemptive action when necessary to defend our liberty and to defend our lives." "Remarks by the President at 2002 Graduation Exercises of the United States Military Academy, West Point, New York," www.whitehouse.gov/ news/releases/2002/06/print/20020601-3.html (accessed June 1, 2002).

6. M. Elaine Bunn, "Preemptive Action: When, How, and To What Effect?" *Strategic Forum*, Institute of National Strategic Studies, National Defense University, 200 (July 2003), 7. This is the clearest statement of the requirements for a doctrine that I have come across.

7. For an excellent treatment of the hazards of preemption during the Cold War, see Bruce G. Blair, *The Logic of Accidental Nuclear War* (Washington, DC: The Brookings Institution, 1993).

8. Daniel Webster, quoted in Michael Byers, *War Law: Understanding International Law and Armed Conflict* (New York: Grove Press, 2005), 54.

9. Elihu Root, quoted in Lawrence Freedman, *Deterrence* (Cambridge, UK: Polity Press, 2004), 90.

10. See Colin S. Gray, *Another Bloody Century: Future Warfare* (London: Weidenfeld and Nicolson, 2005), ch. 1.

11. Uncertainty is highlighted by Clausewitz as one of the four elements that constitute the "climate" of war. See *On War*, 104. The Preface to Secretary of Defense Donald H. Rumsfeld, *Quadrennial Defense Review Report* (Washington, DC: U.S. Department of Defense, February 6, 2006), v, states that "the President [when he took office in 2001] understood well that we were entering an era of the unexpected and the unpredictable . . ." For a full frontal assault on the Bush administration's emphasis upon uncertainty, see Michael Fitzsimmons, "The Problem of Uncertainty in Strategic Planning," *Survival* 48 (Winter 2006–07), 131–146. See also Stephen Fruhling, "Uncertainty, Forecasting and the Difficulty of Strategy," *Comparative Strategy* 25 (January–March 2006), 19–31; and Talbot C. Imlay and Monica Duffy Toft, eds., *The Fog of Peace and War Planning: Military and Strategic Planning under Uncertainty* (New York: Routledge, 2006).

12. In the judgment of Jeffrey Record, "preemption or prevention have their obvious attractions as contrasted with deterrence, at least when they work. But they carry the risk of encouraging a hopeless quest for total security." Jeffrey Record, *The Specter of Munich: Reconsidering the Lessons of Appeasing Hitler* (Washington, DC: Potomac Books, 2007), 121.

13. Recall George Friedman and Meredith Lebard, *The Coming War with Japan* (New York: St. Martin's Press, 1991). Richard Bernstein and Ross H.

Munro, *The Coming Conflict with China* (New York: Alfred A. Knopf, 1997), was a safer bet. The threat industry abhors a vacuum. I admit to being a worker in that industry. See Colin S. Gray, "The Quadrennial Defense Review (QDR), 2006, and the Perils of the 21st Century," *Comparative Strategy* 25 (April–June 2006), 141–148.

14. It is worth noting the phenomenon of the self-negating prophecy. Naturally, it is impossible to know why anticipated wars failed to occur. It is amusing to observe the high confidence that many people place in the proposition that "deterrence works." They are right, at least they are often right. But even just a single failure can spoil a whole decade or longer. Negative evidence is notoriously difficult to document.

15. Bernard Brodie, *War and Politics* (New York: Macmillan, 1973), 452.

16. Societies have frequently declined to accept a verdict of the battlefield which decreed their states' military defeat. Regular warfare often has been succeeded by a popular insurgency in what can be called the warfare after the war. Americans, with their tendency to contrast war with peace and war with politics, have to learn to come to terms with a historical reality more complex than such a binary approach allows.

17. Clausewitz, 87.

18. See Howard, *Invention of Peace and the Reinvention of War.*

19. The literature on war, morality, and law is huge. These books are especially helpful: Leslie C. Green, *The Contemporary Law of Armed Conflict*, 2nd ed. (Manchester, UK: Manchester University Press, 2000); Michael Walzer, *Just and Unjust Wars: A Moral Argument with Historical Illustrations*, 3rd ed. (New York: Basic Books, 2000); Byers, *War Law;* David Kennedy, *Of War and Law* (Princeton, NJ: Princeton University Press, 2006); and Alan M. Dershowitz, *Preemption: A Knife That Cuts Both Ways* (New York: Norton, 2006).

20. A. J. Coates, *The Ethics of War* (Manchester, UK: Manchester University Press, 1997), is an especially fine treatment of just war criteria.

21. Germany declared war on France on August 4, 1914, but the French government was determined that its army should not be the first to violate Belgian neutrality. It was believed in Paris that a first move into Belgium by the Germans would label them unambiguously as the aggressors. See Robert A. Doughty, *Pyrrhic Victory: French Strategy and Operations in the Great War* (Cambridge, MA: Harvard University Press, 2005), 55. Even Hitler sought to confuse the issue of who was the aggressor on September 1, 1939, when the SS staged phony assaults on a few German border installations and provided dead bodies (from concentration camps) in Polish uniform at the scenes of the crimes.

22. Akira Iriye, *The Origins of the Second World War in Asia and the Pacific*

(London: Longman, 1987), is particularly informative. Also see M. Barnhart, *Japan Prepares for Total War: The Search for Economic Security, 1919–1941* (Ithaca, NY: Cornell University Press, 1987); and Colin S. Gray, *War, Peace and International Relations: An Introduction to Strategic History* (New York: Routledge, 2007), ch. 12.

23. Although most historians today agree that Hitler's voluntary declaration of war on the United States was one of his greatest errors, none of Germany's military leaders raised objections at the time. In Berlin, war with the United States was believed to be inevitable and not very important. The war, overall, was expected to be decided in Russia long before America could mobilize a sufficient weight of military muscle to make a significant difference to the course of events.

24. See John Lewis Gaddis, *We Now Know: Rethinking Cold War History* (Oxford, UK: Clarendon Press, 1997); idem., *The Cold War* (London: Allen Lane, 2006); Vladislaw Zubok and Constantine Pleshakov, *Inside the Kremlin's Cold War: From Stalin to Khrushchev* (Cambridge, MA: Harvard University Press, 1996).

25. The most aggressive American move was the Marshall Plan, announced on June 5, 1947, by Secretary of State George C. Marshall. The Plan was intended both to refire the cold boilers of European economies ruined by war, and to counter Soviet influence, especially in East-Central Europe. Wisely, Stalin rejected the American Plan and ordered his burgeoning, but still insecure, new imperium in Eastern Europe to reject it also.

26. Sensible judgments are provided by strategist-lawyer Walter B. Slocombe in "Force, Preemption and Legitimacy," *Survival* 45 (Spring 2003), 117–130. "The interesting and much-disputed legal issues of how the UN Charter, in particular Article 51 (reserving the inherent right of self-defence against armed attack) should be interpreted—and what, to a practicing lawyer is the equally important issue of who has the legitimate authority to interpret it authoritatively—are matters more for scholars than practitioners of international relations." 121.

27. Bernard Brodie, *Strategy in the Missile Age* (Princeton, NJ: Princeton University Press, 1959), ch. 7, is an essential source. Brodie was a participant-observer. Marc Trachtenberg, *History and Strategy* (Princeton, NJ: Princeton University Press, 1991), is outstandingly useful, as is Steven T. Ross, *American War Plans, 1945–1950* (London: Frank Cass, 1996). See also David S. McDonough, *Nuclear Superiority: The "New Triad" and the Evolution of Nuclear Strategy,* Adelphi Paper 383 (New York: Routledge, for the International Institute for Strategic Studies (IISS), 2006), ch. 1; and the ever helpful Lawrence Freedman, *The Evolution of Nuclear Strategy*, 3rd ed. (New York: Palgrave Macmillan, 2003), especially ch. 3.

28. See Robert S. Litwak, "The New Calculus of Preemption," *Survival* 44 (Winter 2002–03), 64–65.

29. There are many contextual differences between the North Korean and Iranian cases. Not only does North Korea have potent WMD and conventional military forces with considerable deterrent value, but also it is not an ambitious rising regional power. Whereas Pyongyang's WMD are primarily in the service of a defensive and commercial statecraft, those being sought energetically by Tehran would have the political potential to undergird a bid for regional hegemony, as well as to deter U.S. intervention. As always, the U.S. defense analysis industry responds to policy demand. For a good relevant example, see Henry Sokolski and Patrick Clawson, eds., *Getting Ready for a Nuclear-Ready Iran* (Carlisle, PA: Strategic Studies Institute, U.S. Army War College, October 2005).

30. Lawrence Freedman, *Deterrence* (Cambridge, UK: Polity Press, 2004), 86.

31. Bush, *NSS* 2002, 84.

32. See David Luban, "Preventive War," unpublished Paper, prepared for roundtable discussion at the American Political Science Association Conference, August 2003, 27.

33. Michael Williams, "Revisiting Established Doctrine in an Age of Risk," *RUSI Journal* 150 (October 2005), 48–52, points out that "the precautionary principle" is cited in more than 14 multilateral agreements. Williams is not entirely to be trusted on his use of concepts, however, since he writes: "Precautionary war, better known as preemptive war, . . ." 51.

34. Kennedy, *Of War and Law,* 79.

35. Ibid., 79–80.

36. Green, *The Contemporary Law of Armed Conflict,* 9–10.

37. Ibid., 10.

38. Kennedy, *Of War and Law,* 80.

39. Robert R. Tomes, *US Defense Strategy from Vietnam to Operation Iraqi Freedom: Military Innovation and the New American Way of War, 1973–2003* (New York: Routledge, 2007), 141.

40. Tirpitz's ostensible rationale for his High Seas Fleet was that eventually it would be so powerful, albeit still inferior to the British Royal Navy (RN), that London would not dare risk challenging it in battle. The damage the German Fleet would inflict in its inevitable defeat would leave the RN inferior and vulnerable to other great navies. It is safe to assume that Tirpitz's real objective was to achieve a High Seas Fleet second to none, not a second-class "risk fleet." For his theory, policy, and strategy to work, the British were required somehow not to notice the Germans coming, since, if they did, they could outbuild Tirpitz's planned force. The High Seas Fleet was a multidimensional disaster for Imperial Germany. Its existence and progress guaranteed British hostility, while it siphoned off scarce raw materials and superior manpower

of which the army was in great need. See Holger H. Herwig, *"Luxury Fleet":
The Imperial German Navy* (London: George Allen and Unwin, 1980).

41. The Russian "Great Program" decided on in 1914 planned a 40
percent increase in the size of the army by 1917 and, thanks to French finance, railroad expansion that should accelerate their pace of mobilization
and military deployment by 50 percent, again by 1917. David Stevenson,
Cataclysm: The First World War as Political Tragedy (New York: Basic Books,
2004), 18. Also see Strachan, *The First World War*, 1: 296–316.

42. Hitler was explicit on the need for war before 1943. See "Minutes of
the Conference in the Reich Chancellery, Berlin, November 5, 1937" (the
"Hossbach Memorandum"), in *Hitler's Third Reich: A Documentary History*,
Louis L. Snyder, ed. (Chicago: Nelson-Hall, 1981), 268–269.

43. The trials, tribulations, but residual value of deterrence, are discussed
in Keith B. Payne, *The Fallacies of Cold War Deterrence and a New Direction*
(Lexington: University Press of Kentucky, 2001); Freedman, *Deterrence*; and
the discussion in chapter 3 of this book.

44. When Serbian military intelligence propelled the hapless innocent,
Gavrilo Princip, toward his suicidal moment of destiny in Sarajevo on June
28, 1914, it did not intend to ignite a powder trail to a general war. See
Strachan, *The First World War*, 1: 65.

45. Luban, "Preventive War," 4.

46. See Colin S. Gray, *The Sheriff: America's Defense of the New World
Order* (Lexington: University of Kentucky Press, 2004).

47. Clausewitz, 89.

48. The largely American authored strategic theory of the nuclear age
was remarkable for its narrowly military logic. See Hedley Bull, "Strategic
Studies and Its Critics," *World Politics* 20 (July 1968), 593–605; and
Trachtenberg, *History and Strategy*, ch. 1.

49. Clausewitz, 85.

50. Record, *The Specter of Munich*, 121.

51. The deployment of reliable anti-ballistic missile defenses should increase tolerance of imperfection in a preventive strike against missiles armed
with WMD.

52. Gaddis, *Surprise, Security, and the American Experience*, 33.

Chapter 8: The Merit in Ethical Realism

1. J. Glenn Gray, *The Warriors: Reflections on Men in Battle* (New York:
Harper Torchbooks, 1967), 24.

2. Daniel J. Hughes, ed. *Moltke on the Art of War: Selected Writings*,

trans. Hughes and Harry Bell (Novato, CA: Presidio Books, 1993), 47.

3. David J. Lonsdale, *Alexander: Killer of Men. Alexander the Great and the Macedonian Art of War* (London: Constable, 2004), 3.

4. Martin van Creveld, *The Changing Face of War: Lessons of Combat from the Marne to Iraq* (New York: Ballantine Books, 2006), 228.

5. See Gray, *Warriors*, ch. 4, for what may be the most penetrating analysis of the warriors' fear of death ever written.

6. Robert B. Strassler, ed., *The Landmark Thucydides: A Comprehensive Guide to the Peloponnesian War*, Richard Crawley trans., rev. ed. (New York: Free Press, 1996), 43.

7. I am grateful to Scott D. Sagan, *The Limits of Safety: Organizations, Accidents, and Nuclear Weapons* (Princeton, NJ: Princeton University Press, 1993).

8. I first tested this argument in my article, "Future Warfare: Or, the triumph of History," *RUSI Journal* 150 (October 2005), 16–19.

9. A famous phrase uttered by Flight Director Kranz to his staff in April 1970 as they struggled to save Apollo 13.

10. See Colin S. Gray: *The Sheriff: America's Defense of the New World Order* (Lexington: University Press of Kentucky, 2004); and *After Iraq: The Search for a Sustainable National Security Strategy* (Carlisle, PA: Strategic Studies Institute, U.S. Army War College, forthcoming).

11. How not to do it (in Iraq) is revealed in Rajiv Chandrasekaran, *Imperial Life in the Emerald City: Inside Baghdad's Green Zone* (London: Bloomsbury, 2008). For interim, multi-authored scholarly reports, see the two excellent works: Thomas G. Mahnken and Thomas A. Keaney, eds., *War in Iraq: Planning and Execution* (Abingdon, UK: Routledge, 2007); and Steven Metz, *Iraq and the Evolution of American Strategy* (Washington, DC: Potomac Books, 2008).

12. Arthur M. Schlesinger, Jr., "America needs history as never before," *International Herald Tribune*, January 2, 2007.

SELECTED BIBLIOGRAPHY

Aron, Raymond. "The Evolution of Modern Strategic Thought." In *Problems of Modern Strategy*, edited by Alastair Buchan. London: Chatto and Windus, 1970.

Bacevich, Andrew J. *American Empire: The Realities and Consequences of U.S. Diplomacy*. Cambridge, MA: Harvard University Press, 2002.

Barnett, Roger W. *Asymmetrical Warfare: Today's Challenge to U.S. Military Power*. Washington, DC: Brassey's, Inc., 2003.

Baylis, John, and others, eds. *Strategy in the Contemporary World: An Introduction to Strategic Studies*. 2nd ed. Oxford: Oxford University Press, 2007.

Beckett, Ian F. W. *Modern Insurgencies and Counter-Insurgencies: Guerrillas and Their Opponents Since 1750*. London: Routledge, 2001.

Betts, Richard K. *Enemies of Intelligence: Knowledge and Power in American National Security*. New York: Columbia University Press, 2007.

————. "Is Strategy an Illusion?" *International Security* 25 (Fall 2000): 5–50.

————. "Should Strategic Studies Survive?" *World Politics* 50 (October 1997): 7–33.

————. *Surprise Attack: Lessons for Defense Planning*. Washington, DC: Brookings Institution, 1982.

———. "The Trouble with Strategy: Bridging Policy and Operations." *Joint Force Quarterly* 29 (Autumn/Winter 2001–02): 23–30.

Betts, Richard K., and Thomas G. Mahnken, eds. *Paradoxes of Intelligence: Essays in Honor of Michael I. Handel.* London: Frank Cass, 2003.

Biddle, Stephen. *Military Power: Explaining Victory and Defeat in Modern Battle.* Princeton, NJ: Princeton University Press, 2004.

Black, Jeremy. *Rethinking Military History.* London: Routledge, 2004.

———. *War in the New Century.* London: Continuum, 2001.

Blanning, T. C. W. *The Origins of the French Revolutionary Wars.* London: Longman, 1986.

Bond, Brian. *The Pursuit of Victory: From Napoleon to Saddam Hussein.* Oxford: Oxford University Press, 1996.

Boot, Max. *The Savage Wars of Peace: Small Wars and the Rise of American Power.* New York: Basic Books, 2007.

Booth, Ken. *Strategy and Ethnocentrism.* London: Croom Helm, 1979.

Brodie, Bernard. *Strategy in the Missile Age.* Princeton, NJ: Princeton University Press, 1959.

———. *War and Politics.* New York: Macmillan, 1973.

Bull, Hedley. "Strategic Studies and Its Critics." *World Politics* 20 (July 1968): 593–605.

Bunn, M. Elaine. "Preemptive Action: When, How, and To What Effect?" *Strategic Forum*, Institute of National Strategic Studies, National Defense University, 200 (July 2003).

Bush, George W. *The National Security Strategy of the United States of America.* Washington, DC: The White House, September 2002.

Callwell, Charles A. *Small Wars: A Tactical Textbook for Imperial Soldiers.* 1906 ed. Novato, CA: Presidio Press, 1990.

Chandrasekaran, Rajiv. *Imperial Life in the Emerald City: Inside Baghdad's Green Zone.* London: Bloomsbury, 2008.

Cimbala, Stephen J. *Coercive Military Strategy.* College Station, TX: Texas A&M University Press, 1998.

Citino, Robert M. *Blitzkrieg to Desert Storm: The Evolution of Operational Warfare.* Lawrence, KS: University Press of Kansas, 2004.

Clausewitz, Carl von. *On War*. Translated by Michael Howard and Peter Paret. Princeton, NJ: Princeton University Press, 1976.

Coker, Christopher. *The Warrior Ethos and the War on Terror*. Abingdon, UK: Routledge, 2007.

Creveld, Martin van. *The Transformation of War*. New York: Free Press, 1991.

Desch, Michael C. "Assessing the Importance of Ideas in Security Studies." *International Security* 23 (Summer 1998): 141–170.

Dombrowski, Peter, and Rodger A. Payne. "The Emerging Consensus for Preventive War." *Survival* 48 (Summer 2006): 115–136.

Dueck, Colin. *Reluctant Crusaders: Power, Culture, and Change in American Grand Strategy*. Princeton, NJ: Princeton University Press, 2006.

Echevarria, Antulio J., II. *Globalization and the Nature of War*. Carlisle, PA: Strategic Studies Institute, U.S. Army War College, 2003.

———. *Toward an American Way of War*. Carlisle, PA: Strategic Studies Institute, U.S. Army War College, 2004.

Fitzsimmons, Michael. "The Problem of Uncertainty in Strategic Planning." *Survival* 48 (Winter 2006–07): 131–146.

Freedman, Lawrence. *The Evolution of Nuclear Strategy*. 3rd ed. Basingstoke, UK: Palgrave Macmillan, 2003.

Friedman, Norman. *The Fifty-Year War: Conflict and Strategy in the Cold War*. Annapolis, MD: Naval Institute Press, 2000.

Gaddis, John Lewis. *The Cold War*. London: Allen Lane, 2006.

Gat, Azar. *A History of Military Thought: From the Enlightenment to the Cold War*. Oxford: Oxford University Press, 2001.

Glenn, John, Darryl Howlett, and Stuart Poore, eds. *Neorealism Versus Strategic Culture*. Burlington, VT: Ashgate Publishing, 2004.

Goldman, Emily, and Leslie C. Eliason, eds. *The Diffusion of Military Technology and Ideas*. Stanford, CA: Stanford University Press, 2003.

Gray, Colin S. *After Iraq: The Search for a Sustainable National Security Strategy*. Carlisle, PA: Strategic Studies Institute, U.S. Army War College, forthcoming.

———. *Explorations in Strategy*. Westport, CT: Praeger Publishers, 1998.

———. *Fighting Talk: Forty Maxims on War, Peace, and Strategy.* Westport, CT: Praeger Security International, 2007.

———. *Modern Strategy.* Oxford: Oxford University Press, 1999.

———. *The Sheriff: America's Defense of the New World Order.* Lexington: University Press of Kentucky, 2004.

———. *Strategy and History: Essays on Theory and Practice.* Abingdon, UK: Routledge, 2006.

———. *Strategy for Chaos: RMA Theory and the Evidence of History.* London: Frank Cass, 2002.

Gray, J. Glenn. *The Warriors: Reflections on Men in Battle.* New York: Harper Torchbooks, 1967.

Gunaratna, Rohan. *Inside Al Qaeda: Global Network of Terror.* New York: Columbia University Press, 2002.

Handel, Michael I. *Masters of War: Classical Strategic Thought.* 3rd ed. London: Frank Cass, 2001.

Hirst, Paul. *War and Power in the 21st Century: The State, Military Conflict, and the International System.* Cambridge: Polity Press, 2001.

Hoffman, Bruce. *Inside Terrorism.* Rev. ed. London: Victor Gollancz, 2006.

Howard, Michael. *The Invention of Peace and the Reinvention of War.* London: Profile Books, 2002.

———. *Liberation or Catastrophe? Reflections on the History of the Twentieth Century.* London: Hambledon Continuum, 2007.

———. "When Are Wars Decisive?" *Survival* 41 (Spring 1999): 126–135.

Huntington, Samuel P. *American Military Strategy,* Policy Paper 28. Berkeley, CA: Institute of International Studies, University of California, Berkeley, 1986.

———. *The Soldier and the State: The Theory and Politics of Civil-Military Relations.* New York: Vintage Books, 1964.

Imlay, Talbot C., and Monica Toft, eds. *The Fog of Peace and War Planning: Military and Strategic Planning under Uncertainty.* Abingdon, UK: Routledge, 2006.

James, Robert R. *U.S. Defense Strategy from Vietnam to Operation Iraqi Freedom: Military Innovation and the New American Way of War, 1973–2003.* Abingdon, UK: Routledge, 2007.

Johnson, Stuart E., and Martin C. Libicki, eds. *Dominant Battlespace Knowledge*. Rev. ed. Washington, DC: National Defense University Press, 2004.

Johnston, Alastair Iain. *Cultural Realism: Strategic Culture and Grand Strategy in Chinese History*. Princeton, NJ: Princeton University Press, 1995.

Jomini, Antoine Henri de. *The Art of War*. 1838. Reprint, Novato, CA: Presidio Press, 1992.

Kagan, Frederick W. *Finding the Target: The Transformation of American Military Policy*. New York: Encounter Books, 2006.

Kahn, Herman. *On Escalation: Metaphors and Scenarios*. New York: Frederick A. Praeger, 1965.

Kaldor, Mary. *New and Old Wars: Organized Violence in a Global Era*. Cambridge: Polity Press, 1999.

Kane, Thomas M. *Military Logistics and Strategic Performance*. London: Frank Cass, 2001.

Keaney, Thomas A., and Eliot A. Cohen. *Revolution in Warfare? Air Power in the Persian Gulf*. Annapolis, MD: Naval Institute Press, 1995.

Kennedy, David. *Of War and Law*. Princeton, NJ: Princeton University Press, 2006.

Kiras, James D. *Rendering the Mortal Blow Easier: Special Operations and the Nature of Strategy*. London: Routledge, 2006.

Kissinger, Henry. *Diplomacy*. New York: Simon and Schuster, 1994.

Krepinevich, Andrew F., Jr. *The Army and Vietnam*. Baltimore: Johns Hopkins University Press, 1986.

Lambeth, Benjamin S. *Air Power Against Terror: America's Conduct of Operation Enduring Freedom*. Santa Monica, CA: RAND, 2005.

————. *NATO's Air War for Kosovo: A Strategic and Operational Assessment*. Santa Monica, CA: RAND, 2001.

————. *The Transformation of American Air Power*. Ithaca, NY: Cornell University Press, 2000.

Liang, Qiao, and Wang Xiangsui. *Unrestricted Warfare: Assumptions on War and Tactics in the Age of Globalization*. Translated by FBIS. Beijing: PLA Literature Arts Publishing House, 1999.

Liddell Hart, B. H. *Strategy: The Indirect Approach*. Rev. ed. London: Faber and Faber, 1967.

Lonsdale, David J. *Alexander the Great: Lessons in Strategy.* Abingdon, UK: Routledge, 2007.

Luttwak, Edward N. *Strategy: The Logic of War and Peace.* 2nd ed. Cambridge, MA: Harvard University Press, 2001.

———. "Toward Post-Heroic Warfare." *Foreign Affairs* 75 (May/June, 1996): 109–122.

Mahnken, Thomas G., and Joseph A. Maiolo, eds. *Strategic Studies: A Reader.* Abingdon, UK: Routledge, 2008.

Mahnken, Thomas G., and Thomas Keaney, eds. *War in Iraq: Planning and Execution.* Abingdon, UK: Routledge, 2007.

McIvor, Anthony, ed. *Rethinking the Principles of War: The Future of Warfare.* Annapolis, MD: Naval Institute Press, 2005.

Mearsheimer, John J. *The Tragedy of Great Power Politics.* New York: W. W. Norton, 2001.

Metz, Steven. *Iraq and the Evolution of American Strategy.* Washington, DC: Potomac Books, 2008.

Metz, Stephen, and Raymond Millen. *Future War/Future Battlespace: The Strategic Role of American Landpower.* Carlisle, PA: Strategic Studies Institute, U.S. Army War College, 2003.

———. *Insurgency and Counterinsurgency in the 21st Century: Reconceptualizing Threat and Response.* Carlisle, PA: Strategic Studies Institute, U.S. Army War College, 2004.

Millett, Allan R., and Williamson Murray, eds. *Military Effectiveness.* 3 vols. Boston: Allen and Unwin, 1988.

Murray, Williamson. "Thinking about Revolutions in Military Affairs." *Joint Force Quarterly* 16 (Summer 1997): 69–76.

Murray, Williamson, MacGregor Knox, and Alvin Bernstein, eds. *The Making of Strategy: Rulers, States and War.* Cambridge: Cambridge University Press, 1994.

Murray, Williamson, and Allan R. Millett, eds. *Military Innovation in the Interwar Period.* Cambridge: Cambridge University Press, 1996.

———. *A War to be Won: Fighting the Second World War.* Cambridge, MA: Harvard University Press, 2000.

Owens, Bill. *Lifting the Fog of War.* New York: Farrow, Straus and Giroux, 2000.

Pape, Robert A. *Bombing to Win: Air Power and Coercion in War.* Ithaca, NY: Cornell University Press, 1996.

Paret, Peter, ed. *Makers of Modern Strategy: From Machiavelli to the Nuclear Age.* Princeton, NJ: Princeton University Press, 1986.

Payne, Keith B. *The Fallacies of Cold War Deterrence and a New Direction.* Lexington: University of Kentucky, 2001.

———. *The Great American Gamble: Deterrence Theory and Practice from the Cold War to the 21st Century.* Fairfax, VA: National Institute Press, 2008.

Peters, Ralph. "In Praise of Attrition." *Parameters* XXXIV (Summer 2004): 24–32.

Posen, Barry R. "Command of the Commons: The Military Foundation of U.S. Hegemony." *International Security* 28 (Summer 2003): 5–46.

Record, Jeffrey. *The Wrong War: Why We Lost in Vietnam.* Annapolis, MD: Naval Institute Press, 1998.

Ricks, Thomas R. *Fiasco: The American Military Adventure in Iraq.* New York: Penguin Press, 2006.

Roberts, Adams. "The 'War on Terror' in Historical Perspective." *Survival* 47 (Summer 2005): 101–130.

Rumsfeld, Donald H. *The National Defense Strategy of the United States of America.* Washington, DC: U.S. Department of Defense, 2005.

Sarkesian, Sam C. *America's Forgotten Wars: The Counterrevolutionary Past and Lessons for the Future.* Westport, CT: Greenwood Press, 1984.

Scales, Robert H., Jr. "Culture-Centric Warfare." U.S. Naval Institute *Proceedings* 130 (October 2004): 32–36.

Schelling, Thomas C. *Arms and Influence.* New Haven, CT: Yale University Press, 1966.

Sondhaus, Lawrence. *Strategic Culture and Ways of War.* London: Routledge, 2006.

Slocombe, Walter B. "Force, Preemption and Legitimacy." *Survival* 45 (Spring 2003): 117–130.

Smith, Rupert. *The Utility of Force: The Art of War in the Modern World.* London: Allen Lane, 2005.

Spykman, Nicholas J. *America's Strategy in World Politics: The United States and the Balance of Power.* New York: Harcourt, Brace, 1942.

Strachan, Hew. "The Lost Meaning of Strategy." *Survival* 47 (Autumn 2005): 33–54.

Strassler, Robert B., ed. *The Landmark Thucydides: A Comprehensive Guide to the Peloponnesian War.* Translated by Richard Crawley. Rev. ed. New York: Free Press, 1996.

Sun Tzu. *The Art of War.* Translated by Ralph D. Sawyer. Boulder, CO: Westview Press, 1994.

Tomes, Robert R. *U.S. Defense Strategy from Vietnam to Operation Iraqi Freedom: Military Innovation and the New American Way of War, 1973–2003.* Abingdon, UK: Routledge, 2007.

Trachtenberg, Marc. *History and Strategy.* Princeton, NJ: Princeton University Press, 1991.

U.S. Army and Marine Corps. *Counterinsurgency Field Manual.* Chicago: University of Chicago Press, 2007.

Vego, Milan. "Effects-Based Operations: A Critique." *Joint Force Quarterly* 41 (2nd qtr. 2007): 51–57.

Walton, C. Dale. *The Myth of Inevitable U.S. Defeat in Vietnam.* London: Frank Cass, 2002.

Walzer, Michael. *Just and Unjust Wars: A Moral Argument with Historical Illustrations.* 3rd ed. New York: Basic Books, 2000.

Watts, Barry. *Clausewitzian Friction and Future War,* McNair Paper 68. Rev. ed. Washington, DC: Institute for National Strategic Studies, National Defense University, 2004.

Weigley, Russell F. *The American Way of War: A History of United States Strategy and Policy.* New York: Macmillan, 1973.

Weltman, John J. *World Politics and the Evolution of War.* Baltimore: Johns Hopkins University Press, 1995.

Wylie, J. C. *Military Strategy: A General Theory of Power Control.* Annapolis, MD: Naval Institute Press, 1989.

INDEX

ABOUT THE AUTHOR

Colin S. Gray is professor of international politics and strategic studies at the University of Reading, England. Over the course of forty years he has combined careers as scholar and government adviser. He taught at Lancaster University in the United Kingdom and then at York University, Toronto, and the University of British Columbia, Vancouver. He worked also at the Canadian Institute of International Affairs, Toronto. In the early 1970s he was assistant director of the International Institute for Strategic Studies in London. In 1976 he moved to the United States where he was director of national security studies at the Hudson Institute, New York, before founding the National Institute for Public Policy in Fairfax, Virginia. He held a presidential appointment in the Reagan administration for five years. In 1993, Dr. Gray returned to England, where he has been teaching at universities (Hull and Reading) and advising government. He is the author of twenty-three books, most recently *Fighting Talk: Forty Maxims on War, Peace, and Strategy* (2007). At present he is writing a major book on strategic theory, *The Strategy Bridge*. Dr. Gray has published extensively on such subjects as nuclear strategy, maritime strategy, spacepower, special operations, geopolitics, arms control, and strategic ideas. He is a dual UK/US citizen and lives in England.